by Sister Angeline Murphy

Mother Florence

A Biographical History

Mother Florence

Florence

A Biographical History

Sister Angelina Murphy, C.D.P.

Foreword by Patrick F. Flores,
Archbishop of San Antonio

AN EXPOSITION-TESTAMENT BOOK

Exposition Press   *Smithtown, New York*

To the sisters who pioneered with Mother Florence

FIRST EDITION

© 1980 by Sister Angelina Murphy, C.D.P.

LIBRARY OF CONGRESS CATALOG CARD NUMBER: 80-67314

ISBN 0-682-49625-1

Printed in the United States of America

Contents

Foreword

There are many reasons why the story of Mother Florence Walter, C.D.P., must be told. The great qualities which we find in her life have powerful possibilities for us today. We need models and heroines whose values we imitate and whose principles we copy: "Let your light shine." The light which radiated from Mother Florence was not only a beacon of hope to people of her own time but has shone through the years to sustain, support, and direct those who still seek meaning and purpose in their lives.

Sister Angelina Murphy, C.D.P., has not merely catalogued the various incidents in the life of Mother Florence, but she has given us the "journey of a soul." She has caught the power, the inner spirit, the faith, and the intense commitment of one person to the Christ she loved so passionately. If the story of Mother Florence had not been told, as it is in these pages, the church in the Southwest would have been deprived of many chapters of its history. Mother Florence was a vital part of that history.

Not only will the archives of the Congregation of Divine Providence be enriched, but all who live and work in the vast areas served by the sisters will hear again the story of their own roots in the Catholicism of this region. In very different circumstances we have the same concerns today as did Mother Florence in her time. We are concerned with evangelization, religious education, family life. We are aware of the tremendous needs. While we have our limitations as to the means to reach these goals, they are not comparable to the obstacles and hardships she had to endure. We can smile today as we read some of the descriptions of those difficult times: "They approached the Medina River, spanned by no bridge but, fortunately for them, with only a bare trickle of water flowing, because no rain had swollen it for many weeks or even months. . . . Sister Florence thought of the many painful waits, marooned in their convent home, for the river to fall enough so that the horses could get across with or without wagons." We question immediately how she could have accomplished so much with so few resources and facilities. We struggle today to find our answer to the needs of the present. We become frustrated at our lack of accomplishment, and yet, when we read the story of Mother Florence, we know there is an answer, there is an explanation, there is something there which perhaps we are missing. We pray that we will be inspired by these pages to find it.

We cannot but be deeply moved by the childhood family life of the Walters in Surbourg, France. We are shouting today about the need for the restoration of Christian family living. We proclaim that it is the faith of the local Christian community which forms and transmits the faith. When we later meet this same great woman of faith, the pioneer and missionary for Christ, we are absolutely convinced that the faith of her own family and community were the high-octane driving force of her entire life and love.

Mother Florence's love of the religious life, and the expression of it in her own congregation, is evident in every line of her biography. Her efforts to recruit and build up the community, her motherly love and care for every sister, her undying attention to them were qualities of a saint. As she traveled all over the Southwest as a powerful leader, an astute business woman, a strong fighter, she remained always a witness of faith, a witness of total commitment to Christ, a witness to the religious life she so deeply cherished. Everywhere she radiated that inner happiness she found in her special calling, perfect satisfaction with her role, convinced that there was, for her, ample opportunity to minister to God's people.

One cannot read these chapters without being aware of the many difficulties, misunderstandings, and conflicts which Mother Florence encountered during her pioneer missionary days. These must be seen as part of her own great spirit, her own imitation of Christ. Jacques Maritain once said, "Christian heroism has not the same sources as heroism of other kinds. It has its source in the heart of God scourged and turned to scorn and crucified outside the city gate."

We take so much for granted today! As we drive so comfortably in our modern transportation throughout the many parishes of this archdiocese, and those of other dioceses and states, does the story of Mother Florence ever come to our minds? Students today complain of the cost of college education, of the demands of study and schooling. Do those who daily rush in and out of the present Our Lady of the Lake University know that not just the education but the entire complex had once to be provided? If walls could talk, would they not shout the story of Mother Florence?

We are eternally grateful to Sister Angelina for giving us this biography of a great and saintly woman. May it not remain merely a historical record for the files of the Sisters of Divine Providence but also heighten the awareness of the values of family living, religious life, evangelization, vocation work, and the basic commitment to Christian living in all who read it.

†PATRICK F. FLORES
Archbishop of San Antonio

Preface

It has been a tremendous experience for me to go back more than a hundred years to the beginning of Mother Florence Walter and to follow her to the end. I went to Alsace-Lorraine, Mother Florence's native country, to Texas, where she put down her congregational roots, to Louisiana, where she accepted the challenge of the bishop to educate the post-Civil War blacks and whites, and to Oklahoma Indian Territory, where she took on the Indians and the emerging state.

Mother Florence, according to and almost in spite of church traditions and the times, was a real mother to her burgeoning congregation, stern and demanding, but warm, loving, and compassionate. I have tried to bring her back to life, to reconstruct her personality, her strengths and weaknesses, her logic and faith, her ambitions and despairs. I have wept with her and rejoiced with her. I feel that I was unfortunate not to have known her more personally during her lifetime. But I believe I have come to know her even better through my research and meditations on her words and actions through eighty-five years.

I have fictionalized this biography to the extent that I invented most of the conversation and many of the actions in order to hold the documentation together in a logical manner. I have also interpreted behavior and events as I believe them to have been. Every event, however, is based on documentation, and even the conversation is sometimes transposed from letters.

Such homey incidents as the apples on the train, the figs from Castroville, and the oranges from Beeville are authentic. I have checked out the characterization of the persons who weave in and out of the story, as well as those of the main figures, with persons who knew them, so that they are true as far as I can determine. I have tried to locate the events within the historical settings and according to the philosophies of former days, which were somewhat different from those of our times.

I have come to appreciate my congregation more than ever, and I hope those who read these pages will feel just a bit of what I felt as I labored lovingly for two years in Mother Florence's footsteps.

I wish to acknowledge at the outset that I leaned heavily on Sister Generosa Callahan's *History of the Congregation of the Sisters of Divine Providence,* which replaced research on my part in the many areas that overlap. I also quoted facts from two of her articles in the *OLL Magazine* dealing with Twenty-fourth Street and the chapel. I am indebted to the archivists of the following places I visited: the Congregation of Divine Providence in France and the one in San Antonio; the San Antonio Archdiocese; the Galveston-Houston Diocese; Our Lady of the Lake University; and Surbourg, France, the birthplace of Mother Florence. I am grateful to the deceased sisters of my congregation who left written memoirs of their early days, and to the elderly sisters living today, who have given me taped and informal accounts of their varied experiences and recollections.

I am grateful to Archbishop Joseph Strebler at Strasbourg for his encouragement, to Gus and Yvonne Vonach, who housed and chauffeured me in Alsace, to Mother Florence's family in Haguenau, France, who helped me reconstruct her childhood and youth. I also appreciate the interest of Mother St. Andrew Feltin's family in La Walck, and Mother Philothea Thiry's family in Saaraltroff. The Sisters of Divine Providence in France spared no pains to help and accommodate me wherever I went. Sisters Rosalie Karstedt and Ann Umscheid in Houston also helped me before and after my European trip and gave me encouragement. I thank the readers of my manuscript, Sisters Lucina Schuler and Rose Marie Gallatin, for their editorial suggestions.

I am indebted to the authors of several books and documents for historical information. They are listed in a brief bibliography at the end of the book.

I am also and especially grateful to my financial sponsors:

the Texas Educational Association, H. B. Zachry, The Oblates of Mary Immaculate, Mrs. Cecile Wolff, Mrs. H. F. Wedelich, Our Lady of the Lake University's Hearst Research Grant, Mr. and Mrs. E. J. Barragy, and others. Without their help, there would be no book.

I thank Sister Charlene Wedelich, my superior general, for allowing me the time and opportunity to research and write this book.

1

A Storm in Castroville

It was August 1886. Sister Florence leaned on the back of the hard, flat seat and wished she had a place to rest her head. Her head was aching and her eyes burned. Perspiration stood in rapidly expanding beads on her face and occasionally one bead spilled over, rolling down her damp wimple. The burden of her responsibility had been so great during the past months, especially the last few weeks, that her thoughts had been limited to the immediate concerns. But now within a few hours the immediate concerns would change; this burden would be lifted and another would face her.

Sister opened her smarting eyes, against which the noonday Texas sun glared relentlessly through the grimy windows of the train. As far as she could see, the parched brown plains stretched on and on, punctuated here and there with scraggly mesquite trees and cacti. Smoke from the engine, wafting in through the open windows, kept her nostrils constantly agitated, and cinders settled gently on her customarily immaculate white guimpe.

The girls, restless with excitement of their approaching arrival in Castroville, had finally succumbed to the oppressive heat and glare and were dozing fitfully, leaning for support against each other. Sister Florence, as was her custom, thought first of the girls.

At her superior's request, and with the permission of her very exacting bishop, Sister Florence had left toward the end of April for Alsace-Lorraine and various places in Germany

1

to recruit girls for her congregation, the Sisters of Divine Providence. With Sister Berthilde Thiel, who wished to return to her familiar and beloved Alsace after having tried the Texas foreign mission for six years and found it beyond her endurance, she went with mixed feelings to her native land, from which she had also been gone six years. It had not been so difficult as she had feared to locate recruits. Mother St. Andrew, her superior general, had been there three years before and had spoken with pastors and parents concerning vocations. Word had spread that she was coming, and the girls were waiting, hoping that she would accept them, hoping their parents could be persuaded— even though some were quite young, wanting to do something deserving of God and His goodness. How her heart beat when she saw them one by one or in groups of two or more as the weeks went by. They were so eager, so joyful, and so determined, but so young. She asked herself, how can they be so sure this is what they want to do to the end of their lives? Can they understand what it means to go away from one's country and one's family and never see native land or relatives again? She had done this herself, true, but it had been, and still was, hard. She was only twenty-eight years old. But she had entered and been trained in her own country among her own people, and she knew from the past six years that that made a difference. Sometimes she thought this back-breaking, heartrending life would go on forever, for a hundred, two hundred years, and nothing would change. Was it right to take these girls away from their homes to a strange and hard land?

Sister Florence sighed softly. God knows she had not put any pressure on any of them, she consoled herself. On the contrary, they had put pressure on her, so eager in their young energy and love of God. They begged to go, received reluctant permission from their parents, and enjoyed every minute of it.

It was hard to believe she was returning with twenty candidates, or rather nineteen candidates and one sister. Sister Camille was professed only three years and was twenty-five years old, one of the oldest of the group, but she had begged to come and had received permission from her superiors. Sister Florence was very fond of Sister Camille, who had entered the novitiate at St. Jean-de-Bassel when Sister Florence made her first profession in 1878. Their meeting this spring had inspired Sister Camille anew to go with her one-time friend to Texas as a missionary. Mother St. Andrew and all the sisters would rejoice! Every Texas parish was crying for sisters—not as in Germany, even in Alsace, where sisters had been taken for granted, and now, under Bismarck's Kulturkampf of 1871, even resented in some areas. In Texas every sister was valued highly—and worked to death!

Her eyes traveled eight seats up the aisle to where Madeleine Pfohl sat, almost overflowing into the aisle. Madeleine was her cousin, jolly, well-rounded physically and psychologically—ready for anything. If she was amused, her laughter rang out above everybody else's; if she suffered from pain, it was nearer a bellow that issued forth. Madeleine was of pioneer stock and would get along all right without being hurt. But she was not so sure about Agatha Pfohl, another relative. How can you help a person discern her future when you have met her only a few short times? Watching Agatha, she was suddenly afraid that this cousin had come for the adventure. If she doesn't show real promise, she determined, watching the girl whimpering in her sleep, she will see that Agatha is returned to her home.

And there was Marie Metz, whom she remembered so fondly meeting as she stood apple-cheeked and eager-eyed with her eighteen-year-old vitality straining at every muscle. With her entry onto the ship, and especially with the disappearance of the coast of France, Marie wilted. She was seasick all the way and was satisfied only when somebody, preferably Sister Florence, sat beside her and consoled her. Even after her recovery and on dry land, Marie was extremely dependent and timid.

As they approached New York, the whole body of passengers gathered on deck to see the new Statue of Liberty, facing them squarely and gleaming a bright copper in the August sun. The girls were as excited as Sister Florence about this statue because it had come from their homeland. The statue itself, designed by Frederic Auguste Bartholdi, and the iron framework, designed by Gustave Eiffel, had been paid for by subscription raised by the French people to commemorate the centennial of American independence.

Nobody knew better than the Alsatians the priceless treasure that independence was, buffeted back and forth as they were by France and Germany every time the two countries clashed. The statue then, shipped to New York in pieces after a long time of planning, financing, and construction, was almost completed. It would be dedicated, they knew, by President Grover Cleveland on October 28 in this year, 1886.

"We will go to see the statue tomorrow," Sister Florence promised them, and they felt very close to this new, free land.

True to her word, Sister set out on an exciting day with the group after a night in a real bed that did not rock and roll, and soaking, soapy baths in real bathtubs. They were in high spirits.

From Battery Park they boarded boats to Liberty Island, although they were told from the start that they could not go inside the statue because the interior of the base, donated by the United States, was not quite complete, and the stairway to the top on the inside was still under construction. But this did not dampen their spirits. They walked around the statue, stroking the shining bronze, thinking of dear France, to which Alsace-Lorraine no longer belonged but which the Alsatians among them still loved.

Back in the city, they walked on the busy streets and went up into the high buildings. Some of the girls purchased small items with the first American money they had ever seen.

They went one afternoon to Benziger Brothers, from whom Sister had often purchased books. There Sister Florence saw a simple German-French reader that she thought would help her teach the girls, even on the ship to Galveston. Being short of funds, she charged the books, because the congregation had an account there.

One of the reasons for lengthening the short stay in New York was that Agatha Pfohl's cousin and a relative of her own, Annie Pfohl, who was in New York, had decided to go to Castroville and enter the convent with them. Sister Florence agreed to take her, but again she asked herself what she actually knew of the girl. Just being a good Christian and a relative was not enough. Father Moye, the founder of the Congregation, had said candidates must be "self-denying and mortified, detached from everything." They must be able, he said, to suffer hardships, and have at heart the salvation of children. She knew what that meant, but it could lose its appeal when it happened day after day after day. So, now, here in front of her was her own selection of twenty young women, some perhaps quite unsure of themselves and some about whom she had some reservation.

But who was sure of herself? Sister asked in the depth of her heart. And for the first time she allowed herself to face the reality that waited in Castroville—a painful, searing reality. Although Sister Florence had been superior of one of the most important houses in the congregation for three years, the only congregational house in San Antonio, she did not yet have perpetual vows, because the sisters were not permitted to make such vows until they were thirty years old. She was not eligible, therefore, to attend the chapter that the bishop had convened for this summer. Because the recruiting trip had been planned before the chapter was convened, she was selected to go to Europe, since she could not attend the chapter anyway. Mother St. Andrew had shown great confidence in her judgment, asking her to be not only superior of a large community but even the representative of the San Antonio district on the congregational board, which helped make some major decisions for the congregation. Mother St. Andrew obviously felt quite secure in sending Sister Florence to Europe to recruit. She was grateful for her superior's confidence in her.

"Bring some more subjects like yourself," Mother told her the day she left, and this was a compliment, coming from the harassed superior.

Sister Florence's heart ached when she thought of Mother St. Andrew. Mother had not been able to keep from her close associates the agony she was undergoing. Her one-time friend Bishop J. C. Neraz, who had come to Texas from Alsace with her brother Nicholas in 1852, had been influenced by several of his diocesan priests to ask for Mother St. Andrew's resignation as superior of the congregation. Whether his antagonistic feelings were personal or whether he was under pressure from his priests, she was not sure. She was convinced that she did not know the entire situation.

Sister Florence knew Bishop Neraz quite well because he often came to St. Joseph's, where she was principal and superior, to check on the San Antonio school and to visit with the sisters and priests there. She could not have asked for better treatment from him than she received, even though she sometimes chafed under his rigidity. She therefore struggled between her love and loyalty for her superior and her respect for and friendship with the bishop.

When Mother St. Andrew told the congregational board that Bishop Neraz had asked her to resign and would formally request this at the chapter, she indicated that if the sisters would elect somebody else to take her place, it would be all right with her. But, because she had done nothing wrong, she would not abandon the sisters as their leader at the request of some priests, if the sisters wanted her to remain. Sister Florence knew that if the two obstinate, self-righteous persons, both convinced that they were doing God's will, pitted their strength against each other, the bishop was sure to win—because of his ecclesiastical position. She knew that Mother St. Andrew's fighting spirit would not be subdued easily. Whatever was to happen at this chapter had already happened by now, and she was completely ignorant of what the results were. When they had stopped over in Galveston, most sisters had not yet returned to the mission; the two who remained in Galveston during the summer and met them there seemed to be as uninformed as she was concerning the outcome.

If Bishop Neraz had succeeded in deposing Mother St. Andrew, who was now the superior? Mother St. Andrew was the one who had given her complete energy, her personal dowry, twenty excruciating years of her life to begin this congregation and bring it through heartbreak, sorrow, failure, and success to this point. There was no one of the new sisters strong enough to take up the struggle, and no one of the tried and true emigrants from the mother house in Europe was courageous enough in her old age to guide the new congregation in the face of storms battering it from every side.

What would she find when she came home with twenty candidates eager to carry on God's work in a missionary country? Would it be to a state of turmoil in the convent with a foundress in disgrace? Would the bishop openly turn the community against their superior? Would Mother St. Andrew be allowed to stay near a new superior, if one was elected in her place, to give her the benefit of her experience? She tried to organize in her own mind just why the bishop wanted Mother deposed at all. It was not clear enough to make good sense. Because they were so much alike, Mother St. Andrew and Bishop Neraz could not understand each other, it seemed to her. Mother said what she meant, and it was not always agreeable. Because the sisters' rules stated that they were not to be "familiar with" the priests, Mother insisted upon this. It was misunderstood or wrongly reported to the parish priests, who protested to the bishop that Mother was ruining their reputations with the sisters and even the laity. They demanded that Mother be deposed and, if not, they would not hear the sisters' confessions, would not serve in the parishes where the Sisters of Divine Providence taught, would not give them Communion, would even leave the diocese. But, if another sister were elected superior general, they would serve as usual in the parishes, working with the congregation and the new superior. Bishop Neraz forthwith initiated an investigation of Mother St. Andrew, during which she admitted to having made certain remarks and denied having made others, maintaining her loyalty and honesty throughout. Because much had happened since Sister Florence's departure, she had to learn of this by means of letters, few and sketchy as they were.

The priests were not satisfied with the results of the investigation, and Bishop Neraz stood by his priests because Mother had not offered any "proof" to substantiate her accusations against them. Neither could they offer any "proofs" against her. Through it all, Mother St. Andrew believed that, as in all the other trials she had passed through, God would also deliver her out of this one. Perhaps He had, Sister Florence mused; perhaps He had, and all was now serene. But she felt uneasy. She forgot her twenty candidates for the first time in many weeks, and she wept for her superior.

The rhythm of the train began to change. Sister Florence looked out the window and saw houses, stores, and grain elevators coming into view. The train whistled, spewed out volumes of steam, slowed, jerked spasmodically, jolting the twenty girls bolt upright in their seats, and then ground to a groaning halt. She looked out the window and saw, about two hundred feet ahead, the station bearing the sign "Schulenburg."

"Can we get out for a few minutes and get a drink of water?" several of the girls wanted to know. She felt her own parched throat and gave them her permission. Sister Camille was to go along. Eagerly but timidly they smoothed their skirts and hair and hastened outside, where she watched them examining everything curiously.

She noticed a priest approach the girls, look at them with great interest, and speak to the conductor, who pointed to the car where she was exercising by walking back and forth in the aisle. The priest came into the car, and she realized with great interest and excitement that he must be the pastor of High Hill, although she had never met him personally. He approached her and introduced himself.

"I am Father Valentin Schmeltzer of High Hill," he said. "You are Sister Florence, returning from Europe with a crowd of candidates, I see."

"I am very glad to see you and to come to the end of my long journey," Sister replied. "It has been a tiresome and warm trip most of the way." She hoped she did not look so tired and warm as she felt.

"There has been great excitement in Castroville," he told her. She felt that this was not the way to receive the news, whether it was good or bad. But she was trembling with curiosity, and she knew that he had met the train and sought her out to convey this news to her.

"Was Mother St. Andrew reelected?" she asked.

"No," he answered, with eyes sparkling. "The sisters elected a new superior, a fine young sister."

Sister Florence's heart sank. Only the older ones, the sisters trained at St. Jean-de-Bassel in Lorraine, were sufficiently formed, mature enough to govern the congregation, she felt. She could not bring herself to ask who this sister was who was presumptuous enough to replace Mother St. Andrew. She looked out the window and saw the girls and Sister Camille returning to the coach.

"I congratulate you, Sister Mary Florence, as the new superior of the Sisters of Divine Providence—in the independent Texas Congregation," Father Schmeltzer said as he clasped her hand warmly. "I understand that Mother St. Andrew recommended you, and Bishop Neraz was pleased with the election."

Sister Florence felt faint. Father Schmeltzer would not joke in a matter of such great moment. He would not joke with her on any matter, in fact, because their acquaintance had been so slight. So it was true.

"Thank you," she said, "for breaking the news to me. Perhaps I can become reconciled to it by the time I reach San Antonio and Castroville."

Having delivered his message, Father Schmeltzer was happy with himself, believing that for once he was ahead of the bishop. He left the train, speaking with the new candidates on the way out.

Sister Florence, unable to control her emotion, chose not to face Sister Camille and the girls yet but turned and walked blindly to the rear of the coach. There she sank down in the farthest corner and drew her veil down over her face while the tears fell. The girls, believing she was asleep, left her momentarily undisturbed.

Unable to think logically, Sister Florence shook with sobs for herself—tired, inexperienced, young—and for Mother St. Andrew—brave, strong, fearless, and now heartbroken. Her storm subsided after a brief time. "Sister Florence," she told herself, "if this is what God is calling you to do, you will obey, doing the best you can. God will help you." She felt better and she thought of the girls. Poor girls! Little did they realize what a weak young thing they would have as their reverend mother. She lifted her veil, wiped her eyes and face, and returned to her customary seat. She took out a bag of apples she had bought in Galveston for their lunch and, walking forward, gave one to each girl.

"Is something wrong, Sister?" Madeleine asked her, seeing her red and swollen eyes.

"Yes," she said. "There has been a storm in Castroville, Father said, and we have lost some of our possessions."

2

La Belle France

To be a leader in a young pioneering congregation, one needed a strong faith, a stable, mature character, vision, and determination. Sister Florence did not yet feel these qualities within herself. She felt very small and very weak, with an unbearable burden placed on her inexperienced shoulders. She flinched from the ordeal facing her and longed to throw herself into her father's strong arms as she had so often done in her childhood, knowing that he would ease the heartache and kiss away the hurt. She needed to return now to the loving presence of her family in the beautiful and peaceful village of Surbourg, as she remembered it so vividly. In order to go back to this nostalgic period of her life, she had only to close her eyes and will it. Thus she lived again the joys and sorrows of her earliest years.

Her father, Antoine Walter, had sought and courted the beautiful Madeleine Langenbronn, not from his native village of Surbourg, or from the adjoining village of Schwabsveiller, but from the larger and more picturesque village of Betschdorf, a few kilometers along the road. Madeleine was as delicate and brilliant as the azure pottery that adorned the stalls and magasin windows of the village, famous throughout France for the perfection and variety of its wares, and its Alsatian-style houses where every window displayed myriads of crimson begonias.

In 1852 at the age of twenty-four he married and brought to Surbourg his young bride of seventeen. Together they had planned and he had already constructed a simple but attractive house, built with colombages that symbolized a family united by faith and love. Madeleine was to make the house blossom with her fertile imagination, her artistic touch, and her sense of order and decor. The garden plot grew lush with vegetables, and flowers of every description blossomed in the borders, in the window boxes, and around the front lawn. Crystal and china stood primly on the tables and shelves along the walls in the airy rooms, where every day she threw back the brightly colored shutters to welcome the sunshine into the house. The walls and floors, the furniture, pots, and stove gleamed with constant polishing, and Madeleine sang as she skimmed the milk in the shining pails that her husband had brought in from the previous milking.

It was not only Madeleine's imagination that was fertile. She soon became pregnant, glowing with life and love. George was born in 1853, a lusty, squalling bundle of joy to his parents. Soon the china and the crystal had to be moved out of reach, and, by the time he was well on his feet, waddling after his father in the yard, Madeleine was carrying their second child. This one was a girl born in 1856, and named, at the father's insistence, Madeleine, after her mother.

While the family grew, so also grew the fields and gardens, the stock, and the henhouses. Antoine, like the other inhabitants of Surbourg, had not far to go to look after his possessions. His house, white with brown colombages, stood some thirty feet from the street that ran through the village, passing the "Mairie," or courthouse, where the post office was also located, the village store, the church of St. Abrogast, one of the oldest in Alsace, and the school off to the side. Then came the homes of the villagers, constructed close together with only a garden or work area between, and the barn, chickenhouse, pigsty, wood and grain storage barns behind the house. Beyond the barns were the pastures and fields, all invisible from the street, but an integral part of the family holdings.

When the husband was busy in the field, the wife sometimes gave a hand by driving the cows home in the evening, right down the main street. Sometimes the wife joined the husband in the field when harvest time came around. She also helped pick the luscious mirabelles, pears, apples, and quetsches from the numerous and generous trees, canning them for the winter months. Although Madeleine was willing to work in the field with Antoine, he preferred that she spend her energies on lighter work and be a constant companion to their lively children.

Soon, in 1858, Francoise, later to be Sister Florence, came upon the scene, which was now quite active and time-consuming. The last child, Antoine, Jr., was born in 1860. It was from this time that Francoise began to remember her family and life at home.

She remembered sitting on her father's lap in the evening to watch the sun set behind the pine trees, and listen to his stories of Jesus and the apostles, walking through the corn fields, sailing in the boat, planting the crops, and making furniture for the people of the village. She listened as he told her of Jesus' mother, much like her own mother, working in the home and helping all her neighbors. She loved the prayers he taught her, and she was soon able to walk the short distance to the old church of St. Abrogast, who had gone into the forest of Haguenau, the largest forest of the plains to be found in Alsace, and lived in a large tree as a hermit. But the Pope had called him to be bishop of his people and he had to leave his solitude.

Her little brother, Antoine, was especially dear to her, and she spent hours with him every day playing with him and teaching him to walk. The family fare, consisting of vegetables from their garden, fruit from their heavily laden trees, meat, eggs, and milk from their yard, was plentiful and tasty, with the aroma of freshly baked bread and mirabelle pie filling the house, which had been enlarged during the past few years.

"Can we help you, Mama?" the little girls asked their mother. She let them churn the rich cream into butter, place the bedding in the windows to freshen it after a night's use, and scrub with a brush the hard and constantly gleaming floor. Outside, they ran and shouted up the long rows of corn, and they carried in vegetables for the family meals. There were always long thin loaves of bread to be broken and dipped into cool glasses of milk. The chickens, cows, and pigs were their friends, each having his or her own name and personality. It was a pleasure to watch their father milk the cows, and sheer ecstasy to ride with him on the horse-drawn mower. In rare moments they invented games to play together while their mother talked with her neighbor over the garden fence.

"Every French mademoiselle can sew and embroider and play a musical instrument," their mother told them as she taught and supervised them in the arts considered appropriate for their culture and station in life.

As the children grew old enough, their parents enrolled them in the parish school across from the church, where the Sisters of Divine Providence both lived and taught. The school stood at the corner, almost as though holding out its arms to the village children who turned in off the main street. Upstairs and downstairs housed the classrooms, girls together and boys together, and the wooden steps creaked with each ascent and descent of the pupils. When Mass time came, they filed into the church, with boys occupying the right front pews and girls the left. The sisters knelt behind them, monitoring their behavior during the Latin Mass, which they did not understand but sometimes felt deeply. The sisters were a profound mystery in their long black robes, gliding silently through the church and the school, lively and friendly on the playground, but stern and firm in the classroom. Like other children, the Walters were sometimes naughty, deserving rebukes and punishment, but they were all bright and loved to learn. As a rule they brought home good reports, which their parents expected but did not demand or praise excessively. Francoise practiced dutifully on her violin.

Reflecting back on all this now, Sister Florence thought warmly of the time the family spent together, growing, loving, laughing, praying, not bound to this house and this family but born for the service of God's people. The house that was built with just this in mind sheltered and protected them, but, when the time came, it opened its doors, letting out the young family and letting in the poor and suffering.

"You must be proud to be French," their parents told them often and fervently. "France is a beautiful country, with many great heroes, whom you should know and revere. French is the most beautiful of all languages. To speak it perfectly is the ideal way to express love and honor for your country." They knew their country's history and loved the flag of France.

News of the world came to Surbourg in rare newspapers and by word of mouth. While the boys were working in the field side by side with their father, and the girls were at home, much more ominous and insidious events were taking place in Europe, including their own dear France, especially in Alsace and Lorraine, which were situated next to the German border. Bismarck was planning his strategy. Napoleon III knew this but failed to acknowledge France's vulnerability. While French statesmen debated endlessly how best to build an invincible army, and Napoleon wavered between what he knew and what he dreamed, the military law of 1818, which conscripted soldiers by lot, continued. This method was ineffective because the "unfortunate" young men who drew the "bad" numbers could buy replacements if they had money. The poor youths who drew "bad" numbers had no choice but to serve. Because army life was not a young Frenchman's ideal, army morale was low. Napoleon made sure, however, that it looked good. He demonstrated with pride, even before his foes, the elaborate uniforms and formations, hoping, no doubt, that this impressive-looking group would appear invincible. The French people as a whole believed in him and lived in security, never suspecting the bitter truth.

Young George Walter wanted least in the world to be a soldier. He loved the peacefulness of Surbourg, the quiet family life, the evening devotions in the church and home. He was a farmer at heart, but physically his heart was not strong. As was the custom in the villages of Alsace, when a young man reached the age to draw his number, the family made a novena of prayers and penance that he would draw a "good" number. And so it was with the Walters. But, while the family waited outside together in prayerful silence, George drew a "bad" number. Gloom descended on the household from that moment. Antoine could not afford to buy a replacement, and he knew besides that every able-bodied man who could go would be pressed into service to preserve the country's freedom. Not being a politician, he did not know the true condition of the country. He had faith in his political leaders, much as he had faith in his church leaders. So he accepted the inevitable, trying to convince himself and his family that George would help keep "la belle France" free. George had no illusions about his prowess. Too upset to eat dinner after he had to kill a chicken for the noon meal, he knew that he would be useless in battle. His mother suffered every agonizing moment with him.

When the family bid him goodbye that gloomy fall morning and watched him depart in the softly falling rain, their tears as well as his mingled with nature's compassion for a sensitive young son of France. For George never saw battle or his family again. After a brief and agonizing period of training and rough life in the army camp, he was confined to bed. His family soon received word that he had died of illness, not in battle. Because the war was going badly, the army was in great confusion; the body was not returned to Surbourg, and George was buried without his family's presence.

Francoise could never blot from her memory the grief of her family at this loss, which was so closely followed by the capitulation of France, and the ceding of Alsace and Lorraine to Germany in the Armistice of January 28, 1871. She was thirteen years old, Madeleine was fifteen, and Antoine was eleven.

While Madeleine helped her mother in the house, Francoise wandered restlessly through the village. She visited the sisters regularly and helped in the church.

"Mama," she reported, scandalized, one day on returning home, "the Germans used the sisters' new chapel at St. Jean-de-Bassel to keep their horses in during the war. Only now can they clean it out and finish the construction." Her mother also felt deeply this desecration.

The time had come for Francoise to make a decision. She had finished school, as far as Surbourg was concerned. But she thirsted for knowledge and service to others. She felt that, much

as she loved her home and family, hers was not to be the lot
of a farmer's wife there. She needed more space, more challenge.
The sisters, teachers, were an inspiration to her in their life and
in their work. She consulted her family. Suffering from the
useless sacrifice of George's death and the humiliation of having
to live under German law and speak German as a national
language in preference to French, they agreed that Francoise
could be of greater service to the church and country as a
religious teacher, if that was what she wanted.

"We have brought you into the world and taught you to be
a person. Every person should serve God and his people in some
way. The right way is for each to decide. It is not for the parents,
who have made their own decision. All we ask is that you do
not waste your wonderful life or be miserable."

It was a heartrending departure in the fall of 1872, and,
for young Antoine, now twelve, a real crucifixion. He and
Francoise had been inseparable from the day he had been born.
"You will give up everything you love but God," he wept, "but,
as long as I live, I will give you anything you ask for. You can
count on that."

Her mother and Madeleine helped prepare her trousseau, and
the family put together part of their savings for her dowry. Then
she kissed the walls of the home, her comfortable bed, the statues
and pictures. She told the cows, the pigs, and the chickens
goodbye. She walked up to the cemetery and down the street
to the post office for the last time. Her family made the long
trip with her to St. Jean-de-Bassel near Berthelming. Here they
placed her in the loving care of the Sisters of Divine Providence.

"We are proud of your decision to follow this vocation," her
father told her as he embraced her in parting, "but, if after a
while you find you have no vocation to this life, we will welcome
you back with joy."

It was a hard parting, and the institutional life she was entering
was a foreign world to her. Never had she seen such large and
high buildings. The dormitory where she was taken on the third
floor was filled with beds where all the postulants slept. Silence
was required there at all times. The huge dining rooms, too, were

crowded with tables and chairs, and no one could talk at table. Long dark halls and winding stairways, dusky basements running from end to end under the main floors, airy attics where occasionally a few novices or sisters slept kept Francoise and the other postulants occupied for a few days while they became acquainted with one another and accustomed to the routine of the convent. She liked best the gardens with flowers and vegetables, the fields and pastures and stock. She felt more free outdoors. She found the patio a bit stuffy, but she loved the forest park with its walkways and majestic trees. Eventually she became absorbed in her studies and her spiritual training, which she took very seriously. Her home training stood her in good stead during the postulate and novitiate when she scrubbed floors, ironed linen, picked and canned fruit, and strove to obey her superiors perfectly. She always found time to study. This was a real consolation to her. Kind as the sisters were to her and much as she loved her companions with whom she conversed and laughed, they could not replace her loving family, who made the long trip to St. Jean-de-Bassel for her special occasions such as entrance into the novitiate and first profession. During these years she developed some enduring friendships—especially the one with Sister Marie Houlne, a brilliant and charming sister who entered the convent in 1878 and received the habit in 1880. These two young women instantly recognized one another's leadership and strong personality. They became lifelong friends and confidantes. Other sisters whom she met at this time—Sisters Arsene Schaef, Berthilde Thiel in her own class, and Camille Karlskind, a few years younger—were to play a part in her future.

Previous to 1871 the sisters had taught in the primary schools, where they were sent with a *lettre d'obedience,* a sort of certificate from the congregation stating that they had completed the prescribed courses required for the grades they were to teach. The "Loi Falloux" of 1852 had given them this privilege. But in 1871 under Bismarck the sisters were required to take the examination at Nancy in French or in one of several other cities in German. Other requirements odious to the sisters were added later. Eventually they were all required to take the German examination and to teach in German.

Francoise came on the educational scene at this time. She began her studies in 1872 and passed her examination first in French at Nancy, by her own choice, and later in Selestat in German, when she saw that it would be required for future certification. But her heart was never in the German language, because it had been ruthlessly forced on the conquered. She resented it consistently.

Two events of 1878 deeply affected the life of Francoise, who was now known as Sister Mary Florence. Her sister, Madeleine, always less aggressive and more domestic than she, fell in love with and married Alois Grüner at the age of twenty-two. The young couple left Surbourg for Reichshoffen to make their home. But Madeleine was homesick for her family, and, when Eugene was born to her in 1879, the birth took place in her parents' house in Surbourg. When she suffered a miscarriage in 1881, it was to Surbourg that she came to recuperate, in the presence of her loving family. Sister Florence was unable to be with her family on either occasion, and she felt the privation.

A second disturbing experience occurred in 1878 as she was preparing for her first assignment. An epidemic of typhoid fever struck the convent of St. Jean-de-Bassel. The sisters had always spent much time in the patio, walled in on four sides by high buildings. The patio was blamed for the epidemic.

"It is the humid, oppressive atmosphere of the patio, often damp under the heavily leafed trees and too low for proper drainage that causes the fever," the superiors decided. Therefore, after a few untimely deaths and numerous cases of serious illness, which affected Sister Florence only slightly, they made some momentous decisions and promises. A number of trees would be removed, the land would be filled in, the top part of one building at each end would be removed to let in the air, and a crucifix would be constructed in the center of the patio. Each year a day would be set aside by the congregation for prayer, penance, and a procession to the cross if the epidemic would cease and no more sisters would be lost. The epidemic ceased and the promise was kept. When she had fully recovered from the fever, Sister Florence went on her first mission to Fegersheim, somewhat similar to the village of Surbourg.

In the meantime the educational system in Alsace-Lorraine, now in Germany, had run into trouble with the people. It ruled that boys and girls would be taught together. The sisters refused to take charge of such schools, and parents demanded that the former state of education be restored. Surprisingly enough, the parents prevailed. However, relations between the religious teachers and the education department remained tense. Sister Florence was qualified to teach in German as well as in French, but, like the other sisters in the "Protestant German schools," she believed it was her duty to keep alive the Catholic and the French traditions for the pupils. This was a delicate situation requiring a great deal of tact as well as a bit of secrecy.

"They can take the religion out of the schools and make us speak German, but they can't ever make us German!" Sister Florence said, remembering her parents' careful training in the French language. "Besides, it gives me a great deal of satisfaction to outwit the department."

The ministers of education, however, were gradually replacing the sisters with lay teachers. Sister Florence felt that the time would come when the sisters would be completely eliminated from the schools. Therefore she began to think of other alternatives. She was not alone with this fear, and it was a real one. Between 1880 and 1888 the congregation lost sixty-one teaching positions, and there were suppression of classes, replacement by lay teachers, a revocation of certificates not valid under German administration. Mother Anna Houlne, not knowing how far this movement would lead, eventually offered the services of the institute to Bishop Maes of Covington, Kentucky.

But, before this step was taken, Mother St. Andrew Feltin came from Texas, looking for volunteers for her community. Sister Florence, like all who listened to Mother, was moved by her stories. She thought of her own Alsatian countrymen in America thirsting for religion and knowledge, and the natives of the country—black, brown, and red—who had no one to teach them.

"How I would love to give myself to this missionary work. I feel that God really needs me in this faraway land where the people have a chance to be free—if only they had an education!"

She prayed long and fervently before making her decision. One day she presented herself before the indefatigable little woman from Texas and looked deeply into the intense dark eyes.

"I feel that I am more needed in Texas than I am here. I am strong and willing to do whatever is required of me. I want to be a part of your community if you will accept me."

Mother St. Andrew studied Sister Florence with a penetrating gaze, which seemed to Sister Florence to examine her entire life and intentions. Then Mother opened her arms and clasped the young sister within them.

"You will add great strength to the congregation and to me," she said, almost in awe as she measured the physical beauty, the regal carriage, and the frank determination of the sister before her, sufficiently educated and experienced to perform great things for the struggling young congregation.

"But how can I tell my family? The time is so short."

Mother St. Andrew arranged for her to spend the last days at her home in Surbourg. It was a happy time but a sad one, for they all believed they would never meet again in this world. As before, her parents gave their blessing, saying that her mission was not to them but to the world, and Antoine promised his support anew. Dear, dear generous and loving Antoine. He had never wavered in his devotion to her.

Fear mingled with excitement as the group, consisting of Mother St. Andrew, four sisters, four novices, and innumerable boxes of statues, vestments, chalices, monstrances, candlesticks, and other chapel objects that Mother had collected to take back to Castroville, boarded the *St. Laurent,* a French steamer, at Le Havre the latter part of July. Besides Sister Florence, those who volunteered were Sisters Berthilde Thiel, Luca Denniger, and Rosine Vonderscher, carrying their violins, which they would need for teaching singing. The novices were Sisters Anna Ehrismann, Mary Buechler, Augusta Rudloff, and Florida Seyler. It was an exciting trip for them all. The young sisters never ceased to be amazed at Mother St. Andrew, so vigorous, ingenious, and uninhibited in her dealing with them and with all others on the ship. She taught them English, sang and prayed with them, and prepared them for life in Texas. Her enthusiasm was infectious. She also arranged for them to spend three days in New York, where they arrived on August 7, an experience Sister Florence determined to provide for the young ladies she was bringing home today.

Then Sister reverted once more to her early summer experience, painful in one respect. When she had been asked to make the recruiting trip, she did not know how she would find her sister. Madeleine had given birth to a baby girl, Mary, in 1883, but her mother wrote that Madeleine was not doing well. In 1885 a third child, Maria Josepha, was born, only to die two weeks later. From this date Madeleine continued to decline. Sister Florence's one hope, when she was chosen to make the trip, was to see her sister in better health once more. Instead, she saw her on her deathbed. Only two days after her arrival in Surbourg in May, Madeleine died, leaving two small children with her husband, who was determined to take care of them the best he could. Sister Florence's mother, not strong herself, she soon discovered, would do all she could for the children, with the help of her husband and Antoine. When she left her home only a few weeks earlier, Sister found her parents the last evening standing hand in hand in the garden, completely oblivious of everything except each other.

They have become so much a part of each other, she thought, that they could not live without one another.

Antoine, now twenty-six, unmarried, and living at home, had told her that he would one day take a wife and have his own family. He deserved his own life, and their parents would be adequately cared for at the same time. It was all she could ask for.

She recalled that seeing the barren, scorched, and brown plains in Texas in 1880 had shocked her, used as she was to the lush green vegetation of Alsace and Lorraine. She could not fathom the immensity of the barren spaces, devoid of tree or dwelling. No church steeple reached into the sky amid red-roofed buildings nestled on the hillside. There were no hillsides, no red roofs, no forests. The heat, like today's, had been overpowering, and she opened her eyes to glance anxiously at the girls. Indeed, she had left Alsace and arrived in Texas for the second time, afraid now for different reasons than she had been on her first arrival, but trusting as she had on her first in an ever-present Providence, who would give her the courage she needed.

3
Mother St. Andrew

Looking out the train window, the weary travelers saw the houses begin to multiply, coming nearer and nearer to the tracks until soon on the scraggly burned lawns back of their houses children stood with hungry eyes as the train passed by. Tired clothes flapped on the lines in the August heat, waiting for housewives to remove their limp privacy from the public scrutiny. The rails began to separate, giving the train some choice, which it seemed hesitant to take. It slowed, stopped, backed, lurched forward, panted to a stop, was jerked violently forward again as the porter entered the car and sang out, "San Antonio! This car has been switched to the Western branch. Stay on this car for La Coste, Del Rio, and points West. San Antonio!"

"Thank God we don't have to change!" Sister Florence said, settling back in the hard seat, which felt as though it had become a part of her.

"Can't we see your school?" the girls asked eagerly, knowing from her conversation that she was very fond of her new building there at St. Joseph's.

"I wish we could!" she said fervently. If she could just walk up Bonham Street and into the front door! If only she could go to the kitchen for a glass of cool water and then stretch her weary body on her own bed one night, she might be ready to face the future. But it was not to be so, and she had learned not to indulge in self-pity. She must get to Castroville tonight with her twenty charges, and plan her life anew from there. If she had known what the future held for her, would she have had the courage to return at all?

The train stopped, and so did her heart, for there on the platform just outside her window stood her pastor from St. Joseph's, Father Henry Pefferkorn, and Bishop J. C. Neraz, looking directly at her. As the coach door opened, they both entered as fast as their combined clerical and pontifical dignity permitted, and came directly to her. Bishop Neraz grasped her hand warmly in both of his.

"Welcome home," he said cordially, "and congratulations! I am here to tell you officially that the sisters have elected you to be their new superior general. I am, as I am sure you know, very happy with their choice. I approve it completely, and I ask God's blessing on you."

Father Pefferkorn also took her hand. "We will miss you sorely at St. Joseph's, but we bow to the greater good."

Sister Florence believed that the great lump in her throat and the tears behind her eyelids would surely strangle her. It took her a few moments with head bowed to control her emotions.

"Your Excellency," she said at last, lifting her head and focusing her large sorrowful brown eyes on his, "you forget that I have not the required age, nor have I yet made my perpetual vows. There must be some mistake."

"Sister Florence," Bishop Neraz answered firmly, "I am your highest superior, and your only one. I dispense you from these requirements."

Sister suddenly recalled Father Schmeltzer's words at the station in Schulenburg, ". . . in the independent Texas Congregation." It had puzzled her at the time, but other concerns had flooded in so fast that she had forgotten it. Now Bishop Neraz had said, "I am your highest superior and your only one."

"What about Reverend Mother Anna at St. Jean-de-Bassel? Mother Adrienne appointed Mother St. Andrew as superior in Texas, and Mother Constantine and Mother Anna renewed the appointment."

"That no longer stands," he said brusquely. "We will talk about it later. Here is my written approval," he said, handing her an envelope. "The sisters are still in Castroville, and tomorrow they will render you their obedience. Don't look so distressed, my child! I will come to help you at nine-thirty in the morning. You will be a good superior general, and the sisters will come to love you as they already respect you."

He held her hand warmly, spoke briefly to the girls, and was gone.

There was no longer any secrecy. Those closest to Sister had heard the entire conversation carried on in French and passed it up the aisle. They were delighted to be the first to know the new superior general. They had no doubt that she loved them in a special way. Already they envisioned themselves as recipients of special favors at her hand. As the train began to move, they were in high spirits, full of questions and suggestions as to what she might or might not do.

Sister Camille was jubilant. "Will you now be called 'Reverend Mother'?" she asked. Sister saw that a great deal of patience was going to be necessary during the next hours toward Sister Camille, who knew her best, and toward the other nineteen young ladies, who had completely revived after their brief stop in San Antonio, and the unexpected news. The day's heat was also lessening, now that the sun had set.

"I suppose so," she answered. "I really don't know how it will be. We shall just have to wait."

"Will you send me to Galveston?" Sister Camille asked. "I liked it there. And Sisters Scholastica and Celestine were very friendly."

"You cannot ask for special favors, Sister Camille, even though I knew you in Alsace and brought you to Texas. God knows where you are needed." She already felt like the superior general, and she did not like what she felt. "Let's not talk about it any more."

The train, interminably slow until now, sped over the flat pastureland, past fields of grain freshly harvested and stacked, giving off an acrid, warm fragrance, past herds of cattle standing in quiet groups, chewing their cud and switching their tails to keep away the flies after the evening milking, past vegetable farms with empty rows and wilted discards strewn through the plots. The dwarfed cotton plants had matured early in the dry summer heat. Already in many fields the pickers were weighing in their sacks, squinting at the scales in the quickening dusk, and heaving the heavy bags over the high boards onto the wagon boxes. Sister Florence felt weaker and weaker as the miles flew by, until quite suddenly and unexpectedly the train slowed and came to a complete stop.

"La Coste! La Coste!" the porter called into the car. He began to take boxes and bags to the door. But his services were hardly necessary for the girls as each one seized her own luggage. Sister Florence had insisted that they carry no sacks or boxes— only their valises. They struggled to the exit. This was the last time they would have to get off the train, they reminded one another with much laughter. Just one more ride and they would be there.

Sister Florence sighed. It would have simplified matters so much for the congregation if Castroville had agreed to accept the railroad station in 1881 when the Texas-New Orleans Railway decided to extend west from San Antonio. But the conservative Castroville residents did not want the kind of traffic through their village that this station would cause. The train therefore went through La Coste, some five miles away. The increasing travel of sisters and students to Castroville required constant transportation from Castroville to La Coste and from La Coste to Castroville, necessary and on call. It was becoming increasingly difficult and burdensome. Mother St. Andrew had really counted on this railroad's going through Castroville when she built up the congregational center here. The railroad continued to expand, until in 1882 it had the longest track in Texas, and by 1884 it was part of the first continental route from New York to San Francisco and many other parts of the United States. It would have made all the difference to the congregation and to Castroville! Looking at the situation with the new eyes of a superior general, Sister Florence knew that the congregational base would eventually have to move to a railroad center.

"What a procession!" laughed Sister Florence, peering through the dark, for there were five carriages and a wagon for the trunks, all lined up with drivers, the sisters' friends and neighbors, ready to help the travelers get themselves and their luggage together into the conveyances. In a surprisingly short time they were on their way, laughing and singing, the cool night air soothing their sweaty faces.

They approached the Medina River, spanned by no bridge but, fortunately for them, with only a bare trickle of water flowing, because no rains had swollen it for many weeks or even months. The carriage procession slowly picked its way down to the riverbed, where the horses waded across the water amid shouts of joy from the occupants, and up the hill on the other side. Sister Florence thought of the many painful waits, marooned in their convent home, for the river to fall enough so that the horses could get across with or without wagons. Surely a bridge could be built, which would stabilize this community and make it independent of the elements for its life.

Coming up out of the riverbed, they saw before them the great house, standing out of the darkness ahead. As the carriages drew up in a line at the main entrance to the convent in Castroville, lights appeared everywhere. Oil lamps and candles sitting in windows and doors began to move, showing their bearers coming down the walk toward the carriages. Speaking animatedly in German and French, the sisters originally from Europe crowded around, not only to greet Sister Florence and the girls, but to hear news of home.

Mother St. Andrew, Sisters Angelique, Ange, and Arsene embraced Sister Florence and asked if she had heard the news. Sister Florence looked anxiously at Mother St. Andrew in the candlelight, but she saw no unusual signs of distress on the face of one who had already withstood so much. Mother said nothing of her feelings. Going to Sister Camille and each girl, she greeted them and tried to recall whose daughters they were and where she had seen them before.

"I didn't bring my glasses out, and it is too dark here to see you properly. Anyway you will look better after a bath and a good night's sleep. So I shall take a thorough look at you in the morning." Each girl was taken in hand by at least one sister and led into the convent, which was to be her future home. Sister Florence went with Mother St. Andrew and a few of the sisters, first to the chapel, and then to the community room, where she told of her meeting with Father Schmeltzer in Schulenburg and with Father Pefferkorn and Bishop Neraz in San Antonio.

"Bishop Neraz said he would be here at nine-thirty tomorrow morning, so I suppose all the sisters must be told," she said.

For the first time, she saw bitterness on Mother St. Andrew's face and heard it in her voice. "Sister Florence, I don't want to spoil your first night's rest, but I suppose you will have to get used to sleepless nights soon enough. I just want to tell you that the bishop has taken over our congregation, and we are from now on to do only what he says. He has forced a separation from St. Jean-de-Bassel and made himself head of the congregation. It breaks my heart more than anything I have undergone so far."

"But how could he take over? We are a branch of St. Jean-de-Bassel, under the government of Mother Anna and the Bishop of Metz. How could Bishop Neraz say that he is our highest and only superior?"

"I have not told you all the difficulties I have been having along that line. I trusted that before I left this office we would have worked out our problems in a satisfactory manner. But now I realize that the one problem, as far as priests are concerned, was simply used as 'evidence' to obtain a point more important in the bishop's mind. It was to separate the Texas branch from the European congregation and make it diocesan, completely under his jurisdiction. I would never agree to this, and neither would Mother Anna. Therefore, the only way it could come about was to depose me and to literally take over the congregation by force, make it diocesan, and declare himself superior."

"Was there no choice, no option?"

"At chapter yesterday the sisters were given two options. I tell you this now, tired as you are after your travels, because Bishop Neraz will be here tomorrow and you need this background information."

"I will listen all night if necessary. I am at a distinct disadvantage, not having been at chapter and not knowing the history of this problem. I cannot accept this responsibility blindly or accede to something I do not understand."

Mother St. Andrew then, as it were, uncorked the bottle, and the explosive contents were absorbed by the small group of sisters present. During the past years Mother St. Andrew had become aware of what she considered abuses in some of the houses of the congregation. She had had experiences previous to this time of seeing some priests in the parishes take advantage of the ignorance and lack of maturity of some of the sisters in the parish school. One example was in the Polish mission of Panna Maria and St. Hedwig in 1874, when the pastor persuaded the sisters to withdraw from the Castroville mother house and become affiliated with the Immaculates in Poland. The superior of the Immaculates in Poland, Mother Marcellena, however, objected to this plan, and Father Felix Zwiardowski had to come up with a new plan.

When Bishop Dominic Pellicer was appointed in 1875, Father Felix had many conferences with the new bishop and they became good friends. Bishop Pellicer made him one of his consultants and "superior of all the missions of the teaching sisters and the clergy, whether secular or religious, and the vicar general for the Polish missions." With these powers, Father Felix set up his own congregation, consisting of Mother St. Andrew's sisters, in his parish, holding investiture on Quinquagesima Sunday, 1875, and clothing them in the blue habit with the rule of the Sisters of the Immaculate Conception.

"If I had failed in their formation, Father Felix failed even more seriously. The project was completely unsuccessful. The sisters returned after a short time to their own homes, and the Polish girls who had come to the Castroville convent from Panna Maria and St. Hedwig's also left and returned to their homes. This loss to the small congregation was very disheartening."

"I recall hearing of this," Sister Florence said. "I often wondered why the sisters could have been so easily swayed by the priest."

"Because they were young and insufficiently formed. I was so pressured to staff the Polish schools that I sent the sisters there because they could speak the language, before they knew what it was to be Sisters of Divine Providence. They were not prepared."

"Did this happen in other instances?"

"Yes," Mother said. "I made the same mistake again and again. I was a long time learning because I always trusted their good common sense and their faith. But they did not have the staunch faith that we knew in Europe. St. Joseph's was another case." She related the story painfully.

"Two years later, in 1877, trouble arose in St. Joseph's, San Antonio, as you have heard, but perhaps not in detail. My brother, Father Nicholas Feltin, was pastor. I sent Sister Virginia Koehler, an annually professed sister, to St. Joseph's, along with three other sisters. Sister Virginia and her sister, Sister Angela, also annually professed, became embroiled in a dispute which they brought back to the convent when they returned. Wrongly or rightly, I believed Sister Angela, and I changed Sister Virginia from St. Joseph's. My brother was very upset by this change. He said that Sister Angela's story was not true. But I felt that she had told me the truth, so I did not change the assignment. The sister's father, Mr. Koehler, learning of the trouble, came onto the scene, also agreeing with Sister Angela. He accused Father Feltin not only of attempting to win the affection of his daughter, but even of trying to poison him. He obtained a warrant for the arrest of my brother. As you can imagine, as soon as the arrest took place, the German and English papers of San Antonio printed the story. Both charges of Mr. Koehler, of course, were false and ridiculous, but the last story was even more false and ridiculous still. It was to cause me much heartache. They said that I had caused my brother's arrest because of our disagreement. The scandal was very great. When the case came before the court, Judge George Noonan dismissed it for lack of evidence. The newspapers acknowledged their mistakes about the story they had released. But it was too late to undo the harm that had been done." Mother was silent for a long time in order to gain mastery of her emotions.

"These sisters left, too, didn't they?" Sister Florence asked gently.

Mother went on to say that Bishop Pellicer delved to the bottom of this case and tried to effect a reconciliation among all concerned. But the two sisters responsible for the commotion returned to their home, and three other sisters, all young and impressionable, also left the congregation. Father Feltin's relations with his sister never returned to normal during the year he lived following this event. However, when he died in 1878, Mother St. Andrew was at his bedside.

"It was painful to me that his last years should have been so unhappy through such foolish mistakes. I tried to make it up to him."

"Were there more such incidents?" Sister Florence prodded her superior.

"There were. However, by this time I knew that I must obtain more sisters who were truly formed in the European mother house, who could also train the newcomers properly and be a solid example to them of religious living. So I had gone to St. Jean-de-Bassel, where I was able to recruit a large number of sisters. This helped considerably, but I will briefly give you the most recent events which brought about the situation we are facing now. It took place this year in New Braunfels."

Sister Christine Fuercher, a young sister, was imprudent, not only in her relations with the pastor, Father Joseph Kirch, but in carrying stories back and forth concerning Mother St. Andrew and her attempts to remedy the situation. She was responsible in this way for involving Sister Ange, who directed the young sisters, by repeating incorrectly the message Mother St. Andrew reportedly sent through her concerning the priest. What she relayed was to be used against Mother St. Andrew in words other than those actually spoken. It was reported to Father Kirch and by him to other priests, especially Father Pefferkorn, and to Bishop Neraz, that Mother St. Andrew had told the sisters and novices, and even members of the laity, that no priest was to be trusted. "Beware of all priests without exception."

"So the priests took this as a personal affront."

"Yes, Bishop Neraz listened to his priests before anybody else. Some of them objected to me because I insisted that the sisters maintain their rule of enclosure and not spend their recreation hour with the clergy." Mother admitted that she was rigid with the sisters, for experience had taught her that, in their youth and innocence, or ignorance, they were easily influenced by lonely priests seeking a bit of diversion. Besides, the rules, incomplete as they were when she brought them from Europe to Texas in 1866, insisted that the sisters devote themselves to the development of their interior life, their religious community, and their teaching or other works, and that they not carry on social relationships with the clergy or laity. They were asked to make hard sacrifices for God, who in turn blessed their lives and work.

"Yes, I understand your position," Sister Florence assured Mother.

"A number of priests who were unhappy with me composed a letter setting forth their grievances. To make matters worse, they dredged up the old story about my alleged treatment of my brother, Father Feltin, although I had long since been cleared of this charge. It was so unfair," she sighed bitterly.

She went on in a moment to tell that they asked the bishop that she be deposed and another sister be elected in her place. Otherwise they would refuse to work in the same parishes with the Sisters of Divine Providence, would not hear the sisters' confessions, and would leave the diocese if they were required to do otherwise. They added, however, that, if another sister were chosen to replace Mother St. Andrew, they would work with the sisters and cooperate in every way. This was signed by Fathers Henry Pefferkorn, John Kirch, Joseph Wack, and Peter Tarrillion, and dated June 29, 1886, while Sister Florence was eagerly going about her recruiting in Europe. Most of the information was entirely new to her.

"Because the priests administer the sacraments and because we are dependent on the sacraments, it seems we are always to be controlled by the priests," Sister Florence mused. "It doesn't seem right, but go on."

On July 28 Bishop Neraz gave a commission to Father Richard J. Maloney, OMI, and Father George Feith, S.M., with Father Pefferkorn as secretary, to act as a committee to "examine a question brought to the bishop's attention by some priests of the diocese." They were told to ask the twenty-one questions listed, write down the answers with proofs, and return the report to the bishop. This they did faithfully. To some of the questions, Mother answered affirmatively, adding that she made such a statement with good reason. But to the question about speaking ill of the priests to sisters, novices, and persons from the outside, her answer was a firm "No." To the question "Did you in private or public tell your sisters or your novices to beware of priests, and that without exception?" the answer was also "No."

Sister Ange, sitting mostly in silence during the narration of this history, interjected here that another of the questions asked was "Did you say that you were not afraid of any ecclesiastical court, even if the Pope were there?" "You know what Mother's answer was because it was so typical of her: 'I would not be afraid of defending my cause before an ecclesiastical court, even if the Pope were present.' "

Because no "proof" was offered either by the priests or by Mother St. Andrew, but only words, it was not an easy case to handle. On August 17, however, after a meeting of the bishop's council, the Sisters of Divine Providence in Castroville received a report of seven statements based on the questions and answers of the trial, the resolutions the four priests had sent to the bishop on July 29, a statement of the meeting of the bishop's council on August 16, and the following four conditions that the Sisters of Divine Providence were to submit to:

1. That the congregation or community must require that Mother St. Andrew hand in her resignation and cease being superior of the Congregation of the Sisters of Divine Providence in this country, and that another sister

be named in her place by those sisters who have a right
to vote;

2. That hereafter, any difficulty between priests and religious must be submitted to the arbitration of His Excellency, the Bishop of the Diocese;

3. That hereafter, any accusation against a priest or religious must be accompanied by solid proofs and be
given only to His Excellency, the Bishop of the Diocese;

4. That these accusations, if there be any, be confided to
no one other than to His Excellency, the Bishop of the
Diocese.

Sister Florence sat very quiet, almost in disbelief at the extent
to which these priests would go to protect themselves from alleged
criticism, justified or not; and the degree of tolerance Mother St.
Andrew manifested. She felt a twinge of shame for her parish
pastor, Father Pefferkorn, for whom not only all the sisters in
his school, but Mother St. Andrew as well, had given so much
physical and psychic energy since its beginning. Mother St. Andrew
continued: "The election date was set for August 26. This did
not leave us much time to prepare for the chapter. It is true that
all the sisters except you and the two taking care of the house
in Galveston were on retreat. Only thirty sisters were perpetually
professed and thirty years old, and so were eligible to vote."

"Bishop Neraz came," Mother continued, "and the thirty
sisters met. Although we had never had chapter of elections here
before, I knew from St. Jean-de-Bassel that at an election the
sisters are supposed to vote according to their conscience, and
the sisters understood that, too."

When the sisters had assembled and the bishop had led them
in a prayer to the Holy Ghost for guidance, he read again the
four conditions stated previously in his letter and called for a
vote. Like bewildered children, the sisters, taken unaware and
unused to making major decisions in a hurry, blindly wrote,
"Mother St. Andrew."

The bishop was visibly angry.

"I read you my statement saying that Mother St. Andrew
should resign and another sister be elected. Since this was not

done, I will hereby depose her. You now have a choice: either elect a sister to replace her, or I will put you under the direction of another congregation."

"I felt sorry for the sisters," Mother St. Andrew said. "I looked from Sister Angelique to Sister Ange, both pillars of the new and old congregations. They could hold the congregation together for a while, I thought. But both shook their heads, indicating that they would not consider taking such a responsibility. I thought of you, Sister Florence. I always thought that someday you would lead the congregation, but I did not know it would be so soon. I could not think of letting all our work, all our plans, all our struggles and sufferings go to someone else, who, as in the case of Panna Maria and the Immaculates, did not even want us. So I said, 'Vote for Sister Florence.' I left the room and the congregation—to the decision they would make. The votes cast were twenty-three for you, Sister Florence, and six scattered, Sister Angelique and Sister Ange receiving four of them. Sister Florence, please accept the cross placed on your young shoulders. It is sudden, but you can learn fast."

Sister Florence wept, taking and kissing the hands of one who had been a mother to her.

"And Bishop Neraz is my highest superior?" she asked wonderingly.

"That will be your biggest cross. In fact, that, it seems to me, is behind everything. A few grumblings from priests are not so powerful as a desire to have a large congregation completely within his authority. Bishop Neraz wanted the Texas branch separated from the European congregation from the time he was named bishop in 1881. I have been against this all the time. As you know, the finest members of our congregation were professed sisters or novices trained at St. Jean-de-Bassel. I saw, after twelve years here, after the Panna Maria and St. Joseph's debacles, that I would not be able to stabilize this congregation without good, mature, educated, and well-trained sisters. I could not find them here, because girls marry at a very young age. I tried accepting the girls too young, but that did not work, as you saw in Panna Maria and St. Joseph's and New Braunfels. So in three separate trips I recruited thirty-two sisters and novices from the European mother house, besides other girls from France and Germany. Mother Constantine Eck, seeing the situation created by the political condition in Europe, was eager to have a branch of the congregation in the United States where sisters might have the option to go if matters worsened in Europe."

"I suppose I might not have come if I had had any idea that the Texas branch would ever separate from St. Jean-de-Bassel. I love our mother congregation," Sister Florence said.

"You know that you chose this option yourself, not to separate from the European congregation but to live and work in an atmosphere more to your liking. Moreover, our roots are there; we are using the rules from there. Bishop Dubuis, whom I always considered our protector and ecclesiastical head here in Texas, did not intend for us to separate. Certainly Mother Constantine did not envision this. And the fact that Mother Anna allowed Sister Camille to come to Texas this summer with you leads me to believe she still considers Texas a branch and not an independent congregation. Did you find this to be so when you talked with Mother Anna this summer?"

"In no way did Mother Anna hint at a separation. It was not even mentioned. She asked for volunteers to go back with me, and Sister Camille was the only one. The sisters were all interested in our community and very favorably disposed toward it. They assisted me in every way. They also wanted to know about you, whom they remember fondly. A separation never occurred to me."

"When I was in St. Jean-de-Bassel in 1883," added Mother St. Andrew, "Mother Constantine said nothing to me nor I to her about a separation. In fact, she enthusiastically asked for volunteers, and many came, as you know, both professed and novices, to make up the fifty-two that I brought back. Would she have let them go if there was a question of separation? And yet Bishop Neraz visited at St. Jean-de-Bassel right after I had left the same year and brought me oral news that we were to become independent of the European congregation. As long as I had no word to this effect from Mother Constantine, or now from Mother Anna, I have held to my original intention of remaining a branch house."

Mother went on to tell that, after Bishop Neraz's visit with Mother Constantine and Mother Marie, her assistant, the latter wrote about the visit. The bishop had asked if the house in Castroville "depended on" St. Jean-de-Bassel. Mother said that was impossible, considering the distance. The bishop knew that Mother St. Andrew had been appointed as the superior of the Texas house, so he suggested that an election ought to be held in the Texas convent. Mother Marie did not say what Mother Constantine's reaction was to the statement about holding an election. She continued by saying that the bishop manifested much interest in and satisfaction with the congregation. Neither Mother St. Andrew nor any of the sisters ever received any word concerning a separation. She therefore believed that, while the St. Jean-de-Bassel administration was content to leave the superior of the Texas branch in complete charge of her community, the Texas group was to remain a branch of the mother house, and this is what she would continue to hold fast to, "although you know that I have always been obedient to the bishop and intend to remain so—unless it becomes impossible for me to do that."

There was a long pause.

"But, Sister Florence, I understand very clearly now that Bishop Neraz will either dissolve this congregation and place the members with other diocesan congregations, or will allow it to remain if it is completely diocesan, with himself as head. Con-. sidering the two evils, perhaps you can go along with this second option for a while until you see your way to changing it. That will have to be your decision. I could not do it. So I have to step down. I will not hold it against you if you decide to accept the diocesan plan. I want you to know this. I will suffer, but I was able only to start this house and not to determine its future—which, I am sure, is in God's hands."

Mother St. Andrew, strong pioneer woman that she was, bowed her head and wept bitterly. The sisters present had never seen her show what they all considered a weakness before. She was always equal to any situation, no matter how searing. They sat in prayerful silence. Finally she raised her head, saying in a choked voice: "I cannot feel myself to be wrong in what I have done. Nor can I think of myself as old and useless for the future; I am not ambitious for myself, but only for God. I have many good years of activity left, and I would like to offer them to God in the congregation."

Sister Florence turned to the other sisters present. "What do you think? Shall we consent to the diocesan plan?" Sisters Angelique and Ange nodded slowly. "Mother is right. We have no real choice. We will have to accept it for now."

Sister Florence rose and placed her arms around the superior.

"You have been a good mother to us all. We would never be here except for you. We will be everlastingly grateful to you for bringing us here and sustaining us through many a dark night and storm. I will do the best I can to carry on what you began. If I have to go against your principles and standards, please remember it will only be for the survival of the congregation, your gift to the church in the Southwest, and only for as long as it must be. Will you please give me your blessing?" she concluded as she knelt before her superior and spiritual mother.

Mother St. Andrew stood up and raised her eyes as she laid her hands upon Sister Florence's head. "May God bless you, my child; may He bring you peace; may He sustain your health and strength in mind, body, and spirit for the work ahead. I thank you, God, for giving us this noble woman to carry on your work here in Texas. May her life be long and fruitful. I ask this through Jesus Christ, our Lord."

All present answered, "Amen."

4

New Responsibilities

When Sister Florence appeared for breakfast in the crowded refectory with the 114 sisters next morning, her demeanor belied the struggle and agony of the previous night. She appeared calm and peaceful, full of joy at being home again, and unworried about the future. But the truth was that she had spent a sleepless night tossing and turning, trying to envision the drama of the coming day and her place in it. Tormented with anxiety, she had abandoned the attempt at rest and sought relief in the chapel, where she pleaded long and ardently for light and peace.

Toward morning, after she had placed herself completely in God's care and surrendered her troubled future into His hands, a calm pervaded her spirit. Suddenly she felt rested and refreshed, as though she had enjoyed a good night's sleep. Thus she was able to face the day with confidence, if not with eager anticipation.

She scanned the faces of the sisters. They seemed less peaceful than she. Some avoided her eyes completely, and she understood their resentment at her for displacing Mother St. Andrew. Others looked and smiled at her shyly, for she was the new symbol of authority and they did not mean to start off in a bad light with her. Mother St. Andrew was, as always, inscrutable, apparently unperturbed. But Sister Florence had had a rare insight the night before into the real person of her former superior, and it multiplied many times her admiration of the older woman's self-discipline.

At 9:30 A.M., according to his promise, Bishop Neraz, accompanied by Father Pefferkorn, drove up into the yard, where the sweaty horses and the dusty carriage were turned over to a local stableman, and the bishop hastily entered the large community room full of sisters, who determinedly suppressed their resentment of his active interference into their lives. They had been completely oriented to venerate all bishops and respect all priests regardless of their individual failings and the unpleasant effects they could have upon others, including themselves.

The sisters stood and bowed toward the bishop and the priest, who had been partly responsible for Mother St. Andrew's dismissal. The members of the administration, including Sister Florence, knelt and kissed the bishop's episcopal ring. Then they were all seated.

Without introduction or preliminary, Bishop Neraz rose and invoked the Holy Spirit upon the morning's meeting.

"This is an important occasion for two reasons," he began. "The members of the chapter already understand these reasons, I believe. But I want to make them very clear before I present you with your new superior general.

"Because of reasons known to myself and the administration, I deemed it necessary that you elect a new superior general. I made it clear then and I repeat it today for all of you, that your only hope of remaining one congregation, the Sisters of Divine Providence, is to accept that new superior whom the chapter members elected. I will now give Sister Florence my blessing and officially present her as your superior general for the term of six years. During this time you will be obedient to her in thought and action, and she will be your spiritual and temporal leader.

"Sister Florence," he said, as she knelt before him, "I pronounce you superior of the Congregation of the Sisters of Divine Providence in the Texas Congregation. I ask God to bless you and lead you in your new office as a true and devoted mother to all the sisters, in the name of the Father, and of the Son, and of the Holy Ghost, Amen.

"Now each sister will come forward to kiss the hand of Sister

Mary Florence, henceforth to be known as Mother Mary Florence. This will be a sign of your acceptance of Mother Florence
and your obedience to her."

The sisters rose silently and, beginning with the oldest, they
came forward hesitantly but passively, and performed the prescribed ritual. Some of her close friends and community members
pressed her hand quietly and flashed her an encouraging glance.
A few did not look at all into her face, and the ritual was hastily
gone through. When the line of sisters came to an end, Mother
St. Andrew, who had not stirred from her chair, rose and approached Mother Florence. Instead of taking her hand as the
others had done, she reached up and took Mother's face between
her hands and kissed her on the lips.

The ceremony is over, Mother Florence thought with relief;
but it was not so. Bishop Neraz rose and faced them again; his
steel-gray eyes were hard and cold. The air grew tense.

"The second reason for this important chapter of elections
is that the Texas branch of the Sisters of Divine Providence is
from this time on independent of the European congregation,
which has been so generous in supporting your efforts up to now
by sending sisters, novices, and postulants to the Texas mission.
In my conversation with Mother Constantine, the superior of
St. Jean-de-Bassel, three years ago, we agreed that distance
made it impossible for the Texas branch to depend upon the
European congregation. I at that time recommended an election.
Moreover, the European congregation is diocesan, under the
jurisdiction of the bishop of Metz. You are in the San Antonio
diocese and must necessarily be under the jurisdiction of the
San Antonio bishop. Therefore, by mutual agreement, the separation is now effective, and you are under my jurisdiction. This
means that I am your highest superior. From henceforth I will
be consulted about all important steps and will approve all major
decisions. I will advise and assist your superior in all situations,
and she will make no major decision without my permission. You
will obey me by obeying Mother Florence, who will speak with
my authority. Respect and obey her and you will prosper; oppose
and disobey her and you will fail; you will be dissolved. May

God bless and prosper you." The bishop abruptly seized his biretta and headed for the door.

Mother Florence rose on weak legs to follow him, saying silently in her heart, "Lord, let me believe that in following the bishop I am following You."

Bishop Neraz, as though hearing her thoughts, stopped on the long front veranda, where he turned to face her. "In following my direction," he said, "you will be doing the will of God." Because he was on his way to another part of the diocese and thus in a hurry to be off, he talked only briefly to her.

"You will choose your assistants," he said, "but do not make a final decision until you talk to me about it. I do not want Mother St. Andrew in any official administrative position where she will influence the sisters. Therefore, I think it will be best to send her as far away as possible, unless indeed, as would be my wish, she returns to Europe."

Mother Florence gasped. The bishop saw but gave no notice. "I will be back on September 4, and we will further discuss congregational affairs. In the meantime you will send the sisters to their missions with as few changes as possible so they can begin work. As soon as Mother St. Andrew is out of Castroville, you will collect all her correspondence, the council meetings, everything except the sisters' personal records and the school records, and we will burn them. I will personally dictate and sign the account of this election, and the congregational records will be kept from this time on, since it is only now that you are truly a Texas and diocesan congregation."

There was no chance to agree or disagree. "God be with you!" he called as he motioned to Father Pefferkorn and then hurried to the carriage.

"Praised be Jesus Christ!" Mother Florence said weakly, recalling her midnight vigil and early morning decision.

"It will be as you said," Mother Florence told Mother St. Andrew later in the day. "I can make no decision without consulting Bishop Neraz. I am not even to have the benefit of your experience in this office. Bishop Neraz believes you should go out, as every other sister, to work on the mission."

Mother St. Andrew was silent for some time. "I feared as much," she said. "I have even given some thought to it. I would like to go either to Galveston or to Frelsburg if it can be arranged. You will find my correspondence and records useful in understanding the history of the first twenty years, which end an era of our congregation today. I have kept them in order."

Mother Florence nodded, unable to reveal the bishop's request for their destruction. Then she went to the privacy of her room to study again from the constitutions that the Texas congregation lived by, printed in French in 1883. They had, as Paul, the bishop of Metz, said in his introduction, some slight changes and updating from the 1867 edition. She had brought a few copies with her from Europe, and she wanted to see now what the description of government said. She felt that she needed to review this section, which had not concerned her much up to this point. She was uneasy with it now. She read in French:

> The principal authority of the congregation is vested in the Bishop of Metz and of Toul, since its mother house is situated in his diocese, and it is governed by the superior general, assisted by her Council.
> 1st. *Higher Superiors*: The Bishop is the chief superior; that is, all important affairs must have his sanction in their final decision, such as the election, the dismissal or resignation of a superior general, and the members of the Council, the admission or exclusion of the professed, and all that concerns the constitutions, statutes, and rules of the congregation. He maintains the faithful observance of the institute and of religious discipline and has an exact account yearly rendered to him in the state in temporalities. . . .
> If the Bishop thinks proper, he may name a delegate superior to represent him in the limit of power he confides to him, ordinary or extraordinary.

As a branch house, the Texas congregation had been ultimately accountable to the bishop of Metz and the mother house of St. Jean-de-Bassel, but Mother St. Andrew had looked upon

Bishop Dubuis as her Texas superior and to Rev. Peter Richard, pastor of Castroville, whom Bishop Dubuis had appointed as ecclesiastical superior of the congregation in his place. Mother St. Andrew had great confidence in both priests and held a real affection for them. But they were both dead now; Father Richard had died in 1880, and Bishop Dubuis in 1884.

Anthony Dominic Pellicer was elevated as first bishop of San Antonio in September 1874 while Bishop Dubuis remained bishop of Galveston. Mother St. Andrew worked under Bishop Pellicer's jurisdiction but still considered Bishop Dubuis her protector. A newcomer to Texas, Bishop Pellicer required some adjusting before understanding the local scene, including the clergy and religious who lived and worked there. But he came to value the new congregation of Divine Providence and asked to see Mother St. Andrew on his deathbed in 1880, when he thanked her and gave her his blessing. It was the same year that she accompanied the ill Father Richard back to Alsace, where he died, and that Sister Florence came to Texas. Mother St. Andrew, as she told Father Richard's parents after his death, truly felt a lack of support now. She had had many trials and hardships during the eighteen years with Bishops Dubuis and Pellicer, but she was always permitted to use her own initiative, and she considered that she had done it responsibly. She felt she knew what the people needed, and she had tried to bring the sisters to fill these needs; she did not want any bishop or clergy breathing down her neck.

So the words of the constitutions on government had never weighed heavily on her until Bishop Neraz insisted that the responsibility accorded the bishop of Metz be transferred to him. Until now this had not officially happened, but with this chapter it was clear that the words in the constitution, "Bishop of Metz," were changed to "Bishop of San Antonio," and he would take them very seriously.

When Mother Florence went to see Bishop Neraz in San Antonio on September 4, she took along a tentative list of council members she considered suitable, as well as a list of the sisters assigned to the various missions, including Mother

St. Andrew to Galveston. Sister Arsene, whom she considered a very knowledgeable person, she chose as assistant and kept in Castroville.

The bishop was expansive. He approved everything and offered his complete support of her. She felt so much better after this visit that she stopped at St. Joseph's Academy for a nostalgic visit with the sisters and students, who were just arriving for the fall term.

This imposing building was a far cry from what she had found on her assignment there in 1881. This tenth school, established by the sisters in 1875, belonged to the congregation. Mother St. Andrew had purchased the property with the two two-room wooden buildings and a barn for $3,300 in gold from Bishop Pellicer, and sent four sisters there. They lived in one of the houses, taught in the other, and converted the barn to a kitchen-dining room area. This is the way Sister Florence had found it in 1881.

After the scandal concerning Father Feltin, Mother St. Andrew, and the two Koehler sisters, the people had lost confidence in the priest and sisters, and the school had suffered. But Sister Agnes Wolf, who replaced Sister Barbara as superior, had restored some credibility to the institution. Father Feltin had died, and Father Pefferkorn, his successor, was a hard worker. Moreover, when Sister Florence came on the scene, Bishop Neraz, a good friend of Father Pefferkorn, took a special interest in this school, which was the first semiparochial school in the city, belonging to the congregation but in and closely attached to the parish.

Sister Florence, twenty-five years old but regal in appearance, with five feet, ten inches of dynamic energy almost completely concealed under her voluminous habit, and large brown eyes that flashed fire or softened with compassion as the occasion required, had spent her first year in Texas studying English. At the request of Mother St. Andrew, who was grooming the promising young sister for the German parish of St. Joseph's, she also perfected her German. She had learned an Alsatian German reluctantly at St. Jean-de-Bassel after the takeover because she had to use it in the school, but her heart was not in it at the time. She spoke French. Sister Florence had already shown herself a brilliant woman of strong personality and deep faith. Young as she was, she had commanded instant respect from the sisters and priests, and Mother St. Andrew thanked God for her generous decision to join the Texas branch.

Arriving at St. Joseph's back in 1881, the new superior and the major superior both knew that the physical arrangement was not a setting in which an effective school situation could be established. By now even the old barn that had been used as a kitchen and dining room had to be used for classes and the sisters ate their meals outside under the trees, bothered by insects, wind, and dust.

Sister Florence began to meet the parishioners, who were impressed with her appearance, personality, academic competence, and ambition for the school. They saw, as she pointed out to them, the tremendous potential of this city school, which could be a cultural center of San Antonio, with a strong music department and an academy with all branches of learning, and eventually accredited. She won them over so thoroughly that, when it came time to raze the three shacks on the property, she had the complete support of Bishop Neraz and Father Pefferkorn and an offer of Meyer's Hall, belonging to a parishioner, F. I. Meyer, to hold classes in. Moreover, another parishioner, Mrs. Ramus, placed her furnished home at the sisters' disposal as a residence for them. Mother St. Andrew hired Henry Pauly and J. C. Dielmann to erect the two-story building, which was later changed to three stories with a cellar and a kitchen in the rear.

Early in the project Sister Florence dreamed of having a bazaar such as she had often helped put on in her Alsatian home town. St. Joseph parishioners raised their eyebrows and said this had never been done here. But she persisted for two reasons, the first of which was financial necessity. She had been brought up to have a strong distaste for debts. The second was her experience of seeing unity and spirit form when people worked and sacrificed together. It was a bonding that gave them a feeling of responsibility for and commitment to one another and the project they were promoting. Her determination and enthusiasm, which also radiated from all the sisters in the community, easily won the sector of the parish who were strongly for the school. Eventually she won with more difficulty those parishioners whose trust in the school had been so shaken that years of patient effort were necessary to convince them that this was a new era and the evils of the past could be forgotten.

Father Pefferkorn, quite excited over the idea of the bazaar, agreed to act as chairman of the three-day fair. Never had the parish seen so much activity, such joy, such imagination. The men worked during the night making sausage and bringing sauerkraut; the women brought mounds of apple strudel and round loaves of pumpernickel bread, fancy work, aprons, and potted plants. Booths went up, and musicians practiced on their instruments. The new three-story building, completed on the outside, stood as proof that what came from this project was already being waited for that May of 1884.

The day of the fair dawned hot and glowering, but spirits soared as the booths bloomed with their wares, and the aroma of spicy food filled the air. As the wind rose, the laughter and shouting rose to match it. Soon dust whirled around the building and through the alley, sprinkling the food with a fine gray seasoning, and the artifacts from the booths flew hither and yon. Father Pefferkorn and the sisters were dismayed at the disarray and feared total disaster.

All day long, and for the three days of the fair, the wind never stopped. What could be moved into the unoccupied building was brought in. And the crowds of people never diminished. Every bite of food was sold, and every article from the booths was gone. The people sang and danced and swayed to the music. They talked and laughed and visited with parishioners they had scarcely met before. Sunday night, after the last person had left and the sisters sat in the unfurnished room of the building where they had taken up residence as soon as the walls were up, they took out the money boxes to count the profit: $800! It couldn't have been a greater success.

All these memories flooded across Mother Florence as she

stood in the door of the academy today. The floor gleamed with its waxed surface, and pride swelled in her bosom when she looked at the shining classrooms and the bright kitchen they had waited so patiently to get into while Sister Antonia had to cook those first days in the cellar by candlelight.

This school really didn't need her any more, she thought sadly. Everything was running so smoothly and they had almost as many pupils as they could take. It had been a challenge, sometimes almost insuperable, but she, with the support of her superior and so many other people, had met the challenge. She felt good.

Now that everything was settled peacefully with the bishop and Mother St. Andrew, she would go to all the houses of the congregation, twenty-one in number, to visit and encourage the sisters, meet the priest and bishops, build a few bridges, and make crooked ways smooth.

She tore herself away from friends and familiar setting, however, with a feeling of sadness. God knows these had been hard years, but, in retrospect, they had been very happy ones and she was satisfied. She had come as a pilgrim to Texas. Now she understood that a pilgrim is without roots, moving from place to place. There was no guarantee that there would ever be a fixed abode where weary feet could rest. But resting her weary feet was the last thing that Mother Florence intended to do now. To a great extent, the congregation and its future depended on her, and she meant to do the best she could for the congregation and, through the congregation, the church in Texas.

5

Dark Days

Mother Florence did not believe that the bishop would actually come to Castroville to burn Mother St. Andrew's records. But she underestimated his determination to rid himself of the troublesome superior once and for all. Early in September he showed up without previous notice and found Mother studying the plans for extending the main building at Castroville. He told her to go ahead and complete the extension that Mother St. Andrew had initiated. Then he announced that they would proceed to the destruction of the records.

"First I will dictate the statement about the chapter of elections," he said as they sat with pen and paper. "By the time we have finished burning the records and correspondence, someone will have this entry written and I will sign it."

"Would we not need these records for the future?" Mother Florence asked. "After all, the congregation has a twenty-year history that we can't ignore."

"What the sisters can recall is all the history that we need," he answered, collecting letters, notebooks, files, financial and business records into two large paper boxes. Taking a small knife from his pocket, he cut out the entire first section from the large council book and crumpled the pages into the boxes. He carried one box and directed Mother Florence to carry the second one into the yard, where he emptied the boxes into a wire burner and lit a match to the papers. His face reflected great satisfaction as the flames licked around the pages, blackened the edges, and eventually consumed them completely, leaving only a cloud of smoke and a few ashes.

"Now, let us begin a new era, free from the encumbrance of the past," he said as he tossed the two paper boxes in on top of the ashes and dusted his hands. Mother Florence felt sick at heart. She found the council book copied and ready for his signature. After he left, she felt she had to get away for a while.

Having lived at St. Joseph's during her five teaching years in Texas, Mother Florence knew that mission life was very demanding, and that sisters, being only weak mortals, needed all the spiritual, moral, and material help that they could get. She suspected that St. Joseph's was not even the most difficult mission, but she did not know this. Therefore, now that all seemed settled around her, she decided to see just where the sisters were teaching and how they were living. For the first time, she felt relaxed and excited about her new responsibility. She chose Haby Settlement because it was the closest.

Being only seven miles from Castroville, Haby Settlement was attached to the mother house at Castroville. Two sisters living in a lonely spot and working with small children all week needed relaxation, companionship, and spiritual nourishment. Therefore, on Friday afternoons Sister Victoria would drive the buggy over from Castroville and pick up the two sisters. Sunday evening she returned them to their mission. Because of these weekend breaks, the two sisters could survive any inconvenience. But Mother learned that when it rained and the Medina River rose, they could not go home, nor could a priest come to offer Mass. Sister Adeline, just professed, suffered through spiritual neglect and loneliness to such an extent that once, after three weeks of high water, the two sisters set out one Saturday at 2:00 A.M. on foot, wading across the river twice to reach home and sisters; this was a tremendous risk. It was too much to expect of them, Mother thought. In their desperation they would drown some day. She would have to see about this school.

From Haby Settlement, Mother went to Fayetteville, a public school that Mother St. Andrew had accepted two years ago.

Here she found a schoolhouse of one room in which all four sisters taught. The sisters' house, a small one-room building, was a half mile away, and they not only walked to and from school in the morning and evening, but went home for a hot noon lunch as well, unless Sister Rosine, who rushed home to cook, carried it back with her. Because the church was far from the public school, neither sisters nor students had the opportunity to assist at daily Mass later in the day. Although the sisters did not complain, Mother was grieved over the spiritual privation, and she spoke to the pastor about the time of services. The sisters were obviously overworked and neglected but apparently happy. She encouraged them to keep the rule and obey the pastor and their superior.

Then she went to Schulenburg—St. Joseph's and St. John's. Everywhere it was the same: privation of every kind, full classrooms, and hard work. Some sisters had not been used to the manual work required of them: drawing water, cutting wood, milking cows, butchering calves, gardening, walking many miles, adjusting to torrid weather in summer and frigid in winter in small crowded quarters. Although a few faltered under these conditions, most grew strong and robust.

It was in Schulenburg that Mother received word that Sister Arsene had left Castroville without permission of Bishop Neraz or herself, and had gone to Galveston, where Mother St. Andrew was. This shocked her, and, with a premonition of worse things to come, she hurried home. The council met without Sister Arsene, the assistant, and informed Mother Florence that Sister Arsene had been restless, resentful over her removal from Galveston, and sympathetic with Mother St. Andrew. Being the mother assistant and the highest authority at the convent in Mother Florence's absence, she had simply announced that she was going to Galveston—to stay. Mother Florence hastened to San Antonio to consult with Bishop Neraz.

Bishop Neraz had just received and finished reading a letter from Sister Arsene dated September 17, as Mother rang his doorbell. He threw open the door with a force that rattled the house, and waved the letter in Mother Florence's face.

"She couldn't stand the way they treated Mother St. Andrew! She wants to continue to live in peace and harmony in Galveston as she has done for the last eight years! They need her! She asks permission to remain there and wants my episcopal blessing!" Bishop Neraz paced back and forth in a rage.

"She will not get my permission or my blessing! It is all Mother St. Andrew's doing. We should have sent her back to Europe. If Sister Arsene does not come home and behave herself, she can count herself out of the congregation. I will write that to her. When and if she comes, you and your council will determine how you will discipline her if she remains. But she must first of all be obedient. She is old enough to understand obedience and not be misled by anybody, whether out of sympathy or otherwise. I will make that very clear in my letter to her."

Mother Florence was not accustomed to seeing the bishop in this state, and she feared he would have a heart attack. She was also frightened. This was not going to be so easy after all. She had thought Sister Arsene was more stable and self-disciplined. She returned to Castroville with a heavy heart.

What followed in no way lightened her burden. On September 24 she received a letter from the bishop, which she slit open and read eagerly, confident that it was news of Sister Arsene. She was surprised to read about Sister Barbara Theis, who had been superior of the New Braunfels community during the last year when trouble arose concerning Father Kirch and the sisters. Mother St. Andrew had added fuel to the fire by making the statement oft misquoted in following days to say "Beware of all priests." Sister Barbara and Sister Christine felt they could no longer remain in the congregation while Mother St. Andrew was the superior. Bishop Neraz had transferred them both to the convent in Victoria. The New Braunfels community eventually dissolved because of talebearing and general misunderstanding. The letter read:

> Dear Mother,
> Sister Barbara, whom I had sent to Victoria, does not feel that she has a vocation to the cloistered life and has asked to come back and return to Castroville, now that Sister St.

Andrew is no longer superior. You may receive her without objection, since it was I myself who permitted her to change communities and since she has done nothing that would deprive her of that favor. If you cannot come to get her and bring her her religious habit, which I sent to Castroville, please send word to one of your sisters here to give her what she needs so that she will be dressed as a religious as formerly. Then you can send her where you want to, either to Castroville or to any other mission that you think proper.

I send my blessing to all.

Devotedly yours,
†Joannes C. Neraz

P.S. I forgot to mention that she is here at her sister's in the city.

Neither Mother nor the congregation was given a choice in the matter. She did as the bishop requested and left for San Antonio with the habit. But, before she went to the house of Sister Barbara's sister, she stopped at the bishop's house to let him know that she had decided with the council that Sister Barbara would be required to remake her novitiate before resuming congregational work. Again she found Bishop Neraz highly incensed. He had just opened a letter from Mother St. Andrew, and he handed it to her. It was dated September 24 and read as follows:

We come to ask a favor of you, namely, of permitting us to start a house here in Galveston. Rt. Rev. C. M. Dubuis's wish and grant was that the seat should be in Frelsburg, Texas; but his lordship, N. A. Gallagher, said it would be better in the city. It could be better tended to than in the country, and we trust that the house in Castroville would not suffer through the separation; on the contrary, we think that both houses will flourish and work for the same aim and end. . . .

"The 'we' in the statement must be Sister Arsene and herself," Mother Florence said in amazement. "That must be why Sister Arsene went there. I recall that Bishop Dubuis had spoken with Mother in 1881 about beginning a branch house in Frelsburg.

But this was not done at the time. Now she wants to do it, but, instead of Frelsburg, Bishop Gallagher wants it in Galveston."

"It will not be done! To establish a branch house in Galveston requires not only Bishop Gallagher's approval, but mine as well," the bishop said. "I will not give my approval, and I will inform Bishop Gallagher with what sort of person he is dealing." He lost no time in seating himself at his desk to dash off this letter. There was no doubt in Mother Florence's mind that it would banish Mother St. Andrew from Galveston. She took her leave to clothe Sister Barbara in her habit and return to Castroville.

As she had suspected, Bishop Neraz's letter to Bishop Gallagher prompted the latter to call for Mother St. Andrew and tell her he would have to withdraw his permission for the branch house in Galveston, and that she would do well to follow Bishop Neraz's direction. Mother St. Andrew, realizing that there was no future for her in Galveston, went, without permission, to Los Angeles, taking Sister Arsene with her.

In her last trip to Europe in 1883, Mother St. Andrew, with the assistance of kind friends, had secured numerous statues and other religious articles, such as chalices, monstrances, and vestments, as Mother Florence so well remembered, which she had hoped to use when setting up a branch house in the Galveston diocese. Because this was now impossible, she took along to California the most portable objects and some money she had obtained for the same purpose. She had used her own patrimony in building the convent in Castroville after all.

In the Los Angeles diocese, she found, as she had expected, a German parish that was in need of teaching sisters. Desperate as she was to establish herself anew, and yet wishing to remain a member of the congregation, she, with Sister Arsene, returned to San Antonio after a few days, full of hope that the bishop would be relieved to have them out of Texas and would give the necessary approval.

Mother Florence, hoping to see all the congregational houses by Thanksgiving, had resumed her journey. It was a relief to her mind to keep busy and tired, so that she would have little time to think of the two dearly loved yet disobedient sisters who were getting themselves more and more deeply into trouble with the congregation and the bishop.

She found the sisters everywhere working in the most primitive conditions. Usually they were by twos and threes, teaching the elementary grades. Except for some of the sisters who came from Europe, they had barely completed elementary school. But they studied every day and were coached by another sister more knowledgeable in the community, so that they were always ready for the next day's classes. It was almost a miracle, Mother thought, how they kept this up; the children learned, and the pastor and parents were satisfied. Many of the schools were public, and the sisters were paid a public school salary as long as the money lasted. But it seldom stretched out over nine months, so the school had to close or the parish made up the remainder of the year's salary—not much to be sure, but just enough to keep the sisters there.

When she learned that the two sisters had returned from California and were in Castroville, she hurried home to see what new situation had developed. She approached the mother house with great misgivings. Well she might have, for she soon learned what the situation was. Asked by Mother St. Andrew for permission to remain until Mother Florence returned, the bishop acquiesced but refused to let her receive the sacraments until she had fulfilled certain conditions: to render obedience to the superior general, to return all articles and money with an account of all that had taken place during her absence, and to go where she would be sent, not as superior but as simple sister. She was not to be permitted to return to California. Sister Arsene, too, could be readmitted only after having repaired the scandal she had caused.

Mother Florence was deeply touched by Mother St. Andrew's plight. She saw the proud independent spirit subdued by the continual acts of humility and submission, by her complete destitution and yet her determination in some way to return a small amount of dignity and self-worth to her life.

Mother St. Andrew could not return the full amount of money

she had taken, $205, because she had used part of it for travel, but she returned all the other objects. Still the bishop would not give her permission to receive holy communion until she had returned the complete amount. Recalling how she had given her patrimony for building the convent, Mother Florence made paper arrangements allowing her the money she needed to make up the balance, and on November 7 was able to write Bishop Neraz that both sisters had fulfilled his conditions completely and satisfactorily.

She longed to keep Mother St. Andrew at the convent, but Mother agreed to go to Clarksville, and she knew she, too, must do as the bishop stipulated. Sister Arsene was sent to teach at Haby Settlement. Her heart bled for Mother St. Andrew that November morning when she left for Clarksville, knowing that it would be well nigh impossible for her to fit into the community and school life there after her many years of administration.

Mother Florence did not yet have perpetual vows, although Bishop Neraz had told her he dispensed her from the age requirement, so now she wrote for permission to pronounce her final vows and to celebrate with a triduum of all-day exposition of the Blessed Sacrament. She invited the bishop to preside at the ceremony. As always, he was agreeable with her, gave her the requested permissions, and appointed a substitute to represent him in case he was unable to be there personally. It was a memorable week in every way. She took time to visit with the girls she had brought from Alsace, so long ago, it seemed. Most were bright and happy, demonstrating their knowledge of English. But Josephine Stocker, she noticed, had lost weight and looked pale.

"Do you eat well, my child?" she asked her gently.

"Oh, yes, Mother. I never ate so much breakfast. And I don't work too hard either. I just get tired."

"You must have extra rest," she said solicitously, and she made a note to tell the infirmarian to give her a tonic.

She also sought out Veronica Huvar, who had just arrived from Alsace. Veronica had not been able to leave with them last summer because of sickness in the family. But here she was, beaming with happiness over her long trip, made quite alone and safely.

She observed with great satisfaction the large number of novices who would be ready to go on the mission during the coming year. She had already received requests for sisters from several places, and she would be able to open some schools next fall. She told the novices and postulants about the schools she had visited, stressing the hardships the sisters had to endure.

"You see, you must learn to be strong, physically, mentally, and spiritually. You must learn all you can and not complain of hardships if you want to be a true daughter of our founder, Father John Martin Moye."

The young people took every opportunity to see and hear her, impressed as they were by her stately bearing, her beauty, and her commanding presence.

Monday evening, at a very solemn moment during the final benediction of the triduum, she pronounced her perpetual vows in the presence of the entire congregation and Father Ad Bruchler, representing the bishop. It was the happiest moment of the turbulent year.

Mother Florence now began to study the congregation's formation program. She saw that the postulants were awakened sometimes at 4:00 A.M. to go into the fields to break the corn. Besides their regular breakfast they ate a good supply of watermelons on their way to or from work, as a special treat. There were no bathtubs and they had to bathe in the nearby Medina River, but in dry weather the water was not very clean and the dust on the road was so thick that their cleanliness was of short duration. The sisters also made their own molasses, one of their most dependable staples. The postulants and novices took turns doing the donkey's work of trudging endlessly around the vat to press and stir the sticky mess.

All the postulants and novices studied every day, and Mother began to plan a systematic summer educational program for all the sisters to continue their study. Requirements were becoming more stringent in the public schools, and certification had to be provided. Also, the only copies of the rule were printed in French, and there were only a few of them. She believed each sister should have a copy she could read and meditate on. And she had a dream that someday as soon as possible the congregation should have its own approved constitutions and become pontifical instead of diocesan.

Then one day in late March the chilling news reached her that Mother St. Andrew had left Clarksville by herself, clothed in her religious habit, and gone to Los Angeles. Soon letters began to come to the sisters, saying that they were needed there, and that a house could be started, as she had learned from the pastor. There were some communities in Texas, she said, where the sisters did not have any spiritual benefits. This would not be the case in California. Mother Florence knew well that various communities were often deprived of spiritual benefits—Mass and the sacraments—and it disturbed her. But this would not be the answer, and Mother St. Andrew, better than anyone else, should know it. She must be distraught, she thought. It would be necessary, as it was in Galveston, to get the San Antonio bishop's approval. He would never give it to Mother St. Andrew for any place in the United States. It was as final as that. Mother would be more hurt than ever when the bishop learned of her plans as he eventually would. But she would not be the one to tell him.

Sister Arsene was one of the sisters who received a letter to come to California. She came to talk it over with Mother Florence, determined to stick with her friend and former superior if possible. Mother Florence was torn by this request. She feared for both sisters' future, once their intention was known. She feared for her own if she sanctioned this move, but her concern for Mother St. Andrew finally prevailed, and she gave Sister Arsene permission to join Mother in California, on condition that she leave her cross, rosary, and ring, symbols of her affiliation with the congregation, in Castroville. At this point her concern was not so much for Sister Arsene as for Mother St. Andrew. She also indicated to Sister Arsene that, if any other sisters wished to go, she would not prevent them. It was clear to her then, if not to Sister Arsene, that this group of sisters in

California would have to be a new community, free of the sisters
in San Antonio, so she advised Sister not to see or tell Bishop
Neraz about her plans, as Sister was ready to do. No other sister
elected to join the two. She waited in trepidation for the news
to reach the bishop. It was not long in coming.

Bishop Neraz ordered California altar wine through Very
Rev. J. Adam, vicar general in the Los Angeles diocese, with
whom he had carried on a correspondence since Mother St.
Andrew's first trip there. On March 2, the day before Mother
St. Andrew left Clarksville for California, Bishop Neraz wrote
Rev. Adam about wine, but in his letter he also mentioned Mother
St. Andrew:

> . . . As to what you asked me about ex-Mother St. Andrew,
> I would state that I cannot recommend her as a good sub-
> ject. I was bound to depose her on a great many complaints
> from most of the sisters and priests who had sisters in their
> parishes. The Sisters of Divine Providence here are giving
> satisfaction and have charge of some of the parochial schools,
> particularly among the Germans. . . . Sister St. Andrew went
> to California without my knowledge after she was deposed
> and after she found out that Bishop Gallagher of Galveston
> would not allow her in his diocese. . . . She has given
> trouble to my predecessor and, as she was a power among
> the people at Castroville, she had her way, but this time she
> could not succeed. . . .

When Bishop Neraz first learned on April 3 that the two
sisters had returned to California, he did not immediately contact
Mother Florence, but he wrote to Rev. Adam, giving further
judgment on the former superior and his own role in the salvation of the Castroville community; he ended with a warning:
"She has no religious spirit, . . . has stolen money from the
community and the people, . . . is not afraid to tell lies . . .
I felt discouraged until, finding an opportunity to act, I did so.
. . . I thank God to have helped me to protect the community
of the Sisters of Divine Providence. . . . It was only by accident
that I found a part of the wrong, and I was bound to act."
He ended this long diatribe with the following:

I think it is a duty for me to let you know these things because I do not like to see a bishop put in trouble for want of
information. . . . Hoping this letter will not reach you too
late, I am, J. C. Neraz.

Father Stoter, who was happy with his sisters in his Anaheim
parish, was told that they could not remain there. He reluctantly
told them. They immediately wrote the vicar general, Sister
Arsene saying she had come with her superior's permission and
approval, and Mother St. Andrew that she was a loyal subject
and would never turn against her congregation. She offered to
start a branch house of the congregation there, where it was so
urgently needed. Father Stoter encouraged her to write her
superior to this effect, and she did. She stated her present condition and work, with the latest development. She said that, if a
house could be officially established in California, everything
would be in order.

The worst had come, Mother Florence saw, and she had to
face the bishop. She took the letter to him, knowing what the
consequences would be. Her only saving feature, as far as the
bishop was concerned (and she in her weakness had foreseen
this), was that she had taken Sister Arsene's rosary, cross, and
ring before she left. The bishop, however, did not spare her for
her part in the proceedings. She was chastened, not on account
of the bishop's censure but on account of her own deception with
Sister Arsene.

"I will write to the bishop," Neraz told her heatedly, "that I
could not in conscience recommend Sister Andrew to any bishop
or priest, and that I told her the only way for her to save her
soul would be to go to Europe to the mother house, if she could
be received, and prepare for death."

"She is only fifty-seven years old," Mother Florence gasped.
"She will live a long time yet."

"I will tell him I have too often been deceived by her, and
she will never be received back in her convent," he continued
with ever-rising voice and increased speed. "She may even take
this to court, but I am prepared for it and then she will be shown

in her true colors. It is my duty, and I will tell him, to protect the good souls in a good institution."

Then, speaking firmly to Mother Florence, he said, "You will answer Rev. Adam's letter, telling him that neither Mother St. Andrew or Sister Arsene is any longer a member of your congregation, having left without permission and giving dis-edification to the community twice." He told her, however, to indicate interest in establishing a house in the Los Angeles diocese, with the understanding that neither of the present sisters would be there.

She wrote this letter with many qualms, knowing that Sister Arsene believed she had gone as a member of the congregation with administrative approval. This letter was to haunt her for many years and to bring both sisters to the end of their membership in the diocesan congregation. They made one last attempt to effect a reconciliation, coming back to San Antonio, where the bishop refused to see them. Sister Arsene stoutly maintained that she went with permission and was therefore blameless. Mother St. Andrew acknowledged her guilt, but appealed to the humanity, the compassion, and the mercy of the bishops of Los Angeles and San Antonio to give her some hope, some place to live, some work, anything—and they would not be sorry. But no help, no hope was given her.

These were dark days indeed for Mother Florence, torn between survival of the congregation and loyalty to her former superior. It was Mother St. Andrew who comforted her in her agony on the day Mother Florence had to tell them to go away.

"Sister Florence," she said sadly, "neither you nor I knew what the full price of our decision would be. I blame myself for my weakness and my mistakes. I never knew the power of bishops over one another and institutions before. Now we both know. Continue to do what you have to do, but work for papal approval of the congregation. It is your only hope."

Both women wept, clinging to each other. "I will pray for you every day until God shows a way to set things right for you," Mother Florence said.

"I will not die from this, I assure you; nor will I return to

Europe. God writes straight with crooked lines, and since I cannot choose what I am to do, I shall simply wait on His call. Don't worry about me. I feel that God still has use for me."

Mother St. Andrew had given her patrimony for the building of the Castroville mother house. The constitutions stated that a professed sister who is dismissed or withdraws voluntarily from the congregation has no right to claim anything:

> . . . any revenue of her property accruing since her taking the vows nor for any gift freely made to the community, nor for any service she may have rendered. It is for the superior to consider what alms they may give her in the way of kindness or charity. . . .

Although the bishop instructed Mother Florence not to extend any help to Mother St. Andrew or Sister Arsene except to send them back to Europe if they agreed to go, she knew she would follow her rule regarding "kindness and charity." Sister Arsene chose to return to Europe. Mother St. Andrew remained in Castroville, in her religious habit, with her brother and his family until a small house was given for her use. And there she spent her days in prayer and waiting.

6

First Term (1886-1892)

When Mother Florence read that President Abraham Lincoln had said, "I claim not to have controlled events but must confess plainly that events have controlled me," she realized that this is exactly what was happening to her. She had been responding to a host of emergencies without furthering the congregation or exercising her leadership in any way. There was so much to do.

In the privacy of her room she took stock of her situation, trying to determine what was to be done and in what order she would undertake these tasks. She had to consider at the same time the liabilities, obstacles to the achievement of anything. The most outstanding were these, as she perceived them: a powerful, paternal, domineering bishop, one that she sometimes disagreed with, whose approval she had to obtain for every action she performed; Mother St. Andrew, a considerable influence with the people of Castroville and the sisters, living alone and in disgrace within sight of the convent—if one looked from an upstairs window (this presence reflected negatively on her, who was powerless under obedience to ameliorate the ex-superior's condition in any observable way); her own youth and lack of administrative experience, coupled with her slight acquaintance with the sisters and the schools in operation.

Formidable as these seemed, she began to think of her assets, and she found six. She had boundless trust in Divine Providence, a healthy optimism, and at least the appearance of self-confidence and authority. She had, so far, the goodwill of the bishop, who often went along with her proposals. She had the word of the

64

influential priests in the diocese who had opposed Mother St. Andrew that they would support her, but she had not tested them yet. She had ambition, drive, ideas, imagination, intelligence, an innate sense of order and beauty, and a strong will, which she meant to use for the church and the congregation.

Next to God, she loved people, with a special compassion for the poor and oppressed. She was a woman of prayer and an indefatigable worker. It seemed to her that the positive considerations outweighed the negative. This was encouraging.

When she had come from Alsace, her chief concern was to be obedient to her superiors in carrying out the assignments given her for her missionary work in Texas. Now she was responsible for governing not only her own apostolic life but that of the entire congregation as well. Although the general thrust was the same, the responsibility had broadened to cover much more than she had ever dreamed of, and it was she who had to furnish the personnel, the atmosphere, and the incentive for all the members. One year had already passed. She would try, during the five remaining years of her term, at least to begin what she saw as imperative needs: to provide intensive and continuous educational and spiritual help for the sisters in their professional and personal lives, to establish and maintain reasonable religious discipline in all the houses of the congregation, to improve and extend the teaching apostolate, to see that the ordinary business of institutional life was carried on with dignity, promptness, and thoroughness, to provide financially and materially for the growing congregation, and to plan for the future as well as the present by seeking vocations to the congregation.

To do all this, she felt it was absolutely essential to win the support of bishops, priests, superiors and sisters, community leaders, businessmen, and bankers, without compromising her principles.

As she began each phase of her plan, she would have to obtain the approval, first of the bishop and then of her counselors —Sisters Stanislaus, Agnes, Pierre, and Paul—along with Sister Angelique, her most valued assistant.

"The congregation is growing," Sister Angelique observed. "You have given yourself a heavy load if you plan to do this, but it is important, and we will all help you."

"Of course. I can plan, but it takes us all to accomplish the task."

As good as this sounded, Mother already saw that she must be the one to initiate and supervise everything. She worked as she thought—fast and thoroughly. She was impatient with bumbling, hesitancy, indecision, failure. She wanted to see results immediately. With the help of the sisters who were most familiar with the educational system in practice, she evaluated the congregation's teaching programs. The majority of sisters had only an elementary education, with additional study provided in the community under the supervision of a sister with slightly higher education. It was not enough.

Conditions were changing in this country; new methods were being introduced. Besides, the sisters needed to be educated beyond the next day's class. Also, in some schools, especially in the academies owned by the sisters, higher education was required. It would also soon be required in the parish and the public schools. The sisters had to be prepared. Mother Florence began immediately to look for and to contract lay teachers to come to Castroville to teach special courses for the sisters. All sisters who were to teach these subjects in their schools were expected to attend. She became acquainted with and engaged Professor J. V. Bradford, teacher in the public schools of Medina County, to teach algebra and geometry at the convent. Because he was also on the county examining board for teachers' certificates, his instruction was considered especially valuable.

Each year the summer classes became better organized and more numerous, so that every sister had an opportunity to study a subject practical for her. Sisters also took the examinations in the counties where they taught for the certificates they needed. This program was to expand considerably during Mother Florence's second term.

At the same time, Mother Florence continued what had already become a custom in the congregation: every sister was to spend the summer at the mother house, not only for school courses but for continued spiritual formation and community building. A part of this consisted of the congregational daily meetings, presided over by Mother Florence, which were to become legend. Besides giving food for thought on spiritual matters, they were an occasion for instruction on many subjects important for sisters to know and practice: food service and table manners, relations with the clergy and people in the parish, social etiquette, housekeeping, travel, discipline of children, self-discipline, obedience to superiors, a spirit of sacrifice and willingness to suffer.

These conferences began gently, and the sisters appreciated them, even though occasionally they hit sensitive chords. From the beginning she insisted that sisters traveling carry only one suitcase and no boxes or bags. They were to walk in San Antonio on the less crowded streets when they arrived there by train, so as not to be too conspicuous to too many people.

"Take time to sit down and eat each well-prepared hot meal, using the correct service," she told them, knowing that the temptation was ever present to seize a cup of coffee and make a sandwich of whatever was available to eat on the run. On the mission where there was no cook assigned, a sister had to leave the classroom early to prepare the noon meal so that it would be ready when the other sister or sisters came. "Spend the full time on your meditation and visit to the Blessed Sacrament without sleeping or planning the day's work at that time. God comes before all. If you are a good religious, you will be a good teacher." She gradually learned that this was not always so. Some good religious were just not good teachers, especially if they had not had time to prepare lessons or were too tired and unsure of themselves to inspire confidence in the children. Sometimes the most "worldly" sisters were the best and most popular teachers. This began to puzzle and annoy her. She would have to study how to deal with it.

Mother Florence's first years as superior general were crucial, not only for the corporate survival of the congregation but for the spiritual and physical health as well. Summer normal was not over when the sisters began to fall ill in 1887. It was not difficult to see that the illness was typhoid fever. Mother was quite familiar with this, as she recalled the days in St. Jean-de-Bassel when many sisters were ill and some died. The water supplied by the well, low from long lack of rain, was probably contaminated. The food supply for the 114 sisters during the hot summer was unrefrigerated; mosquitoes from the stagnant Medina River infested the nearby areas; and intense heat enervated the sisters, already exhausted from the year's work. Some of the sisters became seriously ill and some only slightly. Three young sisters succumbed completely. Among the stricken was Sister Joachim Sweeney, a strong, energetic Irish sister, and a fighter. With strong faith and a will to live, even when death was imminent, she asked the infirmarian to bring oil from the lamp that burned continually night and day before the picture of the Holy Face. Mother St. Andrew had obtained from Rome a copy of the picture of the face of Christ, imprinted on the scarf held by Veronica to the face of Christ on the way to Calvary. The scarf with the picture imprinted on it had had a stormy history, but Christians everywhere prayed with deep faith before the face of the suffering Christ. The infirmarian complied with her request, applying the oil while the sisters prayed for healing. Their faith was rewarded. Sister Joachim began to recover until soon her health was assured.

Mother Florence, truly alarmed for the sisters, but grateful for the relief, promised that, if no one else died and the epidemic ceased, the feast day of St. Veronica, February 4, would henceforth be observed in the congregation as a holy day of obligation, on which the sisters would offer Holy Communion in thanksgiving, make acts of reparation, and refrain from servile work. The epidemic gradually ceased and no one else died. The promise was formally registered to be kept.

After 1887 there was no further death in the congregation until 1890. Among those who had died was Josephine Stocker, now Sister Angele, a novice of twenty-one years, whom Mother had brought the previous year from Alsace. Like a true natural parent, Mother grieved for this young sister, feeling somehow responsible, because she had uprooted the girl from her native country and family. She wrote Josephine's parents:

> I, like you, am a bereaved mother. The only consolation I have is that she was so good and wanted so much to do God's will that she was ready to go. We allowed her to make her religious profession two days before she died. We must rejoice that she is now in Heaven, her true home.

But she wondered how to make the Texas convent more of a home for the new recruits.

In the past the sisters did not have copies of the congregational constitutions. It was no wonder that they had found it difficult to live them. When Mother Florence had returned from St. Jean-de-Bassel in 1886, she had brought with her the latest revision of the constitutions, which had been published in French in 1884. In one of her trips to Gonzalez to determine whether to leave the sisters there, since the parish did not pay their house rent as promised, and they were often deprived of Mass, Communion, and the sacraments, she met the scholarly French Jesuit, Rev. Peter Garresché. He impressed her as the person to translate the constitutions. He was charmed to be asked and immediately set about the task, while promising to provide better for the sisters. She left the sisters in Gonzalez that year.

Before the constitutions were printed in English, Mother presented them to Bishop Neraz for approval. He not only approved them, but he wrote the preface, in which he stated that he had examined, approved, and recommended them to the sisters as the "sole rules, constitutions, and directory" that they were to keep and observe. The English translation was printed and distributed to all the sisters in 1887. There was no question now of sisters or priests not knowing what was required of the sisters.

Bishop Neraz thoroughly supported Mother Florence when it came to implementing the rules. When Mother St. Andrew had tried to enforce the same rules, he had turned against her and taken the part of the priests. Now Mother Florence had only to tell priests, as she did when Father Kirch of New Braunfels requested certain exceptions, that she would consult the bishop.

Father Kirch knew that the bishop would not consent, so the matter was ended. In her first years, Bishop Neraz's self-imposed position as "Father Superior" of the congregation was an asset to her because it absolved her from becoming immersed in personality clashes as had happened to Mother St. Andrew. She consulted him on all matters of importance and usually obtained his approval of her suggestions and plans. That the bishop was pleased with her administration is evident from some of his correspondence. He wrote Rev. Adam in California in 1887:

> Since the new superior has taken charge of the mother house, everything is going on well and the religious spirit is on the increase. The name of the new superior is Mother St. Florence.

Mother had difficulty getting and keeping a chaplain for the mother house. She continually requested this from the bishop, especially for the summer months when all the sisters were there. She wrote the bishop in June 1889:

> The mother house ought to be the center of spiritual contemplation, and alas, my heart bleeds at the thought that it will be otherwise. Will your lordship permit his worthy daughter and all the professed sisters one more communion a week during vacation in order to regain that which we have lost during the course of the year?

But she was not willing to settle for just any priest. When Father Meinrad Lennartz of Temple offered himself as chaplain, she put him off, telling him he was needed in Temple.

Just as she had discovered Father Garresché in Gonzalez, she found in Alexandria, in the process of opening a school there, Father Leonard Menard, whose everlasting friendship she won by asking him to translate the life of the congregational founder, Father John Martin Moye, into English for the sisters' inspiration and instruction. He completed this translation and it was distributed to the sisters in 1891.

The year 1890 would always stand out as the nadir of Mother Florence's first term in office. Just as she was on the point of recovering from one traumatic event, another and another struck her down. Mother St. Andrew, living quietly in her little Castroville house, had never ceased to hope that some day she would begin another branch of the congregation in spite of Bishop Neraz. She was resourceful. She had written, in fact, to Rev. Nicholas Michel, Father Superior of the St. Jean-de-Bassel community, asking him to reclaim her as a congregational member, give her a new name, write a recommendation for her, and send some sisters to work with her in a German Kansas parish she had discovered in need of sisters. He was not to mention anything about her Texas experience, so that Bishop Neraz would not get wind of her whereabouts. Father Michel, after consulting with the superior of St. Jean-de-Bassel, refused, saying that she had withdrawn from that community freely, and he would not dissemble. Indeed the sisters in Europe were now under the impression that she had intentionally separated herself from their community in 1883, her last visit there. Bishop Neraz had fostered this impression with them when he visited there after she had left that year. At any rate, clothed always in her habit, Mother St. Andrew was a continual painful daily reminder that she was a renegade and unwelcome at the convent. In February 1890 Mother St. Andrew's sister-in-law, Louis Feltin's wife, in a period of depression took her own life, leaving the family of seven children motherless. Louis asked his sister to be a mother to them.

Removing her habit for the first time, and laying it carefully away for some future day when she would need it, she put on lay clothes and took the family away from the scene that had produced so much pain for them all. Because Louis had not been able to provide financially for the family, she was to set up a small store in California and care for the children financially as well as educationally and spiritually. Mother Florence saw her leave, with agony and relief. She was unable to help her, hardly able to talk with her amid the tragic circumstances of her departure, but she was relieved that she would no longer see the lone figure going about her religious duties and her small charities in the village. More than this, she recalled Mother's words that she would wait until the Lord needed her. It was clear that the time had come; she would measure up. Mother Florence closed herself away for a few days after Mother St. Andrew's departure, to recover her courage and self-image. Eventually she was drawn by the pressure of events to become absorbed in countless congregational affairs. She was completely involved toward the end of the year with closing some schools and opening others when Sister Jerome Brumpt, one of the twenty girls she had recruited from Alsace, died in her twenty-third year. Sister Jerome had been frail and unable to work hard, had even been confined to bed. Again Mother grieved and wrote to the sorrowing parents. Four months later Magdalen Huvar, another of "her girls," died almost suddenly.

"Perhaps the Lord is telling me something," she agonized. She thought back to the green forests and hills of Alsace, and the cool fresh air nurturing not only vegetation but human life as well. "If I had not taken them away, perhaps they would be alive today." The climate of Surbourg, however, was no elixir, guaranteeing longevity, she was to learn.

Mother and all the sisters were in the midst of Christmas preparations when her brother Antoine wired her that her mother had died on December 21. She went back in spirit to her last home visit four years before, when she had told herself that her parents had become so much as one that they could not live apart. She spent the Christmas in anxious prayer and waiting. She had not long. Again Antoine wired her, this time to say that her father had died on December 26. In her sorrow she rejoiced that they were together. Antoine now lived with his wife of one year in the family home.

Because Mother believed that a sister's family affairs should not absorb the community ("Let the dead bury the dead," Mt. 8:22), she tried not to let her suffering be observed by others. She simply recommended her parents to their prayers, guarding her grief in her own heart as the other sisters did. She had so schooled herself by now to contain her exuberant and affectionate nature that few sisters suspected the partial death she suffered. In her long hours of prayer she read from her worn and trusted book, *The Imitation of Christ:*

> Your discipline has fallen upon me and your rod of cor-
> rection has taught me. Under the rod I wholly submit my-
> self. Strike my back and my bones and make me bow my
> crooked will to your will.

Only she and Antoine now remained of the family. She would
dedicate herself anew and trust in Divine Providence.

In the spring of 1886, when Mother Florence had been on
the ship sailing for France, she had met Bishop Anthony Durier
from Louisiana, going to visit his home in France and make his
report to Rome. During the long hours on deck, they spoke of
their respective missions—Mother Florence of St. Joseph's and
the German, Bohemian, and Polish schools in Texas; Bishop
Durier of post-Civil War Louisiana. He related stories of the
poor blacks, free now but bound by ignorance and poverty, more
helpless in some ways than they had been during slave days.

"If only I had a few sisters to teach them catechism, reading, writing, and numbers, it would be the greatest charity we
could do."

"It would be what our founder, Father John Martin Moye,
would want us to do," Sister Florence had said, full of zeal
and enthusiasm.

"When you go back to Texas, will you ask your superior
to send us some sisters?" he asked earnestly, and Sister Florence
promised that she would do her best to obtain sisters for him.

Now that she was the superior, she began receiving among
the requests from the Texas dioceses the persistent plea from her
friend, Bishop Durier of Louisiana. She remembered her promise
and spoke to Bishop Neraz about it. Bishop Neraz, knowing
Durier, was agreeable as long as the Texas schools did not suffer.
So plans began to form for the coming year, and Bishop Durier
was from the start an ardent admirer and supporter of the young
superior; Louisiana was the first state outside Texas where Sisters
of Divine Providence were to go.

The schools were always her main concern. She continued
to receive requests for sisters almost weekly, although she had
decided to open no new schools the first year. The second year
she had additional sisters so that she could begin three new

schools. The two in Texas were in Sedan and Colorado Line; the third was in Louisiana. Bishop Durier was like a child in his eagerness to have sisters in his diocese. He invited Mother Florence to come to Louisiana. She did. It was a new world to her. Unlike Texas, it was green and verdant. As the horses drew the carriage along the narrow, twisting roads, she saw tall pine trees on both sides reaching into the sky; willows dipped their heavy tendrils into the waters of the bayous all along the road; cypress knees appeared in the dusky woods; and occasionally an alligator glided, half immersed in the murky waters. Black children threw their baited twines into the water and shouted triumphantly at each catch of crawfish they drew out. They were providing the family meal and enjoying it.

Mother saw imposing colonial plantation houses with stately pillars supporting wide verandas. But the buildings were in a sad state of disrepair, and the plantations they sat on were largely untended. Nestled uncomfortably close together in many areas at the edges of the plantations were the small rickety shanties where the Negroes lived. Mother was accustomed to class distinction. It existed everywhere. But segregation was beyond her comprehension. So, too, were the black faces staring at her from the poor little cabins in Alexandria and along the Cane River near Isle Brevelle, Cloutierville, and Natchitoches.

"Why are some quite black while others are almost blond?" she asked Bishop Durier. He told her about the plantation system, when the white masters often had children by the slave women. These children were mulattoes. In time the mulattoes, who were often freed by their masters, became numerous in some areas, not accepted by the white community or the black community. So each school would require segregation three ways—white, black, and mulatto.

"When you take a school, it will mean at least two schools— the white and the black, or the white and the mulatto. But, in the case of Isle Brevelle, it will be only one, because all are mulattoes. In Cloutierville, we may need three."

"That is unchristian!" Mother said. "And a waste of personnel."

"This may be true," the bishop told her, "but we are too close to the War and Reconstruction period. The white population has lost everything with their defeat—their position, their property, their slaves. They are still bitter, and conditions are explosive. We have to move slowly. But we must educate the Negroes so that they can take their place in society with dignity in the coming years. We have to start from the beginning with them." Mother tried to understand.

The first school they decided to open was in Alexandria, from where they would get a feel for the culture and the climate. Then they would move into the other areas—Pineville, Natchitoches, Isle Brevelle, and Cloutierville perhaps. In February 1887 Bishop Durier wrote to Mother Florence:

> It will be a beautiful day when the sisters arrive. I have bought a house in Isle Brevelle from the Commission of Indian Affairs for the sisters if they will take care of the colored school. I need six sisters in Natchitoches and three in Isle Brevelle for the 40 children there. I will give the sisters the title to the property there on condition all goes back to the diocese if they leave.

Because the teaching ministry was the only reason for the sisters being in Texas and Louisiana in the first place, Mother tried to be of service wherever the need seemed to be the greatest, and to respond to as many needs as possible. Her zeal sometimes preceded her caution, so that occasionally she pledged herself to parishes and priests who would cause much heartache later. She always tried to follow this procedure: (1) the bishop or pastor made the request; (2) she indirectly investigated or personally visited the place requesting sisters; (3) she checked with Bishop Neraz and the bishop of the diocese where the request came from; (4) she made sure of housing and spiritual care for the sisters; (5) she asked for a contract.

Often, in contracting with Mother Florence, the bishop or pastor of the place deeded the property to the congregation where the sisters' residence or school was to stand or already stood. If the congregation accepted, the sisters were to furnish their residence and keep it in repair; but, if the sisters left the place, the property was to revert to the parish or diocese, and the congregation would be reimbursed for the expense they had incurred in building or renovation. Seldom was the land an outright gift to the sisters. The purpose of this transaction was to insure the parish of the sisters' permanent investment in the place. It was also to ease the financial burden of the parish.

Thus in 1887 Mother accepted and staffed three new schools: Alexandria, Colorado Line, and Sedan. In 1888 four more schools: two in Natchitoches, Pineville, and Temple. In 1889 six: Cloutierville (two), Isle Brevelle, Many, Longview, and Weimer. In 1890 two schools: Tours and St. Rose, Schulenburg. And, in the last year of her first term of office, 1891, three more: Jefferson, Muenster, and Corn Hill. In all, eighteen new schools, including eight in Louisiana, came into being in a period of five years. Mother personally supervised the sisters' housing, the classroom space, the personnel—superior, housekeeper, teachers, and music teacher—and the teaching program. Often she ordered the furniture for the sisters' residence, and even desks and equipment for the classrooms. For instance, in 1890 she ordered double desks for Schulenburg from Messa Schewood & Co., Chicago, for $2.00 apiece, single desks for $1.75, and teacher's desks for $2.32. Messa was introducing these desks in Texas. She helped select the books when it was not a case of using books prescribed by the public school system. For the books she selected she obtained permission from Bishop Neraz, even when the school was in another diocese. If the sisters' residence or school had to be built, she was consulted or did much of the actual planning, depending on the leadership of the pastor. She also had to provide funds for building, renovation, and repair.

Draining as this work was for her, it was sometimes a welcome distraction to expend mental and physical energy on new beginnings after the incessant small responsibilities funneled in daily and hourly at the convent. On the missions she met people, visited with the sisters, saw the children for whom all this would make a difference. She was quite happy there, putting her hand to everything.

The three types of schools already in operation in 1886 were the public school, which ran from three to five months with public money. Religion was never taught in these schools, but before or after school in parish buildings. Most public schools closed after public monies ran out. But, where the sisters taught in a public school in a Catholic settlement, it continued after public funds ceased, financed by tuition from the parents. In such cases the textbooks were switched at this time to those approved by the bishop and the sisters. Mother Florence did not like these public schools and could hardly agree to accept any new ones of this type.

"I have had experience with publicly supported schools in Alsace," she said. "The state will become more and more demanding, until we are either forced out of them or will have to submit to humiliating regulations." She always negotiated for parish schools, where the parish furnished the facilities and the parents paid tuition for the children. She was not always successful, for sometimes the bishop insisted she accept a public school where the parents could not afford to pay the tuition.

And then there were the few academies owned and operated by the congregation, offering a more liberal education. The academies always had boarders, and sometimes the sisters teaching in parish or public schools even kept boarders who attended these schools, especially the children living too far away to come as day students but needing preparation for first communion or confirmation. Boarding schools were later to offer many difficulties, especially in the Indian territory.

Father Menard in Alexandria and Father M. P. Lennartz in Temple were to consume much of Mother's time and psychic energy. Father Menard was the first pastor to request sisters in Louisiana. With Bishop Neraz's permission and advice, and Bishop Durier's eager interest, Mother Florence took four sisters to Alexandria, where they were warmly welcomed. But when she saw the poor house they were to live in on the waterfront, she had grave doubts. In 1858 this house had been brought on a raft from across the bayou at Clark's Point and set up on First Street. It was almost in an irreparable state, and she left the sisters there with misgivings. During that winter the sisters suffered intensely from the damp cold, and one succumbed. Father Menard asked her to have the house repaired, but Bishop Neraz advised her not to spend money on repairing parish property. Rather than let the sisters leave or spend another miserable winter in this house, Father Menard finally appealed to the people, who built, at great sacrifice, a new residence for the sisters, with some room even for boarders. This was to last through her first two terms of office. Moreover, she discovered Father Menard's scholarship and knowledge of the French language, so that she invited him to translate the life of Father Moye into English, a task he was delighted to do, and one that generated a permanent tie between them.

But, with Father Lennartz in Temple, problems were not so easily solved, and Mother never succeeded in winning his friendship. At his urgent request for sisters to work in his new "fruitful and well-equipped parish," she consulted Bishops Gallagher and Neraz. She went to the place and agreed to staff it. Like many other pastors, Father Lennartz wanted to deed the property to the congregation, and Bishop Neraz agreed, under the usual conditions. When all was settled, Father Lennartz, an exile from his own religious Congregation of the Precious Blood and temporarily accepted by Bishop Gallagher in the Galveston diocese, began to make demands.

"I want kind and able and fair sisters, especially the superior, who will speak English, and then all will be right," he wrote Mother. But all was never right. There was constant need for improvements, constant need for building, request after request for money, and complaints about the delay in sending money. He thought she would "be pleased to have her own place there, but it now sounds like it was a crime." He was persecuted by his own order, he said. He heard that she was looking for a convent chaplain. He would like that even for one year. It would give him "a respectable position." But Mother Florence told him he could not leave the Temple people. By the end of 1889 the congregation had invested $900 in building and repairs in Temple. By July 1890, Mother had spent $1,050 and had received volumes of complaints and recriminations. In 1891 Father was still building, still requesting money, which he said did not come in time to pay the laborers. While Mother Florence resisted his demands as much as possible, she did not intend to oppose any priest and scandalize the parishioners if she could help it.

Mother Florence felt a real excitement about the Louisiana mission for two reasons. First, she thought it was what the founder, Father Moye, would have wanted and what she had come to America to do: to live in poverty with the poor, where nobody else would work. The Third Plenary Council of Baltimore in 1884 had decreed that each parish should have a Catholic school. Bishop Durier was convinced of this necessity in Louisiana, but he could not find sisters even for his white schools now, much less his colored. And there was little money in Louisiana for anything at all. But Mother felt that Divine Providence would somehow provide.

The second reason for Mother's pleasure was Bishop Durier, a faith-filled, energetic, and zealous Frenchman with a sense of humor and a heart filled with love and gratitude. His admiration for Mother Florence was boundless and energizing; it soon extended to the entire congregation, replete with approval and support, which she was careful to believe she did not seek, but which nevertheless lightened her burden considerably. She looked forward to her visits with Bishop Durier and treasured his letters. The tenor of his correspondence ran thus:

> *April 1888:* Jews and Protestants want the sisters also. The Fair will bring enough money to pay them. The Mission Society will help Isle Brevelle. Think of Natchitoches first.

Also:

> *June 1888:* The Cloutierville priest will give $200 to the sisters the day they come. I send my love and blessing.
> *July 1888:* I will add rooms—parlor, refectory, bedrooms, if I can get money. Somehow I will get it. But don't put the mulattoes with the colored.

And:

> *June 1889:* The sisters are at work in Cloutierville and Isle Brevelle. They give honor to the Church and to your congregation. I am proud of them.

The sisters, like Mother Florence, could not understand segregation. The bishop soon got repercussions. He wrote Mother that Sister Helen took the mulattoes who were ready for the seventh and eighth grades to the white school so they could continue their education. The people were incensed. The priest also persuaded the sister, who was sent to cook, to come and help teach in the Negro school. The bishop did not complain. Things would work out.

In November 1888 Bishop Durier wrote:

> I feel the need to say the sisters are giving me the greatest satisfaction. I hear nothing but praise. Natchitoches regards the superior as a person of great capacity. The people say, "They can't fail to succeed; they are so simple." I am so happy. I bless them and you. It is the first time since my return that I am so happy.

Mother's letters were formal and inhibited. She was careful never to put in writing anything that might be misinterpreted. In responding to the bishop's requests about the number of sisters for each school, she wrote, "I will submit to your wishes as I do not want to put any obstacle in the way of the good that can be done."

When Mother was finally persuaded by Bishop Durier in 1889 to send two sisters to Many, Louisiana, she knew that Sabine Parish had been "neutral territory" between Texas and Louisiana in the early days, when desperadoes, fleeing from justice, sought refuge there. It was named Sabine because the Indian tribe occupying the land had lost their wives and daughters to a stronger warring tribe. Although the community was made up at this time chiefly of English and Scotch-Irish Protestants from the Atlantic seaboard, four men named John—three

Belgian and one Irish—had come twenty-seven years earlier. Their numerous offspring made up most of the Catholic population in this hostile community. The church was named St. John by these men. The school where Sisters Lucia and Beatrice taught was one room with boxes for desks and boards for benches. The sisters' residence was a dilapidated tavern, where U. S. Grant, a captain in the Mexican War, had dined while surveying the road between Natchitoches and San Antonio. Behind the tavern was a cemetery against a backdrop of heavy pine forest. In front were two huge oak trees on which, as tradition had it, desperadoes were hanged. Rev. A. Anseeuw, pastor where an earlier attempt to establish a mission had failed, helped sustain the missionary spirit of the two brave pioneers for the first two or three years while they accustomed themselves to the poverty, climate, and people. There were no Creoles or mulattoes here, but the black community held their nightly fetes within earshot of the convent.

In May 1889 the bishop wrote, "I found the sisters in Many cheerful, happy, like fishes in the water." And in August of the same year, "People along the Cane River are being evangelized." In 1890 he wrote, "The union between the people and the sisters is very good," and, later, "Messages from the Sisters of Divine Providence are like messages from the angels."

In the last year of her first term the Sisters of Divine Providence were firmly established in Louisiana and in Bishop Durier's heart. He continued to be grateful and to express his gratitude. Invited to Castroville, he wrote:

> I would like to see that beautiful convent, that blessed beehive with so many happy bees. Sure they would not sting me but would welcome me with some of their honey and would cheer me up with the cheerfulness that God gives to His beloved ones. But mind you, I am sickly since ten days, and so are the other priests. All is gloomy enough around here. We are waiting for our little sisters to come and laugh at us and make fun of us and give us some sunshine. Cotton is splendid along the Cane River. That means for the sisters a fair prospect of having square meals this year, chicken and butter three times a day, and molasses all over the table.

In his Christmas message of 1891 he said, "The old bishop of Natchitoches blesses the Sisters of Divine Providence one and all, and especially good Mother Florence, whom we all love so well." He had a special story to tell at this time:

> Even Sister Florentine contributes to give us that blessed cheerfulness in spite of the dark prospect hanging overhead. What is the dark prospect? A pipe organ is coming from France for her, with pedals and a blower managed by the organist. She will have her ten fingers busy at the keyboard and she will play on the pedal with one foot, and blow the organ with the other foot, and sing with all her lungs, and mind a dozen giddy-headed girls who sing with her, and look at the book with one eye, and do all those things at the same time. You might think she is like Mother Goose, "who had so many children she didn't know what to do." Well, not at all. She is ready to master the situation and laugh at all the dark clouds hanging over her head.

Except for Temple and Muenster, which wanted sisters to teach in the public school, the opening of the ten Texas schools was routine. But Mother had some difficulty with existing schools. This was true in Palestine, where the sisters were spiritually deprived and physically overworked, even though financially they were offered an increase in stipend. "Money shall not lower my feelings in regard to the hard toil of the sisters in Palestine. Doubling the expenses would never pay for their sacrifices," she wrote the pastor. But she always gave the priests another chance. She decided to lend money from the mother house to build a decent house there. Palestine, an academy, was to pay this back to the congregation.

Marienfield had to be closed, she wrote Bishop Neraz. First of all, there were too few pupils. "Furthermore I have other reasons sufficient for me to act thus, which I will offer you, my lord, orally," she wrote, not being willing to provide a permanent written record of her complaint. Although she had considered removing the sisters from Columbus because of poor spiritual and physical conditions, she likewise gave the pastor a chance to get them better accommodations and spiritual assistance.

When the Fayetteville trustees complained about the superior, whom they wished changed, Mother was noticeably annoyed:

> I believe she is doing a very good job and I do not intend to remove her. I am surprised that the trustees of Fayetteville allow themselves to be ruled by a poor sister. No one bound you to obey her. If your opinion is contrary to hers, simply declare the fact and I am confident that if reasonable, she will not be opposed thereto. She is, however, going there soon and will see you.

She also wrote Bishop Gallagher requesting to see him about the situation in Fayetteville, where the pastor did not want the sisters, and was making it difficult for them.

Mother Florence saw very early in her administration that with the urgent requests for sisters from all over Texas, and even outside Texas, she was not going to be able to take care of all needs, or even the most pressing ones, without additional personnel. It was true that the novitiate was large now because of previous recruiting in Europe; and this would give her quite a large number for the missions for the first two or three years. But she had to look ahead. It took several years to train and educate the young women after they arrived. So, much as she felt personally about recruiting in Europe, it had to be done for the church in Texas. From experience she knew that the most effective method was to cultivate the pastors, inspire confidence and missionary zeal in them, and let them study and encourage young women in their parishes. This she began to do immediately with the help of the Irish and European sisters who knew the pastors in their home towns and surrounding parishes. Some of the pastors in both Ireland and Europe were very responsive. Mother Florence's brother Antoine, apprised of the need, also kept a lookout for prospects. Sometimes his judgment was more accurate than the pastors', for several girls, encouraged by their pastors and thus accepted by the sisters, seemed to him entirely unacceptable as religious. He was usually right, for these girls soon left the convent.

In 1888 one young lady came from Ireland and four from

Europe in order to enter the convent. Others indicated that they would come the following year, so in 1889 Sisters Angelique Decker and Gonzaga Mosser brought twenty-six prospective members from Germany and Alsace. Four of these girls left, as Antoine had predicted. Antoine was now actively involved in aiding his sister, as he had so often promised her he would. If a young lady was financially strapped, he and his wife helped to supply her trousseau. If her family was unable to pay her complete fare, he helped obtain funds. He often accompanied a group of young women to Antwerp or Le Havre, wherever the ship was leaving from, and he gave the sisters who came for the girls his wholehearted cooperation. Three young ladies came independently and alone in 1890 and 1891, but these came from Germany and Austria on their own. In all, thirty-four aspirants came to Texas from Ireland and Europe between 1887 and 1892, of whom twenty-nine remained. Sister Clementine Marquis, one of "Mother's girls," asked in 1891 not to renew her vows but to return home, because this life was not for her. It was Mother's fourth loss from her group of twenty in six years, and she was still uncertain about Annie and Agatha Pfohl. But they would have to decide for themselves, she knew.

Besides the European recruits, twenty-nine American young ladies entered the convent and became sisters during those same six years. Mother Florence received each future sister with loving tenderness and solicitude. She tried to ensure that they would have companionship, encouragement, and sufficient training to ease the pain of separation from their families and homeland. She was a true and compassionate mother to them.

The Texas congregation had been from the very first poor and frugal. The fare, whether at the mother house or on the mission, was the food of the poor. Their lodging was simple and spare. A small coin went a long way, for there was little money coming in. The sisters, however, were industrious and talented in needlework. Such objects as they produced helped to increase the income. There was constant building and repair work going on in the mother house and the other houses of the congregation. Some pastors could not pay the sisters when the time came.

Others asked loans from the mother house for school construction. If there was money on hand, Mother Florence loaned it. Each Christmas she sent the bishops a gift, usually liturgical vestments or altar linen that the sisters had made. On special parish occasions, she made presentations to the pastors. She had a constant urge to have all the Lord's dwellings properly furnished and the Lord's ministers adequately cared for. Whether she planned it this way or not, she won the respect and love of practically all priests who in turn were ready to help her when she needed them.

Already she had asked her lay friends in St. Joseph's parish to lend her money for purchasing land near St. Joseph's. This was to become her practice: to borrow first from priests and friends before she went to the bank. She hated borrowing and debts, but she had to accept it as the only way to accomplish the Lord's work. If a loss were suffered, it was the congregation's, not the benefactor's. Mother had plans for larger projects in the back of her head. If she were reelected in 1892, she would proceed with these plans. Before this election, however, she believed that the number of sisters eligible to vote in chapter was becoming unwieldy. A representative system such as was being used in larger congregations would be more effective. She wrote to Bishop Neraz asking for his approval to devise a representative system and to prepare the constitution, including the new section that he had sent her, forbidding compulsory manifestation of conscience of sisters to their superiors, to Rome for approval. Bishop Neraz refused her permission for both. As long as he lived, he meant to keep the congregation as it was; he was pleased with it and discouraged her from moving the diocesan congregation toward pontifical approval. There was nothing further that she could do. She prepared for the chapter of 1892.

Looking back over her first term in office, she sighed. It had been harder than she had ever feared it would be. If she were reelected, she would know how to proceed. There were large plans in her head, and she now had the support that she had set as one of her goals in the beginning. In fact, her track record looked good—if she could erase all the heartbreaks.

7

Second Term (1892-1898)

Mother Florence had mixed feelings about the upcoming election. There was no doubt that she would be reelected. She and all the sisters knew that Bishop Neraz would want it so; that was enough reason. But besides that, she had governed successfully during her term in office, and the sisters were pleased. As for herself, although she knew it would be hard, it could never be so hard as what she had already experienced. There were also certain things she now wanted to do and knew she could do. So in her heart she already anticipated a second term. She sent out the notices to the sisters, all fifty-five of them who were eligible to vote, since Bishop Neraz had not approved a representative system; then she wrote Bishop Durier that election would be held that summer. He was quick to reply:

> You spoke of the election of superior general. Does it mean that you are in danger of tumbling down the mountain top? I hope it will not be the case, but I suppose it would be so. All right. Nevertheless our gentle and loving Mother Florence, who founded our convents on Cane River, and Red River, in spite of every and any difficulty, shall have a special place in our hearts.

This time there was no tension as the sisters, already at the mother house, prepared to meet for chapter of election. On July 13 Bishop Neraz, Rev. J. B. Weimer, Rev. J. Lagleder, and Rev. Wm. Fuhrwerk arrived at the designated time, the bishop to preside and the other three to observe. The atmosphere was comparatively relaxed as the bishop and clergy chatted informally with the sisters.

Bishop Neraz greeted Mother Florence warmly and spoke to the sisters in glowing praise of her first term, "getting the congregation on its feet," with his help. Then the voting took place. The first ballot showed Mother Florence with fifty-four votes and Sister Angelique one. Mother Florence had already selected her council, which she submitted to the bishop for approval. They were Sister Angelique, first assistant; Sister Flavienne, second assistant and directress of the boarding school; Sister Gonzaga, mistress of novices; Sister Stanislaus, secretary; Sisters Ange, Pierre, Mary Agnes, and Scholastica as delegates of districts. Bishop Neraz approved the selection, and the announcement was made. There was little business to discuss, so the chapter was soon over, Mother Florence installed, and a congregational Mass and special dinner held for the entire congregation.

Mother Florence had long since established the custom of celebrating special occasions with elaborate dinner, the best china, silverware, crystal, linen, food, and wine available. The long tables were festively decorated, the cooks had outdone themselves, and the novices in long white aprons served at table. A prepared message of congratulation and praise was read and later presented to Mother with a bouquet of flowers. She thought of the unhappy day six years ago and felt indeed that God had blessed the congregation and her in spite of her ignorance and blunders. She wrote to her friends in St. Jean-de-Bassel, telling them of the election.

By 1889 the congregation at St. Jean-de-Bassel knew for sure that the American branch was independent from the root house. They had counted on the American foundation as a possible alternative should they be denied a place in the schools of Alsace-Lorraine. Many of the sisters had already been released from their former teaching assignments, and the congregation had large numbers of novices. Mother Anna Houlne had to look elsewhere than Texas for an American foundation that would remain dependent on the mother house. In deciding on a place to apply, Mother Anna, after fervent prayer to Divine Providence for guidance, opened the *U.S. Catholic Directory* by chance to the name of Bishop C. P. Maes of Covington, Kentucky. She wrote to him in part: "The situation in our dear country is so that the religious congregations, teaching especially, are more or less menaced in their existence, and already are hampered in their actions and development." Bishop Maes was delighted to have them in his diocese. The three sisters sent set up a provincial house in the diocese, where they opened a boarding school in Newport.

Sister Camille, the former Sister Arsene Schaef and devoted friend of Mother St. Andrew, was one of the three. She had returned to St. Jean-de-Bassel in 1887 and reentered the novitiate, where she was given the new name. Also in the American province was Sister Marie Houlne, a friend whom Mother Florence remembered well from Europe. They began a correspondence that was to grow and deepen into a lifelong friendship. In 1891, when Sister Marie opened an orphanage in Providence, Rhode Island, Mother Florence occasionally contributed financially to this worthy cause. She later managed to visit Sister Marie several times. She was glad that Sister Arsene was well and happy.

Mother Florence came to her second term with great enthusiasm. Her two main dreams, simmering for a few years now in the back of her head, were to move the mother house from Castroville to San Antonio and to start the process that would eventually lead the congregation to the status of a pontifical institute. Bishop Neraz was in poor health and aging rapidly. The plans for both projects must be ready to move before he should die. In the meantime she meant to expand the sisters' education program both in the summertime and during the year.

She decided immediately after election in 1892 that she had to do something about the Temple situation before the sisters could return there for the year. Bishop Gallagher had already left for Rome, but before his departure he had expressed great dissatisfaction with Lennartz's handling of the parish, and his property dealings. Father Lennartz was determined to get everything settled to the bishop's satisfaction before he would return. He wrote Weimer, V. G., a highly exaggerated letter, asking for his support in the action proposed—to evacuate the sisters and hire lay teachers. He then wrote Mother Florence, telling her that since the congregation had failed to honor the terms of the deed, she should return the deed to him. He ended his letter with this clinching statement:

> I would call your attention to the two sisters here, that sit here, not going to confession and without Holy Communion. You better see whether you have authority to place sisters in such a position of obedience or bitter tyranny. *Before God and man you cannot do this.*

Because Bishop Gallagher was in Rome, there was no recourse to him. Mother therefore wrote attorney H. B. Sanders of Belton about the Temple affair, giving the exact day of the legal transfer of property to the congregation and the amount spent in improvements. She said she must remain under ecclesiastical government and would legally protest the evacuation.

Mother invited Father Lennartz to come to San Antonio for the investiture ceremony and to talk the situation over with Bishop Neraz and herself. Neither Bishop Neraz nor Mother was prepared for his outbursts or able to calm him. "I want the sisters out of Temple! They are incompetent and independent." On August 11 she wrote Bishop Gallagher details of this visit:

> His Lordship is well acquainted with Father Lennartz' dissatisfaction with the sisters which in the absence of my Lord has risen to such a point that Rev. Father Lennartz commanded the sisters to leave Temple, alluding that his Lordship had given his opinion to replace the sisters by secular teachers. As Rt. Rev. J. C. Neraz presided at the ceremonies of investiture of profession in July here in Castroville, an invitation was extended to Very Rev. J. B. Weimer and Rev.

Lennartz to which both priests responded. Our intention was to come to the conclusion "to leave matters until the return of his Lordship to Galveston." Father Lennartz being asked in presence of Bishop Neraz what charges he has against the sisters, he said, "They act too independent." I once more begged him to tell me in what, but he remained silent, as in conscience he could not accuse them of anything, the sisters having fulfilled their duty regarding church, children, and people; besides they had referred to the pastor as to giving picnics to the pupils, exhibitions, etc. Rev. Father continued saying he wanted a Parochial School. Rt. Rev. J. C. Neraz answered, "Let the sisters teach Parochial School in your house and everything will be all right." But he persisted to have the sisters leave Temple. Rev. J. B. Weimer took the word: "Leave everything until his Lordship's arrival." But Father Lennartz was not to be contented.

Mother continued:

I received a petition signed by the most prominent men of Temple, begging to have their sisters back for September. Moreover, I am happy to inform his Lordship that since the sisters' stay in Temple, the school was never as prosperous as last season. The sisters are trying their best to keep as quiet as possible, although Rev. Lennartz leaves nothing undone to oppose them wherever he can. For about one and a half months he has been refusing them absolution, although I had replaced the old teachers by two other sisters during vacation. I referred them to Father Hennessey as being their manager in spiritual affairs during his Lordship's absence.

Mother had this to say to the bishop about vacating the property:

A few days ago Father Lennartz told the sisters to vacate the house; in case of refusal he would use force of law. The sisters are still in the house only waiting for his Lordship's decision. I therefore humbly ask you, My Lord, to favor with a few lines, as also to tell Rev. Lennartz your opinion about the affair. I will try to be in Galveston for his Lordship's arrival in order to clear matters. But I must acknowledge my reluctance at leaving Temple, as we have sacrificed $6,000 for improvements. Very Rev. J. B. Weimer will more enlarge on the subject as he is well acquainted with it.

When Bishop Gallagher returned, he evidently took Lennartz to task. What with the bishop's disapproval, complaints from the parishioners, and petitions from the people for the sisters' return, Lennartz was finally forced to resign.

For a moment it looked as though the trouble might be over. Father Pius Heckman was appointed to replace him. Mother told Bishop Gallagher, however, that the lawyer said the deed was somehow incomplete, as she had pointed out to Bishop Neraz at the time it was given to her. She now sent it to him for completion and recording. He acknowledged receipt of it, saying he was sending it to the new pastor to have it recorded in Temple.

If Mother Florence now thought the matter was ended, she soon learned otherwise. Lennartz was assigned to Frelsburg, where he again had Sisters of Divine Providence in his school. He then went to La Grange, where he employed a lawyer to look after his interests, to the chagrin of Bishop Gallagher and Mother Florence, who hated legal proceedings. Lennartz continued to claim the Temple property and sent threatening letters concerning it.

Mother wrote Father Weimer in July 1893 saying she would give up the property since there seemed no way of keeping it. But he said no; it was legally the congregation's, and she should go to court, or both she and Lennartz would be humbled. Lennartz had no such qualms. He sent an emissary to Mother, saying he was resigning the priesthood and leaving the diocese,* but keeping the Temple property. If she wanted the property, she would buy it from him.

*Lennartz did not leave the priesthood or the diocese. He remained in La Grange twelve years and was then assigned to St. Joseph's, Galveston, in 1912, where he again had Sisters of Divine Providence in his school. Bishop Christopher Byrne, the successor of Bishop Gallagher, appointed him to his council. He spent the remainder of his life in Galveston, dying there in 1932.

Mother wrote Bishop Gallagher:

> I will relinguish the property if I can. All I ask is the $900
> paid in notes. We will not buy the house 1) because the
> walls are already cracking, 2) I think there is no blessing on
> the house. I would prefer to have things settled peacefully
> than go to court and improve on our property.

As in all painful situations she concluded her letter with "At the
foot of the Cross."

Bishop Gallagher, thinking of the school rather than of the
congregation, wrote, "Take it to court if necessary. If Lennartz
gets it, it will break up the school."

Bishop Neraz agreed with Gallagher: "Lennartz is forcing
you to go to court. Such a man has no conscience, so ask all
the sisters to pray. You can get nowhere with him except by
force." There seemed no way out of this endless mess. She made
an appointment with Bishop Gallagher for the end of August,
inviting Lennartz to meet with them. "I hope to have satisfaction
given to his Lordship, yourself, and our institute," she wrote him.
Lennartz came, sullen and determined.

"I am requesting you to pay the sisters the $900 that they
so justly claim," the bishop told him.

"I will pay them nothing!" he answered, hardly giving Mother
Florence a second glance. He left and the bishop confessed his
powerlessness to deal with him. But he insisted that she take
the case to court.

By November, having put off the unsavory ordeal as long
as possible, Mother looked into it and found that she would
have to pay $500 in fees, plus lose the $900 if she did not win
the case. The price did not seem worth the effort. She wrote the
bishop: "Since the chief purpose is to save the school, will the
diocese be willing to pay part of the cost?" If she would give
the church property to Lennartz and keep the school, she would
let the school be used for services on Sundays. The sisters would
arrange everything Friday after school. The bishop did not respond.

Because the bishop failed to take any further interest in the case, she decided to give the property to Lennartz. But she could not do this without obtaining a quitclaim, which she had a notary draw up. This, too, needed the bishop's approval. When no reply came, she wrote impatiently, "Kindly inform me whether you have placed my deed of last year to you on record or not. I need it now. Mr. Ellinger threatens to sue unless he hears from me by Dec. 2." This brought the indifferent reply "I do not consider this matter the interest of the Church, but only your own."

By December 1 Mother had no reply from the bishop and no quitclaim to send Mr. Ellinger when she wrote him: "I am tired of that continual worry and do not wish to possess for one minute longer not even one inch of that property."

The final step was taken just prior to the letter of January 10, 1894, from Bishop Gallagher, saying that the parish priest was forced to vacate the church and residence, that Lennartz sold the property to Mr. Ellinger, and that the church would be rebuilt at another location. "Your property is your problem," he ended.

Neither Bishop Neraz nor Gallagher had been of any real help to Mother in this continual ordeal, which was initiated with the approval of both bishops in 1888, and had yielded nothing but humiliation, expense, loss of time, and mental stress for herself and the sisters stationed there for six years. One thing she learned: that she would do well to seek legal aid herself and not depend on ecclesiastical help in congregational matters now that she had learned how to do it. It was obvious, too, that the first introduction to a parish was not an indication of what might develop there. The true condition is not always evident in the beginning. Mother was aware of her tendency to trust all priests and bishops and to try to cooperate with them even at great sacrifice to herself and the congregation. She also knew that her warmhearted sympathy and missionary zeal would probably lead her into other difficult situations. She would try to be prudent without losing her basic trust in people and Divine Providence— even when this meant taking risks.

Mother Florence hoped that she would be able during this

term to begin proceedings for approval of the constitutions and pontifical status for the congregation. She knew she could not put it exactly this way to the bishop, however. She would have to be more subtle. She planned her strategy. She would continue her attitude of concern for his health and happiness and submit to his decisions. But she would prepare the drafts and present them to him as a practical step for supplying additional needed copies of the constitutions, with the section on manifestation of conscience and holy communion as part of the book. The constitutions would also contain in the historical introduction a statement regarding the time of and reason for the Texas branch becoming independent of the European mother house. She would mention sending, as a formality, a copy to Rome for approval. In November 1892 she wrote Bishop Neraz telling him what she proposed.

From Eagle Pass, the bishop wrote to her:

> Your favor of the 8th is received. I do not understand well the meaning of your letter, as one copy of the document you sent me and the letter you wrote treat of two different subjects. As to the separate house of Castroville, I am not the one who asked for it and established it. When I was in St. Jean-de-Bassel, I asked the Mother Superior if she could help Castroville by furnishing some subjects and in recognizing your house as a branch of the mother house. The superior answered me that it was impossible for her to do so on account of the distance. But I understood well that her refusal was on account of Mother St. Andrew, so I did the best I could to keep up your house, and thanks to God I succeeded.
>
> The second object is your rule. I think you have the same rules as they have at St. Jean-de-Bassel; in that case there is nothing to be done as Rome will not examine them if they have been examined before. If there are some changes, which I do not think or remember, then it is only since I acted on the words of Mother Superior at St. Jean-de-Bassel; in that case Rome will not pass an opinion on the rule as it takes a longer time to prove that they are good and sufficient. As a general custom Rome requires 20-50 years experience to find out how they fulfill the aim for which they have been made. . . . When we take such

> steps, we must act prudently and according to the laws of the Church . . . so I advise you not to be in a hurry about it, so no false steps are made or taken.

Of course, the rules at St. Jean-de-Bassel had never been approved by Rome, but Mother saw that this was a final response from the bishop: that she would never know how the separation came about as far as the bishop and St. Jean-de-Bassel were concerned, and that, as long as Bishop Neraz lived, there would be no progress toward attaining pontifical status. She would simply try to be patient a few more years and make the remaining days of the bishop's life as pleasant as possible.

Whenever an occasion arose, she sent him affirming messages. Immediately after his refusal concerning the constitutions, he highly recommended the Sisters of Divine Providence for the school in Aransas Pass. She wrote him:

> I cannot but express my warmest gratitude for your kindness as this is one proof more to convince the Daughters of Providence of the great interest my Lord and venerated father takes in the welfare of our poor congregation.

And later she wrote him near Christmas time:

> May the shattered health be strengthened and sustained to the contentment of your humble daughter; and when your revered forehead shall be browned and wrinkled by the heat of the day, may your noble soul rest in the bosom of the Sacred Heart.

In October 1894 Mother Florence sent a monetary gift in gratitude for all his services to the congregation. In his last letter to her a few days later, he wrote:

> You have always helped me enough for all that I have done for you. Moreover, I thank you—I send my blessings to all the sisters.

He died November 15, 1894. Mother Florence wept tears of sincere sorrow over his passing. He had indeed been a true father and friend to her in his own way. When the funeral was over, she sat down and composed a telegram to Mother St. Andrew in California:

> Bishop Neraz died Nov. 15. May he rest in peace. Please feel free to come home now, if you can. We want you here.

But Mother St. Andrew could not come. Her brother's children needed her, and she could not abandon them. She was educating them to be self-supporting, good Christians and she had not completed her labor of love. She was grateful beyond words for the message, and she looked forward to the day when she could accept the welcome invitation.

The year 1894 was very special to Mother Florence for several reasons. It was the year the final decision was made to select a site and begin construction on the new mother house in San Antonio. It had been clear to her from the day she first took office that the convent would have to move. Now was the time.

With Sister Angelique, her first assistant, she set out to view the places that had been suggested to her by her friends in the city. She had obtained with no difficulty permission of Bishop Neraz for the move. He had been indeed happy to know that his congregation would be within reach, because he was less and less able to make the long drive from San Antonio to Castroville. He was not to live to see this take place. The most likely site they could find was on Government Hill, east of the city. Mayor Henry Elmendorf, learning that she was contemplating a move, recommended an elevated plateau of eighteen acres in the Lake View addition, touching Lake Elmendorf on the southwest.

She mentioned this to a friend, Miss Nora Kelley, who immediately hired a carriage to take Mother Florence and Sister Philothea Thiry, the superior of St. Joseph's Academy in San Antonio, to see it. They drove out West Commerce, past the end of the trolley line on Hamilton. They continued on the dirt road through the mesquite prairie until they came to within a block of Lake Elmendorf. The eighteen acres lay beyond the lake and were encircled on almost two sides by the lake. The party got down from the carriage and walked across a footbridge to reach the plateau. The lake was wide and deep on both sides of the bridge. It was spring. The plateau and the land sloping to the lake were covered with thick green grass and Texas wild flowers: wild verbena, Indian blankets, bluebonnets, and primroses. To the southwest lay Castroville Road, which both Mother Florence and Sister Philothea had traveled many times on their way from Castroville to St. Joseph's. It would be convenient to get to and from Castroville from this place. Mother meant to keep the house in Castroville as a girls' school and a home for the old sisters. She liked the suggested place immediately and decided this would be the site of the new mother house and the academy for girls.

On the way back to San Antonio, she had the carriage stop on Prospect Hill, where she turned and looked back at her future home. There, in her mind's eye, across the lake she saw a large four-story building with turrets on each side of the broad entrance, and wings on either side. Beside it she visioned a tall chapel with two spires reaching into the blue Texas sky, and other buildings spreading in both directions. All were reflected in the waters of the lake, which lay before them. Her breath came softly through parted lips, and her large brown eyes glowed as she sat in reverie, to be nudged gently by Sister Philothea.

"Come," said Sister Philothea, "it will take a little doing before we see in reality what you are dreaming of."

But when Mother exuberantly reported to Mayor Elmendorf about her decision, he offered to donate the entire eighteen acres to the congregation on condition that she spend $75,000 on construction within the next ten years. She accepted his gift without hesitation, knowing that it was the right thing to do.

With the approval of her council, the hiring of James Wahrenberger as architect, the drawing of plans, and contracting of the firm of Schaumm, Flaig, and Wagner for the sum of $40,000, the construction was under way. The complex was to be a worthy tribute to Divine Providence, with none like it in San Antonio or perhaps in all of Texas. Because it was to be a training center for those who would bring Christ into the highways and byways of Texas, it must be a worthy symbol of its purpose to the locale. This meant more than bricks and mortar. It meant heart and soul, grace and dignity, beauty with endurance. It would be built at great sacrifice to all the sisters for years to come, because there was very little money on hand. It was God's work and He would see it through. It would be built step by painful step, perfect, beginning with the central part, the entrance area of the main building.

Ground was broken August 15, 1895, the Feast of the Assumption of the Blessed Virgin Mary. By December 8, the Feast of the Immaculate Conception, the cornerstone could be laid. This was set for two days after the feast, December 10. Bishop J. A. Forest, who had succeeded Bishop Neraz to the San Antonio see on October 8 of that year, blessed and laid the cornerstone in the presence of Mother Florence and her council and several other sisters. The document deposited in the cornerstone began with the dedication:

> Confiding in God's help, we, the Sisters of Divine Providence, and humble daughters of Father Moye, our saintly founder whose beatification is now expected, erect this building in honor of the Blessed Trinity, under the protection of our dear Mother Mary and St. Anne our patroness . . . on the 10th day of December, being the 18th of the pontificate of Leo XIII, Most Rev. Francis Janssens, Archbishop of New Orleans, Rt. Rev. J. A. Forest, Bishop of San Antonio, Grover Cleveland, President of the U. S., Charles A. Culberson, governor of Texas, Henry Elmendorf, mayor of San Antonio. The 27th anniversary of the Sisters of Divine Providence in Texas. . . .

At the dinner that followed the laying of the cornerstone, Bishop Forest suggested that the projected name of "St. Mary's of the Lake" be changed to "Our Lady of the Lake" because of other "St. Marys" in the city. Mother accepted his suggestion.

For weeks and months Mother lay awake part of each night planning and dreaming. Often during the week she watched the men work and inspected the construction brick by blond brick. When she was forced to be absent for a while, she became impatient and irritable. She became sterner and more demanding of the sisters, from whom she asked hard sacrifices in order to save money. The workmen knew and respected her, realizing that if any flaw appeared, it would mean real trouble for them. On Sunday afternoons she walked through the shell with Mother Philothea, whose opinion and advice she had come to respect highly, planning the interior and the impressive entrance that would wind around the lake from Nineteenth Street, lined by majestic pine trees, as was the entrance at the convent of St. Jean-de-Bassel.

According to Mother Florence's established procedure, she had contacted her friends for loans first. Among those who made large loans were the priests who had opposed Mother St. Andrew but had promised to support another sister elected in her place, each pledging about $2,000: Fathers Pefferkorn, Kirch, Tarrillion, and Wack, who could afford the least. There were other priests and laymen who also made loans.

In the spring the building neared completion and Mother spent much time supervising the interior finish and the furniture. She was afraid it would not be ready in time for the sisters to stay there that summer. But she trusted that it would be, and she sent out a letter to the sisters in April:

> It has been decided by the Council that all professed sisters will spend the vacation in the Mother House of Our Lady of the Lake, San Antonio, while the sisters not having pronounced their vows will pass theirs at the house of the novitiate, Castroville. No community trunk will be forwarded to the House of Novitiate, but all must be directed to Lake View. The sisters destined for Castroville will simply pack the clothes they need in a satchel, while no valise will be allowed for those who meet at San Antonio.
>
> Each sister shall have a strong leather valise, well strapped. Communities of three or more may have a community trunk. All trunks and valises must be checked and transferred to Our Lady of the Lake, paying 45¢ for each. I do not wish that any sister should carry bundles or valises through the city.

She also wrote Bishop Forest at the same time, requesting a chaplain for Our Lady of the Lake for the summer: "I hear that Father Pefferkorn is about to retire. We know and highly respect him. Will you allow him to be our chaplain at Lake View?" The bishop gave permission and Father Pefferkorn served as chaplain for several years.

It was an exciting summer for all concerned, but not an easy one. Many of the sisters wished themselves back at Castroville. There was no entrance, no water supply, no gas, no sewerage system, no power lines to the new construction. Though near San Antonio, it was more isolated than Castroville in many ways and the inconveniences that first summer were greater. Besides the footbridge there was no road to West Commerce. The only way a carriage could approach or leave the grounds was to cut across the prairie east of the site to or from what was later to be Nineteenth Street around the lake and then to Commerce, or cut across the prairie to the south and reach Castroville Road. That was what they did. But in June 1896 Mother Florence's influence in San Antonio had so grown with the support she enjoyed from the mayor, the bishop, the priests, and the business community, that she wrote with confidence to Mr. H. Weiks at the Street Car Company as follows:

> Please have the street car run as far as Lake View to afford adequate accommodations for about 100 sisters and the same number (of students) all year. Have it run every hour.

And he did as she requested.

The teacher education program that Mother Florence began with the sisters in Castroville spread and increased throughout the country, and the teachers' institutes started in earnest in 1892. The first such institute in Medina County was held in the study hall of Divine Providence in Castroville. Later it was held several times a year, usually in Castroville or Hondo. When it was in Castroville, Mother always offered the large study hall. It took place on Friday and Saturday, at which times certain subjects were presented, sometimes by the sisters, in which all teachers participated. For instance, different aspects of arithmetic, grammar, reading, physiology, and spelling were presented. Teachers could actually make as much progress by attending these institutes as they could by attending the summer normals. The sisters did participate, both as presenters and as students at the Medina County institutes and those of other counties where they taught. It was a real treat or a real cross for them to travel to institute centers, sometimes having to spend the night in a hotel and dine on restaurant food, which they brought to their room, because they did not eat in public. The summer normal was still held in Castroville even after the mother house was moved to San Antonio, until 1900, when it was also transferred to San Antonio.

During her second term of office, Mother did not send any sisters to Europe to recruit. She needed every penny for the new mother house and other buildings she had to construct on the missions; besides, she believed that girls from Texas would be entering. During these six years only ten girls came on their own from Europe, and one of them was her niece, Mary Grüner, her sister Madeleine's child. Antoine wrote to his sister that their niece and nephew were finished with the local schooling and were not being trained for any work. Mary, he said, really missed having a mother, but she seemed to have a strong leaning toward the religious life. Antoine had a child of his own at last; she was now two years old and the apple of his eye. His devotion to his sister, however, was only slightly diminished financially, but still active otherwise. She wrote him in 1896:

> You must do something for the children. Have Eugene educated for some trade, and send Mary to me in Texas. I know that you cannot afford this expense all at once, but you can use my part of our parents' inheritance, my patrimony, for Mary's expenses. Later, if it can be done, you can replace it for me. I will see that Mary is educated properly, and if she has a vocation, I will accept her into the convent.

Mary came, thirteen years old, and was put in school. She did, indeed, want to enter the convent and was accepted into the postulate immediately, received the habit two years later, and was professed in 1902. From Texas and Louisiana sixty-eight girls entered and remained in the convent during Mother Florence's second term, plus the ten from Europe. Mother realized that she would have to actively recruit again in Europe if she were elected for a third term.

Because Mother was deeply involved in two or three congregational projects, it did not mean that all other regular activity stopped. It was the small crises, joys, and sorrows, the monotonous routine trivia that made up the large portion of her busy days. They wakened, wearied, and worried her, but kept her in contact with the sisters and mission conditions. When the superior in Muenster overstepped her authority, Mother made it clear that the pastor and not the superior was responsible for the parish. When Don Beatty in Washington, from whom she had ordered a piano, wrote for payment before shipping, she wrote a scathing letter:

> The reputation we enjoy is dearer to us than a fortune; still this will teach us not to deal with firms who take no account of a word given.

She opened no new schools in 1892, but she kept in touch with those already established. Sister Dominic wrote from Tours:

> As you know, I was sent here to teach Bohemian, which I didn't know very well, although I would not tell the pastor so. I now have to translate the pastor's sermons from German to Bohemian, as he doesn't know it either. Regulations for Lent, sermons for weddings, advice for confession, and many other topics. I read it to him several times so that he will know how to say it. To do this translation I have to look up in the dictionary almost every other word. If you could see me standing in the middle of the room, half in despair, wringing my hands and saying, "My God, it is for you; help me." Sometimes it is 2 o'clock before I get to bed, but I am up at 5 with the rest. After Mass Father came to me overjoyed to tell me that the people came in crowds to thank him for the nice sermon. "If you only knew what it cost me!" I felt like telling him. You see, though, how everything turns to profit.

Every week the sisters in Selma were driven in a wagon to Weimer in rain, snow, wind, or sunshine. Once the driver, being angry, drove furiously. The seat jumped high with the sisters until one final jolt landed them head down and feet up in front of the seat, where they stuck. It required several mighty shouts to bring the driver to a halt in order to set the sisters upright again.

A variety of trials faced the sisters there. One of them wrote:

> One evening a young man decided to spend the night in the schoolhouse by entering through a window.
> "You can't stay there!" I called to him.
> "What will you do with me?" he called back, proceeding with his plan. I set off across the corn and cotton fields to our neighbor's house, beginning over and over again the "Sub Tuum" but never being able to finish it. I feared that any moment a bullet would fly through the corn rows from the man who might be following me. When I arrived back at the school with my neighbor, a six shooter sticking out of his pocket, my guest was only too glad to be off.

One morning a sister discovered a five-foot snake in the middle room of the second floor of the convent. It set the tone for the day.

In Fredericksburg the living quarters were so poor that there was no ceiling in the bedroom, only canvas stretched across from wall to wall, but the sisters were grateful for the protection this afforded when they heard the rats scrambling back and forth across the canvas at night. In Colorado Line the house was even worse. There was no canvas ceiling. It was merely a box with cracks so large the rain, snow, and wind came and went at will.

One day the sisters were on their way to the railroad station in the wagon when the horses became frightened and set off at a gallop. Sister Hildegarde fell out of the wagon, hitting her head on a stone. The horses ran on. Some time later, when she was picked up, she had to be taken to the hospital, where she remained for quite some time before she recovered enough to return to work.

At home, too, there were difficulties. When a postulant for whom the congregation paid the fare from Europe, kept gratis, and educated, left the order, her mother asked the congregation to pay various expenses in addition to her ticket and pocket money. "A bitter chalice she has prepared for me which I have not refused to drink," Mother lamented.

In 1895 Bishop Durier looked forward to going to Europe. Before he set sail, he wrote a nostalgic letter to Mother:

> Off I go. Will soon rock on the Atlantic. Last time, in '86, on those blue waves, Divine Providence presented me with a great blessing in the shape of a gentle sister. Six convents have been the outcome of that blessing. How I cherish the memory of the gentle sister! May she live long and happy and keep on doing good to the poor bishop of Natchitoches. . . . In my written report to the Holy Father I gave a glowing report of 1) their superior and 2) their devotedness.

Sister Dominic wrote from Dubina in 1897, after the parish priest was changed from that place, that, as she was going to church on Sunday morning, an angry woman "shook her fist in our faces, saying, 'You black swine are the cause that we lose our good priest.' "

Sister Florida, who had perpetual vows, had asked for a dispensation and left the congregation. After some time, however, she appealed to Bishop Forest for permission to return. Mother Florence was firm in her refusal: "She left of her own accord in sound health and was a scandal to her community for some time." It was no longer as in the days when Bishop Neraz requested her to take back Sister Barbara.

In 1893 Mother opened six schools: St. Henry's in San Antonio, Lindsay, Pilot Point, Pisek, Praha, and Windthorst, all in small country places. In 1894 there were two in Campti, one for the whites and one for the colored, and two others in Moulton and Industry. In 1895 there were two: Denton and Gainesville; in 1896 four: Our Lady of the Lake, Beeville, Cameron, and Cleburne. In 1897, one, Quero; and in 1898 one, Westphalia. In all, eighteen schools were opened during her second term, only two of which were in Louisiana.

Pastors wrote and asked her about such trifles as paying for the hammer that a sister broke while ringing the church bell in Schulenburg; she responded:

> Had I followed the bishop's advice last Sept., this would not have happened; but in future the sisters will no more ring the bells, and such breakings will never more occur.

Mother borrowed money to build in St. Henry's parish on condition that the school community would repay the mother house. To the pastor in Palestine, she advised that in painting the interior of the house, he use graining instead of hard oil finish and the color should be light green or blue. She sought and obtained permission of the bishop for two sisters dying of consumption to pronounce their perpetual vows.

Bishop Durier was as effusive as ever: "The people are well pleased. . . . In Cloutierville the priest and the superior get along well. . . . Your sisters are friends in need. . . . Sister Xavier directs the colored children very well in Campti, . . . and Blessings to all Sisters of Divine Providence, and especially to their gentle mother."

Sister Elizabeth Schuehle, formerly a Lutheran from Baden, Germany, who had entered the convent on the day of her baptism, died of measles in Fredericksburg. The people requested that her body be allowed to remain there for burial. Mother acceded to their request. And Sister Stanislaus Kuechly, who had been left an orphan at the age of three at St. Jean-de-Bassel and later brought to America, where she entered the convent, died at twenty-nine. Mother Florence wrote about these deaths to Mother Anna and added:

> We have 20 young sisters in the novitiate . . . but alas, the number is too small to suffice for the needs of Texas and Louisiana.

Indeed, she had lost fourteen sisters by death by the end of her second term, and eleven annually professed sisters had left the congregation, including Annie Pfohl, one of "her girls." Sister Angele (her little Marie Metz from Alsace) was not able to cope. The rapidly increasing educational demands with study, supervisors, and examinations frightened and intimidated her beyond endurance. She gave up more each week, until she became almost helpless. Mother wrote to Marie's brother in Alsace that she would have to send Marie home. He replied in haste: "In your big convent there do you not have place for one helpless little sister? I cannot take care of her here, nor do I have someone else to do it. Please remember that she was a beautiful healthy girl when you took her away." It was true. Cost what it may, Mother decided to keep her. She later had her clothed in a complete religious habit and took her to a photographer to have a photo made. This she sent to the family in Alsace so that they would have it to look at and show their friends with pride. But Mary became as dependent as a little child and could do only the most simple tasks. Mother requested that all the sisters treat her with respect and see that she was given love and attention. In ten years Mother had lost seven of her girls by death, departure, and mental failure. It tore at her heart.

As her second term came to an end, Mother realized she had not yet devised a representative system for voting. There were now ninety-nine perpetually professed sisters eligible to vote. She realized, moreover, that her intensive drive to erect and move into the new mother house had taxed her disposition. Her naturally volatile temperament sometimes withered the sisters (but not the priests, who always saw her at her charming best). Her loving motherly heart soon melted with tenderness, however, so that she completely forgot that she had been upset and had made others suffer.

Sister Scholastica Schorp, a representative of one of the districts and a council member, on the other hand, was always cool and in complete control of her feelings. It was true that she was extremely exacting, often unsmiling and unemotional, but, at the same time, frank and kind. She was predictable. She exercised some influence over the sisters in her district. Mother admired these qualities in her and often wished that she possessed some of them herself. She would cast her vote for Sister Scholastica this time. As much as she hated to think about it, she felt that other electors would do the same. She was quite sure, however, that she would be reelected, even without Bishop Neraz to give his support. She was becoming aware of other strong women emerging in the congregation—with minds and leadership of their own. The future would be more difficult for a superior. Even ten sisters voting for somebody else would make her feel uneasy and unaccepted. She blamed herself for failing to get the representative system going. A smaller number of voters would be more discriminating perhaps than the entire group, some of whom would simply vote as their friends did. She had such vivid dreams about the coming years that she could hardly wait to be about their fulfillment. The congregation would support her in carrying them out, even though a few would grumble at the changes. This would always be so, she knew, and yet it was very important to her that the sisters be united as one for the good of the church and the congregation.

Mother suddenly realized that being elected to a third term was very important to her. Just thinking about life without the tension and responsibility seemed dull and unendurable.

8

Third Term (1898-1904)

If Mother Florence had accepted a second term as superior general without pain, she accepted her third term with a great deal of pleasure. It was true that, as she had anticipated, Sister Scholastica received nine votes, and this upset her—not because she had anything against Sister Scholastica, however. In fact, she herself had voted for Sister, and she now moved her into the position of second assistant and treasurer, keeping Sister Angelique, her closest associate during the last twelve years, as first assistant and superior of the house in Castroville. Sister Scholastica's popularity made Mother aware that there were sisters in the congregation who preferred Sister Scholastica's method of handling congregational matters and therefore did not fully support herself as superior general. She expected full support from all sisters; she began to understand more and more how Mother St. Andrew had felt about her position as congregational leader. If Mother St. Andrew had brought the congregation to birth and nurtured it for twenty years, she herself had saved it from destruction and set it firmly in six dioceses, including the one in Louisiana. She had won the support of six bishops and most of the priests, whom she now felt she could count on to continue the growth and expansion of the work.

Mother was now forty years old, not old in fact, but old in experience. She felt that never had she been more able to handle the multitude of duties and responsibilities and at the same time enjoy living as now. Still sensitive to the sisters' needs and sufferings, she had learned to be a bit more objective, she thought. With Sisters Scholastica and Philothea as her close associates, she could steer a calm and straight course. She had retained Sister Angelique as first assistant and Sister Ange as mistress of novices, but, because Sister Ange was becoming very feeble, she appointed Sister Philothea as assistant mistress of novices. District delegates were Sister Philothea, Diocese of San Antonio; Sister Mary, Diocese of Galveston; Sister Joachim, Diocese of Natchitoches; and Sister Margaret Mary, Diocese of Dallas. She pinpointed those sisters who had voted against her and kept an eagle eye on them, so that they sometimes squirmed. This office, she couldn't help feeling, really belonged to her, and she had her finger on everything inside and outside the congregation. She knew every sister personally; she felt that most respected her and even loved her. Although something new was always cropping up, she felt fairly good about things.

It was during this year that matters came to a head in Alexandria. Father Menard, who had begun construction of a new school off the waterfront near St. Francis Church, ran so heavily into debt that he told Mother Florence he would have to let it go to the creditors, and the sisters would have to remain in their old convent and school.

"I can't let Alexandria go," she told her council in distress. "This school is so important for the people and for us that we must keep it. If we stay in Louisiana, we need to maintain a number of houses, for the morale of the sisters, if for nothing else. All the schools must be good. Bishop Durier depends on us and we can't let him down." Her council agreed.

When Mother Florence had accepted the first schools in Louisiana, Bishop Durier had insisted that she accept the title to the property and establish private schools so that he could get money (from the Commission for Indians and Negroes) for his Negro schools. She had not been in favor of setting up independent establishments, especially in such faraway places, because it tended to make the congregation, and even houses in the congregation, independent of one another and of the parishes and dioceses. But she had already done this in Texas and she would continue to do it when it seemed the only way. She liked the feeling of independence almost as much as Mother St. Andrew had liked it, but she was not sure what it would do to the unity of the congregation.

"We will buy the incomplete building if the bishop agrees. It has to be another debt for us, but if God wants it, as it seems He does, He will provide. We will make it an academy similar to the one in Natchitoches." She paid $4,000 for it, and Father Menard was immensely relieved.

Once the decision was made, Mother threw herself wholeheartedly into the project. With apron on and active involvement in every phase of the construction, furnishing, and planning of schedules, she never seemed to tire. Bishop Durier applauded her success.

Back at Castroville, she saw that something had to be done with the young women in formation. Sister Mary Ange, tiny and old but saintly and powerful, had been training the novices now for many years. The novices were still in Castroville. The novitiate was loosely organized, with novices putting on a veil and going out to help in the schools as soon as they had a bare foundation. They received in-service training on the missions where they were stationed. Much of their spiritual formation went on during the summers. Mother decided that there was room in the San Antonio mother house for the novices to move in but not so much as would soon be needed. She therefore prepared to construct a south wing in 1898, with August Fuessel as contractor, at a cost of $8,600.

The moving was a joyful adventure for the novices. They made it a picnic by stopping under a tree to eat their lunch. When they arrived at their new home, they found the building was not so spacious for the large group as they had hoped. They crowded together in the dormitory and the refectory and bathed in the washhouse in the back. They were instructed in hygiene and personal care by Sister Flavienne Braun, who had received her nurse's training in Europe. She had taken up residence at Our Lady of the Lake as soon as it was occupied. She had her own office with bottles of medicine lining shelves on two sides of the room and the third wall displaying an array of diplomas attesting to her competence. Here she sat at her desk in state, clothed in a voluminous white apron, until her presence was required elsewhere. Her homemade potions were said to "kill or cure," and young women not accustomed to such potent medicine hesitated to confess their illnesses. This hurt her. "When you feel bad, my child, you come to me," she would tell them. "I am the oldest one here. I am the mother of them all." But in 1899 an epidemic of consumption and other illnesses struck the congregation, and eight sisters, mostly young ones, succumbed. These included three of Mother Florence's "girls": Sister Felicity Becker, who had always found obedience hard but had nevertheless submitted; Sister Lima Vonderscher; and Sister Sebastian Hinterlang. Mother felt these losses deeply but was powerless to prevent them.

Moving the novices to San Antonio gave them more educational opportunities and gave the new convent more helpers. Sister Scholastica oversaw them as they maintained the high polish on the wood floors and stair railings. Holding her skirt up with one hand, as was her custom, she ran her finger over the woodwork distastefully, indicating their slipshod work. Then came a few harsh words, enough to deflate the more timid among them. Mother Florence, however, seeing the hurt looks on the novices' faces, would put her motherly arms around their shoulders and tell each one: "It's all right, my child," and they felt much better. They watered the young trees carrying buckets of water long distances, for no well had yet been drilled on the campus.

To exercise her literary ability, one of the novices, Sister Digna Egan, composed a jingle that her companions soon took up:

> *In the evening*
> *When we are free*
> *We carry three buckets*
> *Of water to every tree.*

Mother Florence had already named Sister Philothea assistant mistress of novices although she was still superior in St. Joseph's. She would soon call her in to assume her duties. This happened more quickly than they dreamed. In the summer of 1899 Sisters Benedict Fenelon and Madeleine Sheltein were sent to Ireland and Europe to recruit young women, some of whom had been waiting several years to come. The response was beyond anyone's fondest dreams. Sister Benedict gathered together thirty lively, intelligent, young Irish girls, and on October 26, returned with them, plus one whom she added in New York. Mother Florence was overjoyed when she saw their smiling rosy faces and heard their easy laughter as she fondly embraced each one. Sister Madeleine's group of sixteen was slightly delayed by a storm at sea and arrived November 8. Nine more came alone or in small groups throughout the year. By the end of 1899 the fifty-six Irish and European postulants, along with those already there (seventy-five in all), were truly an awesome crowd. Sister Mary Ange, veteran that she was, quailed before them. It was then that Sister Philothea was called in.

Sister Philothea Thiry, who had come to Texas in 1883 with Mother St. Andrew at the age of fourteen, had developed into a spiritual force over the past years. No matter what her assignment, she worked until she had become expert in it. First, of course, was the spiritual base, not too narrow and not too broad for her day, but solid and constant. She became a talented musician and music teacher. As superior of St. Joseph's, she proved an able administrator and educator; as representative of the San Antonio District on the congregational council, she was an excellent resource person for Mother Florence, and a levelheaded businesswoman. Mother Florence felt that, in assigning her as mistress of novices, she was providing the future members with the best foundation they could get.

In spite of her virtue and experience, Sister Philothea was awed before this unmanageable group of intelligent, mischievous, imaginative, homesick young women, speaking various languages and possessing different cultures. She was not able to restrain her tears even in their presence as she, not so much older than they, sat helplessly before them. No one can say how she finally mastered the situation to such an extent that eventually they came to respect and love her throughout her and their lifetimes.

When summer came and all the sisters and novices returned from the missions, it was impossible to house them all at Our Lady of the Lake. Mother Florence, who knew well that this was an unusual situation, decided to keep the novices who were ready to make profession at the mother house and send the others to Castroville. Sister Philothea was assigned to the mother house group, and Sister Mary Ange had charge of the others. Sister Ange was hard put to manage them, and Sister Philothea went out occasionally to give her support. In the double desks where they studied, an Irish or American girl was placed with a German-speaking girl. This arrangement also held at table, to enable the German girls to learn English faster.

Into this melting pot came a distinguished and attractive, self-assured young lady from Texas, Claudia Ayres, a native of Mississippi now living in New Braunfels but educated in Austin by the Holy Cross Sisters at St. Mary's. From the beginning she commanded the love and respect of her superiors and her companions, by whom she was often chosen as mediator and spokesperson. She was gifted with a rare sense of humor, and an experiential knowledge of the aesthetic and the useful. She had a way with words, both written and spoken, that won her many admirers. But, in spite of her "aristocratic" upbringing, appearance, and abilities, which included musical accomplishment, she neither claimed nor accepted any exceptions from the regular household duties. She scrubbed and waxed floors, washed and ironed clothing, and took her turn in the scullery with the others. Even Sister Scholastica, exacting mistress of the boarders, sought and followed her suggestions in many instances when they pertained to boarding accommodations and procedures. Sister Philothea, her novice mistress, respected her intellectual prowess, her eagerness to accept spiritual direction, and her independent spirit, which gave her originality and ingenuity. In receiving Miss Ayres, the superiors know that they were fortunate.

This group of young women developed into fine teachers,

superiors, administrators, and leaders in a few years.

In 1900 a second wing was added to the mother house at a cost of $8,000, and in 1902 further additions were made, amounting to $17,300, for both the academy and the congregation were growing rapidly. Working closely with Mother Florence, who was continuously making plans, adding ideas, and supervising all aspects of the construction, Mr. Fuessel received a real education. He said later in his career, "I learned most of what I know from Mother Florence."

When young women came to the United States from Europe and Ireland to enter the convent, they envisioned wild pagan Indian children running about the forests. They hoped that they would gradually win them for Christ, sitting under the trees in the great outdoors of Texas. Most of them never saw an Indian, for they were soon missioned to the German, Czech, and Polish parishes of Texas. Mother Florence was among them. Some went to Louisiana, where they taught Cajuns and other people of French extraction, and the Negroes, who spoke English.

In 1889 Old Oklahoma, or Indian Territory which had not been assigned to the Indians by the U.S. government, was opened for settlement. Hordes of people, mainly Protestant middle-class fortune hunters from the Midwest, made the "Run" for the free new territory to be had. They immediately staked their claims, built their houses, cultivated their land, and set about establishing a community with church, school, and government. Very few were Catholic, but those who were were under the jurisdiction of the Benedictine Fathers, in Oklahoma since 1880. In 1891 the whole of Oklahoma and Indian Territory, occupied by the five civilized tribes—Cherokee, Creek, Choctaw, Chickasaw, and Seminole, assigned there by the government—and various other tribes, was made into a vicariate apostolic. Father Theophile Meerschaert was the first vicar apostolic. There were few railroads in the territory, no large cities, and the missions were stretched out over long distances.

Three secular priests and some Benedictine Fathers served the people. Father Meerschaert had a dominant personality and spoke with "fire and music." His life was simple. He lived with

Mother Mary Florence Walter in 1892, when she began her second six-year term as superior general of the Texas congregation of the Sisters of Divine Providence

Mother Florence, in 1907,
as the sisters remember her
looking for many years

Mother Florence after her
thirty-nine years as superior
general were ended—the
picture was taken in 1930,
when she was superior of the
convent community. She
looked like this to the end
of her days in 1944.

Antoine Walter, Jr., brother of Mother Florence, his wife, Madeleine, and their daughter Françoise, named for Mother Florence *(Photo ca. 1900)*

Françoise Walter, now Mme. Françoise Kauffmann, born in 1894 and now living in Haguenau, France

The first part of the new San Antonio convent, constructed in 1896, into which Mother Florence moved the congregation from Castroville

When Mother Florence left the office of superior general in 1925, the buildings shown—in addition to St. Ann's Hall and the laundry not visible in the photo—the convent, chapel, main building, Moye Hall, and rectory remained as her legacy.

Mother St. Andrew Feltin was the first superior of the Sisters of Divine Providence in Texas. She began the convent in Castroville shortly after she arrived in Texas in 1866. Mother St. Andrew was deposed by Bishop J. C. Neraz in 1886 and, soon after, Mother left the San Antonio congregation, returning to the convent in Castroville in 1900, where she died five years later.

The spires of Sacred Heart Chapel are seen for miles in every direction in San Antonio. The bells chime on every quarter hour and on every hour.

The interior of the Sacred Heart Chapel—it was the longtime dream of Mother Florence and was completed during her last term in office in 1923.

Sister Philothea Thiry arrived in Texas in 1883. She was named mistress of novices in 1899 and eight years later was elected to the council. Sister Philothea became superior general in 1925.

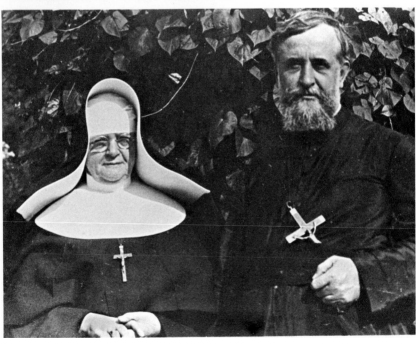

Mother Philothea Thiry, superior general from 1925 until three years before her death in 1946, worked closely with her brother, the Reverend Ferdinand Thiry, OMI, when he was in San Antonio.

the pioneers, breaking bread with them, sleeping in their homes or under the stars. He drove his ponies the length and breadth of the land, spending the night under the wagon with only a blanket, swimming across streams with his horses, visiting Indian villages, eating homemade soup in dugouts, and ruffling the hair of his future church builders.

Perry was one of the cities that thrived and grew, with a parish directed by a progressive pastor. Father Willibrord Voogden, OSB, wanted by all means to build up a first-class parish with a twelve-year graded school for his thriving community. There were a few sisters in Oklahoma and Indian Territory already: Sisters of Perpetual Adoration of the Blessed Sacrament in Atoka; Benedictine Sisters at Sacred Heart, Oklahoma City, Lehigh, and Vinita; and Franciscans from Philadelphia in the Indian schools. Father Willibrord, in his travels, had met Father Pius Heckman from Temple, who told him about his school and the Sisters of Divine Providence who staffed it. Father Willibrord looked into the school and decided it was what he wanted. In 1898 he began negotiations with Mother Florence, who had a large novitiate just beginning. With brown eyes sparkling, she told her council, "This is what our founder would have wanted us to do. It is very hard for the bishop to find sisters for the Indians. I suppose some are afraid. But there is nothing to fear if God is with us. Do you agree to taking the risk?"

Mother Joachim was especially excited. Here was a place, a cooler and greener spot than Texas, where the Irish sisters, who did not speak German, Polish, or Czech, would like to teach the Indians. "I am for it," she said, and the others agreed.

Perry did not have an Indian school, but, on the advice of Bishop Meerschaert and Bishop Forest, Mother came to believe that the small Catholic population in the predominantly Protestant territory needed the Catholic foundation and support they would get from a good school. So, with her eye on the Indians beyond, and her heart in accord with the fearless Bishop Meerschaert and the people, she agreed to staff Perry in 1900.

Father Willibrord was not modest in his expectations or in

his preparations. He constructed for the sisters on his own initiative (Mother Florence usually accepted without objection what the pastor offered) a new frame building with adequate apartments for the sisters, a small chapel (something they had never had before), five classrooms, and a music studio. His school was to be equal to any public school in Oklahoma. He did not keep this school a secret. In July he wrote to Mother Florence:

> The public school board has engaged a smaller number of teachers than usual in view of the Sisters coming here. They have a great idea of the Sisters.

Father Willibrord was a businessman and he wanted to know what his responsibilities were to the congregation. Mother had trusted this to him in spite of past sometimes disappointing experiences. He wrote:

> You have never submitted any conditions on your part as how to fill the financial part of the running of the school, etc.

Later that month he wrote:

> Father Metter of Norman, O.T., wrote to me that he feels delighted to see four sisters come to the Territory.

The Perry school became a model educational institution, a showplace. Pastors throughout Oklahoma came to see it and discussed it with Father Willibrord. In October he wrote:

> The people, Catholic as well as non-Catholic, seem to be highly satisfied with the institution and bestow great praise on the sacrificing Sisters.

Father Renier Sevens, pastor of St. Felix Church in Ponca City, was the next to request sisters. He said he was very much pleased "with the ability, the order, the piety and tact" of the sisters in Perry and had therefore decided to employ them in preference to all others. He would have a school ready by fall

1901 if Mother could send sisters. She had already spoken to Bishop Meerschaert; she could and did send sisters. She also sent a piano and some furniture for the sisters' quarters. Father Sevens modeled his school after the one in Perry and was greatly pleased with Sister Raphael Miesch and the four other sisters who came. The school grew so fast that he had to add on to it in 1902 and 1903, each time asking Mother Florence for loans. When he asked for $200 to add a wing so that boarders could be housed, Mother said it was only right that she should pay this, because it was the sisters who profited financially from the boarding school. When he asked for $800 in 1904, she remembered Temple. Father was shocked to receive a written contract that stated that the diocese would return the $1,000 should the sisters leave Ponca City. But both he and Bishop Meerschaert signed it. When Father Sevens asked to take his meals with the sisters because there was no room in the rectory for a housekeeper, he was denied his request and continued to eat in the restaurant. "One can never be too careful of the temptations offered the priests and sisters when they are thrown together so frequently," Mother said. Besides, she had to guard against scandal to the people.

The school directory in the early days gave this description of the educational program offered:

> The pupils have also a chance to take extra studies of German, bookkeeping, stenography, plain and fancy sewing, each department being in charge of competent teachers. A complete course of vocal and instrumental music can also be had at the school, special attention being given to instruction on the piano and all string instruments. The music teachers are fully able to give to their pupils the best that can be given.
>
> In connection with the school is also a boarding school in charge of the sisters. Special attention is given to the children placed in charge of the sisters, that they may grow up, not only well educated, but refined and with well-informed characters.

Although Mother was gratified over the success of the two schools, she was not really happy about the situation until the bishop asked her to staff the Indian school in Antlers in 1902. This is what she had envisioned in the Indian Territory from the start. Father William A. Ketchum, the first priest ordained for service in the vicariate, and a missionary to the Indians, built St. Agnes School with a donation from the Honorable W. R. Grace of New York. It was a private school for Catholic children of the Choctaw tribe, built in 1897. It was named St. Agnes in memory of Grace's daughter. Although this was not a government school, the superintendent of the schools for the Indian Territory paid two dollars a month for Choctaw children whose parents wanted them to attend St. Agnes. They were residents, the girls living with the sisters, and the boys at the rectory with the priest. There were also nonresident white students, both Catholic and non-Catholic in the school, with three sisters, one being a music teacher. This was always to be a difficult school to maintain, requiring heroic labor of the small staff and students, with little financial and no personal assistance. But the sisters, missionaries that they were, loved the Indians and were willing to do what was necessary to maintain the school. In the meantime Father Ketchum was made director of the Bureau of Indian Missions in Washington, and Father Dupret was assigned to Antlers. As in the other Indian schools, financial support was always indefinite and unpredictable from year to year.

In 1899, Bishop Meerschaert, looking for sisters for Tulsa and Vinita, had met Sister Apoline of the Sisters of Mt. Carmel in New Orleans, with whom he made a contract for both schools. The contract was binding for five years. It was similar to the ones the Sisters of Divine Providence would later live by. It stipulated that the sisters were to take charge of the Catholic schools at Tulsa, Indian Territory, and Vinita. In addition to the school, the sisters agreed to take charge of the parish choir, "provided it be composed mostly of pupils of the school and not of the ladies and gentlemen of the parish." The parish was responsible for providing a furnished convent for the sisters plus light and fuel expenses. Each sister would receive $20 a month, plus the fee for music lessons and the "extras"—painting, drawing, fancy work, and foreign languages.

To finance the schools, the bishop wrote to Mother M. Katherine Drexel, heiress to the Drexel banking fortune in Philadelphia and active missionary among the Indians and Negroes. The interest on her invested fortune was said to amount to $1,000 a day, and for sixty years she spent $1,000 a day on the missions. She sent the bishop $1,500 on May 27, 1899, for the erection of a school in Tulsa, Indian Territory, to be used for the benefit of the Indian and colored people of the Territory of Oklahoma and Indian Territory. And $1,700 for Vinita.

Hearing, as pastors had a way of doing, even without telephone, radio, television, or airmail, that Tulsa would be getting Sisters of Divine Providence the following year, the pastor of Vinita rushed a letter to Mother Florence:

> My school is older and better supported than that in Tulsa. It would be a sin to let it fail now. It has cost me eight years of hard work to build it up, and ruined me financially, and it would truly break my heart to see it abandoned now. . . . I feel certain that the school will improve considerably under the management of the Sisters of Divine Providence, at least judging from the reports I have heard of their work. Besides, Tulsa and Vinita, being only 60 miles apart, would be, in my opinion, a great advantage to the sisters to take charge of both houses at the same time.

Both were Indian schools, but not completely. Of course, Mother Florence had no choice in her own mind but to accept Vinita along with Tulsa.

Father Charles Van Hulse, who had worked so hard to establish the Tulsa church and school, was assigned to Muskogee and replaced by his brother Theophile. There was a third Van Hulse brother in Oklahoma, Father Joseph. In 1903 Mother Florence selected her cousin, Sister Laurentia, and three other sisters for Tulsa, while she sent Sister Elizabeth and four other sisters to Vinita. She accompanied the sisters to their new homes. St. Theresa's in Tulsa was in the middle of the city, bounded by Third and Fourth Streets and Elgin and Frankfurt Avenues. The school was parochial and elementary, with school and convent in a single very plain frame building with just sufficient space to accommodate the number of sisters and pupils.

The sisters in Vinita were installed in Sacred Heart Convent and School at the same time. It was understood that Indians would continue to be admitted free, because Mother Drexel had financed the building. This was agreeable to both the pastor and the sisters, and things began to move smoothly, under the watchful eye of Father Ketchum, who was now in the Indian Bureau in Washington.

In the meantime, Mother St. Andrew in California never forgot the invitation she had received from Mother Florence to come home. She was ready now. Early in 1900 Sister Eugenia Kaiser received a letter from Mother St. Andrew, who had just undergone a serious operation without an anesthetic, her niece was later to say, "in order to atone for the suffering she had caused others." Mother said she would love to come home if Mother Florence truly wanted her. Sister Eugenia wrote to her immediately saying that Mother Florence had prayed for this every day, and that she was to have no hesitation. Mother St. Andrew forthwith wrote Mother Florence asking permission to return.

Mother Florence's great heart overflowed with joy as she hastened to Castroville to the old home with the letter. Assembled in the refectory for dinner, the sisters listened as Mother read the letter. "You all know Mother St. Andrew's history, and you know her. She asks to join you here. Do you accept her back?"

There was loud, enthusiastic applause, mingled with tears of joy and pity as the sisters voiced their approval. It was with extreme peace and happiness that Mother Florence, after having obtained approval of Msgr. Audet, administrator of the diocese in the absence of Bishop Forest, sent Mother a telegram saying, "Come. We await you with joy."

Mother did come, met in Hondo by one of her old friends, the grandfather of Sister Mary Alma Marty. Mother Florence, along with the entire community of the old home, was in Castroville on October 27, 1900, to receive her. Mother St. Andrew had gone away strong and healthy, determined and capable. Ten years had taken their toll. She was pale and stooped, using a cane for walking. But she wore her religious habit proudly, the one she had kept in her trunk through the years, waiting to wear again. Her humility and gratitude were touching as Mother Florence, with tears flowing freely, clasped her in her arms. Each sister greeted her affectionately, and she was taken to chapel, where she pronounced again her perpetual vows.

If, as Mother St. Andrew said, she had wet her pillow with tears each night since her departure because of her transgressions, Mother Florence had not grieved much less over her own.

"Would we do it again?" they asked each other as they sat for hours reminiscing. Mother Florence showed her what the congregation had become now, fruit of the seed planted thirty-nine years ago right here in Castroville, and Mother St. Andrew's pride was as great as her own. "I think we would do it again," they agreed as the former superior settled down to a happy and peaceful life with the sisters she loved. She wrote home to her little family, who were now able to manage their own lives, "I have never once had a heartache since I returned." One day she handed Mother Florence $700 in cash, saying that, if the children needed money, each was to receive $50, but that the rest was to remain in the congregation. The Castroville people, whom she did not encourage to visit her, sometimes managed to see her anyway. The children in school venerated her as a saint, imitating at times even her shoulder stoop and halting gait.

Each time Mother Florence visited Castroville, she went into the garden to pick fresh figs. The plants at the convent were not yet large enough to produce, and figs were her favorite fruit. Moreover, anyone making the trip from the old home to the convent in San Antonio always carried a generous supply of figs in season. Mother would take a dish heaped with the carefully washed fruit and sit in a comfortable chair, slowly savoring every swallow. This was a rare luxury she allowed herself.

This same year, Bishop Durier, complaining of age and weakness, discussed with Mother Florence the disposition of the greater part of his money. Would she agree to a contract by which he would give her $10,000, from which she would pay him $800 a year while he lived and have a hundred Masses offered for him when he died? Of course she would. In the meantime she would invest this money in building a wing to the academy. It was agreed. Miss Christine Tarrillion, her former student, made a similar contract on a smaller scale.

In the summer of 1900 Mother Florence moved the summer normal, which she had held in Castroville for the past two summers, to San Antonio, with Professor W. T. Calmes in charge. Here the normal was more extensively planned than it had previously been. Each following year the teaching faculty and course offering widened, coming to include Professor John O'Shea, who continued his association with Our Lady of the Lake until his death; John Martin and Bernard Steinfeld; Mrs. Emma Heilig Rice; Professor Walter Romberg; and Rev. Henry Constantineau, OMI. Mother Florence had applied in 1903 for state approval of the summer normal, but she was too late to get it for that summer. In the summer of 1904 state approval became effective, with the state issuing certificates after successful examinations at the end of the summer. The summer normal was now under the direction of Professor T. E. Colson, who, along with P. H. Underwood, had been added to the staff. Mother Florence, realizing the necessity of good teaching, was highly pleased with the San Antonio summer normals.

At peace with herself finally, and with the approval of Mother St. Andrew, who never lost the determination for this cause, Mother Florence decided to move for papal approval of the constitutions and the congregation. Bishop Forest had not the same desire to control the congregation that Neraz had had. Moreover, he had no time to function as an ecclesiastical superior.

Mother Florence was largely on her own now, with more than twice as many sisters as she had had when she first assumed office, and with numerous diocesan, private, and public institutions in six dioceses.

"I am torn," she told her council, "between visiting the sisters on their missions and making plans to move the congregation forward. The constitutions must be rewritten, changing the government structure, the formation program, the method of choosing chapter delegates, and some other things."

She met with her council August 1903 at which time they made two proposals: (1) to ask for the appointment of an ecclesiastical superior and (2) to build a new mother house for the sisters and leave the academy building for academic work and a boarders' residence. For ecclesiastical superior they voted to ask the bishop for Very Rev. Henry Constantineau, OMI. They had already received valuable assistance from him for several years and recognized his spiritual and business acumen.

Father Constantineau had graduated from the University of Ottawa, taught business subjects there, became secretary and finally rector of the University. Laval University had conferred a Ph.D. upon him. His health began to fail him, so he came to Texas as a simple priest. Here he was asked to direct the building of the Oblate seminary, which he did. He also taught courses, gave retreats, and helped work out a religious program of study for the Sisters of Divine Providence. The academy and congregation had been employing Oblates for teaching religion courses and giving retreats and highly valued their expertise. Oblates also served as chaplains at Castroville and Our Lady of the Lake. The sisters requested Bishop Forest to name Father Constantineau as delegate superior, and he did this.

Father Constantineau was progressive, energetic, and thoroughly devoted to Catholic education and the religious life. Mother Florence invited him into the life of the congregation, sending him as troubleshooter to missions where she thought he would probably be more effective than she, or even having him accompany her at times. She sought his advice on matters of business, law, and contracts.

Father Constantineau became a significant figure in the congregation, spending much time with the administration and with the sisters at home and on the missions. He wrote circular letters, gave spiritual direction, counseled, served as extraordinary confessor, and in return received respect and obedience. Mother Florence, already adept at business, was an eager learner from this master. She became bolder in congregational endeavors, insuring buildings, buying property, and especially altering the constitutions that the congregation had tried to follow all these years. She wanted it brought into what now seemed reasonable and practical, while at the same time, adhering to canon law. Sister Philothea entered more and more into the administrative planning, working closely with Mother Florence and Father Constantineau.

This time, after Sister Scholastica issued the call to meet for chapter with the note appended, "No person outside our religious family has any right to be informed of what is transpiring there," members of the chapter of elections were selected as the original constitutions had specified: the superior general and counselors, delegates of districts, the two oldest members of the mother house, and the local superiors who had perpetual vows and were thirty-five years old. Bishop Neraz had included all professed sisters and was unwilling to change. Last time there were ninety-nine delegates; now there were only forty-five. Neither of these systems, it was decided, however, would be the one devised for the new constitutions.

During her third term, Mother had staffed eighteen new schools, of which five were in Oklahoma and Indian Territory, and one in Louisiana. She had built at congregational expense of $5,978.68 the school in Plaucheville that had been destroyed by fire and that the parish was unable to rebuild. In 1901 she purchased from the Ursulines the school in the Polish St. Michael's parish of San Antonio, this besides building three wings onto the academy and doing numerous repairs on mission schools and residences.

In September 1901 Sister Mary Ange Decker, first assistant and close associate of Mother Florence for fifteen years, died of a paralytic stroke after having performed her usual duties of the day as superior of the Castroville community. Sister Mary Ange had come to America in 1878 after holding the responsible position of treasurer general at St. Jean-de-Bassel. With the exception of several years in the school in High Hill, opened in 1880, she spent all her time in Castroville in responsible positions. With Sister Angelique gone, Sister Mary Ange and Mother St. Andrew failing, it seemed to Mother that the old order was passing. Before returning to San Antonio she sat a long time with Mother St. Andrew, reviewing the events of the past, as they sat laughing and weeping together.

But business went on as usual. Father Weimer wrote Mother Florence in 1903 stating that Bishop Gallagher wanted to build an academy in Palestine. Bishop Gallagher, he recalled, had not always assisted the congregation too well in the past:

> Very likely his conscience pressed him to accord some favor to the humble daughters of Providence, moreover, they never asked for particular favors. . . . He wishes not to make it a one-horse institution.

Before closing his letter, he added:

> I can offer you another barrel of pure and strictly pure wine for altar use and perhaps some for some sick sisters. The wine is fully seasoned and worth every cent.

In 1903 Mother Florence was delighted to see the construction of the Castroville bridge over the Medina River by the S. A. Oliver Company. As she rode smoothly over the long, wide, beautiful bridge, with walks on either side, she thought of all the inconvenience and actual physical suffering this bridgeless river had caused the members of the congregation and the people of Castroville in the past. It seemed incredible to her, after her own successful constructions, that it had taken all this time to bring this into being.

During this last term seventeen sisters had died. From Ireland and Europe had come ninety-three young women, and from the U.S. sixty-five, making a total of a hundred and fifty-six entries, a few of whom left again. With the change in the constitutions, which would become tentatively effective this summer if the chapter approved them, eighty-four novices would be permitted to make their first vows.

Sister Ange Huvar, who had assisted Mother Florence ever since 1886 in the administration and as mistress of novices, died on February 2, 1904. Sister Ange, tiny and frail, was truly what her name signified, an angel. Looking at her as she lay in the poor simple coffin, Mother touched her hand lovingly and whispered, "Why are you all leaving me just as we are about to get what we have wanted all these years?"

Mother St. Andrew, too, came in silently and stood beside Mother Florence. "I am ready, too," she said, "but I only want to see the document of papal approbation in your hands first. Then I will, as Simeon said, 'depart this life in peace.'"

"Partings are so difficult. Don't go yet. I need my old friends."

But more was to come. For some time Bishop Durier had been in poor health. In the spring of 1903 he had suffered a stroke that left him partially paralyzed. Mother Florence herself was attentive to his needs, for he was a very social person who valued his friendships, and Mother Florence was one of his oldest and staunchest friends. When Mother left Natchitoches, she urged the sisters to care for their bishop the best they could. They never failed him.

He died on February 28, 1904. He had been bishop for nineteen years. He was the first to organize work among the black population and to provide Catholic schools for them. By 1894 he had already six schools for the blacks, all taught by Sisters of Divine Providence. In all academic areas education had begun to flourish in the diocese. There were twelve parochial schools, five academies, and one college for boys, all taught by four brothers and sixty-seven women religious.

His funeral attested to the love the people had for him. Mother Florence was there with a large delegation of sisters to pay her loyal friend of eighteen years a last farewell. She did not know how things would go in Louisiana now. The new bishop was not appointed until six months later, and she had never heard of him.

Mother had begun the custom a few years ago of writing circular letters to the superiors, who held a privileged position, and to the sisters. *The Imitation of Christ* was Mother's constant companion, as it had been that of Father Moye, the congregational founder. She referred regularly to advice she found therein and meditated on it. Some of the admonitions she swallowed were as bitter as gall and left her weary and discouraged, but

some she accepted readily and passed on with a feeling of owner-
ship. One such was the following:

> It is a much surer way to stand in the state of obedience than
> in the state of authority. . . . Go here and there where
> you will, you will never find perfect rest save in humble
> obedience under the government of your proper superior.

This was true for the sisters. As for herself, she did not dwell
too long on whether she always found "perfect rest" under the
government of her proper superiors. Whether the state of authority was less sure than that of obedience or not, she preferred
it for herself. So to both groups she continually stressed obedience,
to the superiors obedience and loyalty to her in order to assist
her in carrying her burden, she always reminded them, and to
give good example to the sisters:

> Oh, if you could read the wishes of this poor heart of mine
> for you the most chosen portion of my flock, the Local
> Superiors of each community! . . . It is you, my dear daugh-
> ters, that have to lend a helping hand to your Mother to
> bring about this progress (in our profession) which should
> instill new life and vigor in our institute.
> It shall be the sacred obligation of your office to esteem
> and love your superiors and your Motherhouse and plant
> the same in the hearts of those confided to your guidance.

And:

> I desire that you increase in love and respect towards your
> superiors—towards those whose awful responsibility it is to
> answer for your souls. . . . be always penetrated with this
> deep and humble conviction that you are unworthy to be
> superior, that God could have provided your community with
> a member that would be a more fitting instrument in
> governing it than you. Fear that your sins and imperfec-
> tions may check the blessings of God upon your community.

To the sisters she gave spiritual nosegays and urged perfect
obedience to the superior, who held the place of God for them.

She also spent some time on directions for studying, obtaining certificates, and sublimating their suffering. The homecoming instructions remained much the same:

> All trunks and valises must be checked and transferred to Our Lady of the Lake, paying 35¢ for each. I do not wish that any sister should carry bundles or valises through the city.

In 1903 she announced the publication of a Necrology:

> Desiring to remember in a special manner the deceased members of the congregation, a Necrology has been compiled. This anniversary of a Sister's death will be mentioned on the eve and the Sisters will recite the De Profundis.

Powerful, awesome, charming, and efficient everywhere, Mother Florence yet suffered more than anyone realized, for the requirements of her office were in many ways diametrically opposed to her natural temperament and inclinations. She was highly intuitive—grasping the situation and climate in an instant. Without explanation, information, study, or consultation, she saw what to do, how to act, what was right. She was ambitious for the Lord, for the congregation, for the church in the United States. She had great dreams and the ability and drive to carry them out. But she was temperamental, volatile, impulsive, and compassionate. She was loved greatly and feared greatly, for she could devastate with a few loud and searing words, but then she would dismiss the event from her memory and be her warm, loving, charming self again.

This was not the model way of religious life, however, in her day. The office she had inherited required utter submission and complete dependence on the bishop, reverence for and obedience to priests. It required intellectual and measured decisions in which feelings had little part. It required deliberate, calculated action, which often had no bearing on compassion and human relationships. It required rigid self-discipline to show an appearance of strength and dedication while the psyche was starving for warmth, affirmation, and friendship. She read in *The Imitation of Christ:*

> Who wages a stronger battle than he who labors to overcome self? And it should be our daily desire to overcome ourselves so that we may be made stronger in spirit and go daily from better to better.

It was her deep and violent faith that allowed her to maintain her sanity in this schizophrenic world. She spent hours each day, in spite of her grueling schedule, in intimate union with her Lord in the tabernacle. Eventually she came to require of the sisters what she herself had such great difficulty achieving, that which in faith she thought religious life was asking of them: utter self-discipline, dedication to duty, obedience to authority, and perfect decorum.

The strength to preserve her temperament as strong and even as it was came partly from the persons she chose as her counselors: Sisters Ange, Anne, Scholastica, Constantine, and Philothea, who were undoubtedly sincere in their devotion to the system. When she saw sisters suffering under the strain, however, she immediately and sympathetically allowed them some temporary or even permanent relief.

Try as she would, she was never quite able to reconcile what her nature required with what her religious life demanded. In bringing the sisters into line, she was at the same time struggling with herself; and, in berating them for their shortcomings, she saw herself in them and chastised herself. As her position and power grew on her, and when she found herself drained and exhausted, she came to the point of allowing herself some exemptions from the general law. Her numerous allergies, for which there were no known remedies, required certain foods, occasional periods of recuperation and purification of the bodily system. The heart-to-heart talks that she so longed for she did not feel were appropriate to share with her sisters, her lay friends, nor even her confessor. Again she meditated on St. Thomas à Kempis's book:

> Open not your heart to every person but only to him who is wise, discreet, and reverent.

She saved these intimate talks for rare occasions when she permitted herself to visit Mother Marie Houlne, now Provincial Superior of the Kentucky province of St. Jean-de-Bassel since 1898. It was a meager diet for a healthy, active woman.

Chapter of elections took place June 22, 1904, giving Mother Florence a sweeping victory. She received forty-three votes, with Sister Scholastica one and Sister Philothea one.

9

Fourth Term (1904-1907)

In some ways Mother Florence's fourth term, only three years, was the most exciting one yet; but in some ways it was the saddest.

There was no question in her mind that this was the time to obtain papal approval for the constitutions and the congregation. Bishop Forest was favorably disposed and he had appointed, at the request of Mother Florence and her council, Rev. H. A. Constantineau, OMI, as delegate superior to the congregation in his place. Father Constantineau, Mother truly felt, had been sent by Divine Providence at this time in history. With his experience in organizing religious communities and his wide and liberal dealings in higher education and theology, he was exactly what the congregation needed.

For the first time Mother had a person near her in whom she could confide even personal problems and concerns, for he was understanding, sympathetic, and personable, without being rigid or dictatorial. He had compassion and a rare sense of humor. He respected Mother Florence very highly, and they could exchange ideas and plans freely without inhibiting each other. He was in favor of obtaining papal approval for the congregation and he knew how to go about doing it. Bishop Forest had presided at a chapter with Father Constantineau, Mother Florence, the council, and the district delegates December 27, 1903, at which time they decided to apply to the Holy See for approval and to make some changes in the rules. Then the chapter of election was held in June, at which time the delegates approved the changes that had been proposed.

Just as history repeats itself, so in the case of Father Constantineau. Almost without exception the priests loved and respected Mother Florence, and they looked with suspicion on this new Oblate in their midst, who almost immediately was "promoted" to the honored position of delegate superior of the congregation in place of any of them who had been in the diocese now for many years. They felt jealous and slighted, and they lost no time in telling the bishop so. To discredit Father Constantineau, ten priests went to the bishop with the latest canons of the church to prove that the election of Mother Florence was not valid. Later, eighteen priests came to him, requesting that he remove Constantineau from the favored position.

Like Neraz before him, Bishop Forest was swayed by his priests and sent a letter to Father Constantineau:

> You know, as well as I do, that your appointment as Superior General of the Sisters of Divine Providence has caused bitter feelings among the Secular Clergy, against their bishop, against yourself and against the Sisters. I have been told several times that I have more confidence in the Oblate Fathers than in my own priests, that I place more confidence in you than in any one of them, and this itself has caused a little trouble amongst our Oblate Fathers.

The bishop thanked Father Constantineau for all he had done for the sisters, saying that for the good of all concerned he would have to remove him from this position and himself be the only superior of the sisters. Neither the bishop nor Father Constantineau mentioned this decision to Mother Florence, although some of the sisters were aware of the ill feelings on the part of several diocesan priests.

Father Constantineau, on his way to Rome for the chapter of his order when he received this communication, took it very philosophically. Actually it mattered little to him whether he held this position or not. He also was not concerned whether the secular priests approved of him or whether they won their case.

He was somewhat concerned that the bishop should bow to such pettiness, and he deplored the setback this would cause the Sisters of Divine Providence. He realized that he had contributed significantly to the congregation, which would be at a loss without him. But he wrote to the bishop that as bishop he had authority and the sisters were responsible in all things to him, that the bishop had appointed him as delegate superior, and that, as a representative, he had reported everything to the bishop. "If you remove me, that is your concern. I shall count on you to be the first to communicate to the Sisters of Divine Providence the decision you have taken with regard to the delegate superior. They have a right to know."

The bishop listened to this reasoning and advice. He did not inform the sisters, however; on the contrary, he reappointed Father Constantineau as delegate superior. Mother Florence accepted this trial as another test of the congregation's steadfastness. When Father Constantineau returned to San Antonio in late October, he came as the appointed provincial of the newly created Southwest Oblate province, which was to have its administrative headquarters in San Antonio. In spite of his new responsibility, he retained the office of delegate superior to the Sisters of Divine Providence and never slackened his interest or work in their behalf. But trouble with the local clergy had not finished. They were out to get Constantineau one way or another, and he paid them no more heed than if they had been a few gnats buzzing around his head. Mother Florence and her council, following the example of their delegate superior, did not allow these petty jealousies to interfere with their plans or their work.

"Now that Bishop Forest approves and we have an able director in our midst who can push our cause, we cannot be deterred," she told her new council: Sisters Joachim Sweeney, first assistant; Scholastica Schorp, second assistant and directress of the boarding school; Philothea Thiry, mistress of novices and secretary; and the district delegates: Sister Mary Buechler, Eugenia Kaiser, Constantine Braun, Liboria Thiemann, Blandina Schaffer, and Raphael Miesch.

In the general chapter of December 29, 1904, the new councillors were given an opportunity to express their views on the upcoming projects. After they had signified in the affirmative, Father Constantineau secured Rev. Albert Antoine, OMI, who had a doctorate in philosophy from the Gregorian Institute in Rome and a doctor of divinity from the University of Ottawa, and had just been appointed as rector of the new theological seminary in San Antonio, to help with the work of writing the constitutions for the sisters.

Looking at the times, it is not surprising that papal approval was so necessary to the congregation. In the pre-Vatican II institutional church, it was the province of the hierarchy to govern all aspects of the church, and the congregations to obey. It was deemed better to obey the head of the whole church, who legislated for all congregations the same, than the head of a diocese, whose governance fluctuated according to the personality of the reigning bishop. In the case of this congregation, which had been so autocratically ruled by one bishop, it was especially important that this autocratic treatment not be repeated.

Mother St. Andrew, who kept herself free from all congregational business except this one item, gently but persistently reminded Mother Florence not to lose time, because the present bishop approved of the step. Mother Florence realized the value of her advice.

After painstakingly perusing the former constitutions of the congregation, works of the founder, the latest canons of the church, and the guides for the writing of constitutions, a committee finally completed the rules and translated them into French. Mother Florence joyfully took the manuscript to Castroville, where she read it item by item to Mother St. Andrew, now quite weak and visibly suffering. Mother St. Andrew forgot her pain during the reading and praised God for the completed work. "I would like to see the document of papal approval in your hands," she sighed, "but I doubt that I will. However, I am satisfied it is coming at last."

While the work of completing the constitutions had gone on intensively, Mother Florence was busy about many other congregational matters. There was constant activity in the Oklahoma and Indian Territory. Sometimes Mother wondered why she had ever considered accepting schools in Oklahoma Territory in the first place. There was no end to the requests and demands made upon her and the sisters, no end to travel, danger, and expense. Father Ketchum, whom she now knew rather well and whose zeal she admired, asked for three sisters for the Indian school at Quapaw. There was only one Sister of St. Joseph's there now with some lay persons, she found out on visiting this mission in the extreme northeast corner of the Territory. The Quapaws were mostly Catholics and had in 1893 requested of the Commission of Indian Affairs

> A Catholic school or schools to be placed under the direction of Catholic religious teachers. . . . We believe our children will improve faster in learning and morals under the supervision of Sisters or other Catholic teachers than under the present system of instruction.

The school, begun in 1893, had to close in 1895 because of lack of funds, but a new petition brought $500 for the education of ten Quapaw children. It had been operating more or less on this basis since then. Mother sent Sisters Aurelia, Cordula, and Columbkille there, with Father D'haenens (known as Father Dennis) as pastor. Although they were never in danger from the friendly Indians, the poverty they experienced, the strange, primitive setting of the school, the lack of congenial associates all contributed to a constant uneasy feeling. They rode across the prairie to Baxter Springs or to Miami for supplies.

Near Quapaw many legends connected with the scenic spots lived among the inhabitants. Lovers' Leap was a high rock from which two lovers of enemy tribes, and unable to marry, bound themselves together and leaped, dressed in their best finery, over the cliff into the water below. In a Romeo-Juliet epilogue, the parents of the star-crossed lovers came to the rock to look over and saw the bodies of the two young people floating together just below the surface of the water.

The Devil's Promenade was the place where the devil came, because of its inaccessibility, for a little peace and quiet by himself. The Devil's Biscuit was a rock hollowed out where the devil was said to have attempted to bake biscuits. But the water always rose and filled the space and washed the biscuits away before he had a chance to eat them. The Ghost Dance was kept alive and actively participated in. Because the sisters had once seen it, the weird music rising from the valley recalled to them the strange ritual. The "Spiritual Dance" was held in the middle of the stamp grounds, where a dead white dog was decorated with beads, ribbons, bells, and other finery. Each dancer went up and whispered in the dead dog's ear some message that he wished to be carried to a departed relative or friend.

While accepting the Quapaw school Mother was considering withdrawing sisters from Antlers, where the few Choctaw children present did not make it a worthwhile effort. But she decided first to make an all-out attempt to recruit or solicit Choctaw families to make use of the school.

Father Emil Depreitre in Enid also wrote for sisters for his school in 1904. Like Perry, it was to be a model school, with the finest of everything. It even had, as he stated July 15, "indoor toilets and other modern conveniences. Send me the cream of the crop, including a good music teacher." Mother Florence entered into the spirit, telling him that the teachers would harmonize with the favorable surroundings. For the sisters' living apartments she ordered six iron bedsteads to be delivered from St. Louis.

"There is every hope," she wrote him, "that Enid may be one of the most flourishing schools in Oklahoma."

Also the question of buying the land in Vinita presented a problem because Mother Katherine Drexel had paid $1,700 into the place, which began as a school for Indians. She feared that, if the land were sold, the Indians could no longer attend school free there. Negotiations carried on by Mother Florence, Father Van Hulse, Father Ketchum, and Mother Drexel continued into the next term of office without being finally resolved. It was understood and decided that Indians would attend school free, and the agreement stated this; but Mother Drexel continued to hesitate over the sale, or over the Indians, or over the refund of

$1,700, so that no closure could occur. In the meantime, the congregation acquired more property there and improved the building.

In accepting the school in Nada, Texas, Mother made her characteristic statement in regard to the sisters' residence: "In regard to the dwelling we have no request to make; this will be left entirely to your judgment."

In the Cuero school there was difficulty, which came to the attention of Bishop Forest. Father Mathias Mertes, the pastor, was displeased with the operation of the school. In order to rid himself of the sisters, he demanded of them that they pay him a salary, they pay him rent on the schoolhouse, and they pay the insurance premium on the school and the residence. Bishop Forest looked into the situation for himself and wrote Father Mertes that the sisters were not to pay any of these fees, and that he would be the person with whom Father would henceforth deal. The enrollment, he pointed out, had more than tripled during the school's short life. He did tell Mother Florence, however, that she should send one English-speaking sister instead of three Germans.

Reviewing conditions in Louisiana and Texas, Mother decided that the school in Norma, Louisiana, would be closed because of scarcity of pupils, and the colored school in Alexandria was too far away from the convent for the sisters to walk.

In Texas the congregation would purchase more land in Clarksville, construct a new building in New Braunfels, make repairs on the Temple building, and send sisters to Nada and Ammansville for the coming term. Insurance policies, something never before considered, were now taken out on the buildings belonging to the congregation, and building improvements were approved and supervised in three states.

Toward the end of January 1905 Mother St. Andrew's suffering became intense. She knew the end was near and asked for the priest. Father Quinn, OMI, chaplain, anointed her. Then she asked the sisters to lay her on the floor. In spite of all protests, her strong will prevailed. Just as she had undergone major surgery without an anesthetic, so would she die without physical comfort in reparation for her sins and in petition for blessing on the congregation. She bade Mother Florence and the weeping sisters farewell, and suffered with Jesus on the cross from 12:00 to 3:00 A.M., when she gave up her spirit.

The sisters had at first planned to have her funeral in the convent chapel. But, when the people of Castroville learned she had died, they tolled the church bell, one gong for each of her seventy-five years of life. Then they requested that she be buried from the parish church. So strong were their appeals that Mother gave in. Father Kirch was now pastor of St. Louis Church. It thus fell to his lot to speak some words about Mother St. Andrew at her funeral.

During the past five years Mother St. Andrew had met Father Kirch on several occasions. But never once did she mention his part in her sad deposal, and, while he treated her with all kindness and respect, he had not spoken to her of it. Mother Florence, therefore, had some misgivings about the coming funeral. The entire parish, however, was involved in making plans to include friends and pupils who remembered her. Mother Florence left the arrangements as much as possible to the superior of the house and to St. Louis Parish. She sat beside Mother's coffin for hours, praying for her friend and speaking to her as she had so often done in life.

Finally the moment came when the pallbearers carried the casket across the street into St. Louis Church. She followed with a long procession of sisters, children, and parishioners, thinking how Mother St. Andrew, when she was quite alone after her deposal, would have been gratified to have followers.

Father Quinn's homily was a beautiful tribute to this woman of great faith, but, when Father Kirch stood up to say a few words, he gave a brief account of the life and labors of the deceased and ended by saying that she had volunteered to go "to the labors of far-off Texas, where the hardships, trials, and humiliations she encountered are known to Him alone for whose sake they were borne so generously. She was a woman of strong character, imbued with a true missionary spirit, which no obstacle, however harsh, could crush."

"So true! So true!" Mother Florence told herself, and she was sure Father Kirch had for many years realized what a noble woman Mother was. She knew he, too, had suffered for his part in Mother's deposal and subsequent struggle to maintain a place in the church.

The old order now had truly passed, and its final passing left Mother Florence utterly weak and ill. For days and weeks she forced herself to go about her duties and to regain her interest in congregational affairs.

Father Constantineau, who was no stranger to ill health, had established for himself a practice of going off to Hot Springs, Arkansas, to recuperate when his body demanded a respite from mental and physical strain. Mother Florence had observed this practice for a few years, but had not taken the advice to follow a similar practice. By the end of 1905, however, when she found herself unable to function effectively without great violence to herself, she listened for the first time to her delegate superior, who insisted she spend a month at Hot Springs under the care of one of the best doctors. When her council seconded this proposal, she reluctantly gave in. Here she completely put from her mind all business responsibilities and gave herself over to the care of the physician. Father Constantineau took charge of the situation, even to the writing of letters home in January 1906:

> I am sure that all the members of our dear congregation will return thanks to God for having brought Reverend Mother here. The terrible suffering which she has undergone for the last 15 years would soon have had a sad termination. She is now under the care of a first-class doctor who understands her case. It was high time for her to undergo the treatment she is now following. May the results of her stay be her restoration to complete health.

Later in the month, when Mother Florence returned to the congregation, strengthened in body and spirit, the reception given her was a triumphal one of celebration and thanksgiving by all groups in the congregation. Converted now to the necessity and effectiveness of occasional periods of rest and recuperation, she consented to "indulge" herself more in the future.

She found on her return that her problems continued to pile up and increase. In Tulsa, Oklahoma, Father John Heiring had replaced Father Van Hulse, at the request of the people, who wanted a pastor who spoke without a Belgian accent and had a more nearly perfect grasp of the English language, so they could understand his sermons and directions better. Father Theophile Van Hulse, outraged and belligerent, left Tulsa unwillingly, and Father Heiring came there almost as unwillingly. But, once he did come and establish himself, he left no doubt in anybody's mind that he would be in complete control of the parish. Concerning this move, he wrote in his diary on October 29, 1906:

> I found the residence locked, and since I could rouse no one, I went to the sisters residing in the school and made inquiry there (after introduction) and found that my predecessor had left on the early morning train, much to my regret.

Father Van Hulse had left the keys with the sisters. Father Heiring took the keys and went to church, where he offered two masses, for it was All Saints' Day. Then he set out to become acquainted with his parish. He wrote in his diary:

> I found everything too small. The church could not hold its membership, if they had all come at once; the school was too crowded, the Sisters sleeping in the attic; and the parochial residence would not permit housekeeping as it had only four rooms. . . . There were some $400 debts to be attended to, but this was an easy matter, for the bank account had enough credit to wipe it out.

Ever since the coming of Father Heiring, things had been moving in Tulsa. Mother began to receive colorful letters with brisk requests and strong opinions, but these were not particularly alarming the first two or three years. It was evident, however, that this man was a person not easy to deal with. His conversations, visits, and letters were never the mild, friendly, conciliatory, polite requests that came from other pastors. They were written when necessary, straight to the point, blunt, and imperious. But Mother Florence knew how to be firm, too. "No, the Sisters cannot cook for you, only breakfast after Mass," she wrote him.

Sister Philothea, now secretary as well as mistress of novices, enjoyed the assistance of one of her former novices, Claudia Ayres, who was now Sister Angelique and one of the teachers at the Academy. With Sister Angelique's initiative, imagination, and writing ability, and with the encouragement of Father Constantineau and Mother Florence, it was decided to publish a monthly *Family Circular,* for the exclusive use of the congregational members. In spite of her music teaching, her business and English classes, and her work as assistant secretary, Sister Angelique assembled the first edition of the *Family Circular,* printed in a 5½-by-11-inch booklet. The editor entitled herself "The Administration" and referred to herself as "It," neither masculine nor feminine. Its opening letter stated:

> We hope that it will be a powerful means of keeping alive in our midst that beautiful family spirit which was so conspicuous during our vacation days at home. . . . We cannot insist too much upon the fact that the publication is for the members alone. No other person, whether layman or priest, whether friend, pupil, or pastor, should be informed of its contents.

In her foreword to the first *Circular,* Mother Florence wrote:

> I entirely approve and sanction in every respect the statement made in the opening letter of the *Family Circular* and sincerely trust that not a single member will be found guilty of breach of confidence.

Besides containing news of the mother house and novitiate, it gave chatty news from the old home in Castroville, and all the houses of the congregation. From issue to issue, the members, like a true family, picked up on items of interest from other communities, exchanged recipes, and related humorous incidents. There were contests with prizes, spiritual messages from Father Superior and Mother Florence, and occasional flights of fancy.

It was very warmly received in the beginning and the responses overflowed the paper. "The Administration" was clearly enjoying itself, along with the rest of the members, although it was never quite clear to the readers who "The Administration" was, that is, who the actual editor was. Printed requests for this revelation resulted in a promise of exposure during the summer. But, as summer approached, The Administration announced the need of an "airship flight" around the world in order to recuperate after a strenuous year. The identity was never revealed.

The *Family Circular* announced in the October issue that certain improvements were projected for the coming year:

> All the sisters will be pleased to learn that the projected improvements for the coming year are: (1) a new artesian well, which will supply us with all the water necessary so that we may introduce into the house and grounds all modern improvements and thus do away with a couple of "historical buildings" that are an eye-sore to our beautiful convent home; (2) the erection of a new building containing a laundry, bath house, trunk rooms, etc.

And the last item was a wistful bid for appreciation and sympathy:

> Rev. Mother, who is always anxious to accede to all requests, sacrificed one of the Academy Sisters to meet the demand for an additional sister on the Mission of Solms. Without wishing to criticize, the Administration feels as though it should make a public statement that, considering the size, the importance and the work to be done at the Academy, our staff is the smallest and most overworked in the congregation; but, dear sisters, we are pleased to do the work since we know that good example must come from "headquarters," and the Administration, being a part of the Academy staff, would be the last to complain when there is a question of work. We might state incidentally, that many demands are made upon us by outside schools, who require assistance in one way or another. We are always pleased to oblige them, and shall always do so whenever the time at our disposal allows.

Mother Florence never spared herself when it came to work and devotion to duty or the spreading of good example. She literally demanded the same of all members of the congregation. When she learned of a sister not carrying willingly her full load of work and responsibility, she did not spare her in private or before the entire congregation. She made her point clear in the *Family Circular* in November 1905:

> How can a religious be filled with the true spirit of her vocation when she allows worldly things, and that which is still worse, creatures, to distract her from her daily duties? All the Sisters of the different communities are expected to be so much taken up with these duties that no time can, in conscience, be found for anything or any person or persons foreign to their work. Nothing is more deplorable in a religious than the wilful waste of time.

About this time, Mother Florence and Sister Scholastica were summoned to court to settle the case of the closed road leading to the academy. When Mayor Elmendorf died in 1901, his wife took charge of their property. She had it fenced in with a gate at the corner of Nineteenth and Durango, the entrance to the academy in 1905. The gate now had to be kept closed. Mother Florence, who hated to go to court, had no choice. She had to have the fence obstructing an alleged public road removed. Before the hearing came up, the two parties settled the question by compromise. Mrs. Elmendorf presented to Bexar County a deed for the strip of land for a public street as well as deeds from other owners of land along the so-called Buckingham Road. The county now had a deed for property to build a street from south of Elmendorf Lake to Castroville Road. There was no bridge across Elmendorf Lake, so the road could not be extended to Commerce Street at that time. It was to come about two years later. Concerning the preliminary hearing, The Administration wrote in the *Family Circular,* with a touch of humor:

> It was found to be almost as difficult to get Buckingham Road opened in front of the Academy to connect with Castroville Road as to pass teacher's examination. Rev. Mother was

liberally cross-questioned for an hour and a half, and although she had failed to get such important data as the color of certain padlocks, the side of the gate they were placed on, etc., the occasion passed quite satisfactorily. Sister Scholastica who accompanied Reverend Mother to the court house has been suffering from a bilious attack. . . .

In June 1905 the decision was made, after much investigation by Father Constantineau and the council, to accept St. Joseph's School in Dallas, a parish in which the Oblates served, in preference to St. Patrick's, which was first considered. The property, with a sixty-foot front, cost $5,300, and the brick veneer school built on the lot cost between $7,000 and $8,000. Five sisters were sent there in the fall of 1905; they lived in a wooden building on Texas and Floyd. Reverend Mother and Sister Joachim were present at the blessing of the new "German Church" in Dallas on October 15. The school, built by the congregation facing Swiss Avenue, was finished, and school was in session. Besides being in a thriving city, the Dallas school was a good bridge between Texas and Oklahoma, so that the investment in money and personnel seemed worthwhile to Mother Florence.

One of the projects of the year 1906 was the drilling of an artesian well. "We are sitting on top of a huge underground body of water which supplies San Antonio and surrounding areas with abundant water. We have no idea how far or through how many strata of rock we will have to drill to reach the water, nor what its force will be once we have found it. But it should be an artesian well," Mother told the council. "We will have to pay an engineer $5,000 to drill the well. And let us all pray that we will find water and that it will be an artesian well that will supply the campus for the rest of our lives." It was decided to drill west of the new laundry, termed, as stated in the *Academy Review*, "the second Alamo, which it notably resembled during the course of its construction." So great was the faith of the sisters that water would be found that, simultaneously with the beginning of the well, a laundry and bathhouse and a steam heating system were being built or installed at a cost of $27,250. Even a "natatorium" was envisioned in the near future.

The only question about the certainty of striking water was the possibility of striking oil instead. Although an oil well would indeed have merit, it did not compare in importance with water. Therefore the sisters and the academy students stormed heaven for water from March until August, when the prospect began to dim. As Mother Florence and Sister Scholastica stood beside the drilling rig day after day, they dropped many blessed medals into the depths below, asking the saints and Our Lady of the Lake to provide the water so desperately needed.

Then one day, August 8, as all the sisters were at prayer in chapel, it happened. Reaching a depth of 1,380 feet through varicolored and varitextured limestone, the drill pierced the final strata, and water flooded the grounds at the rate of 1,000 gallons per minute. The sisters ran from the chapel to observe the miracle that had come to the campus. No longer would water be carried to bathe, cook, water the lawn and trees. The campus kitchen, bathrooms, lawns, gardens in sun-baked Texas would never suffer again from lack of this most precious commodity. The tank erected to hold the water could not contain it all. A permanent rivulet found its way into Elmendorf Lake to augment that body in days of drought as well as days of floods. Our Lady as well as her institution would profit for untold years from her favor.

The constitutions were now on the way to Rome. To prepare the congregation for living this new document better, it was decided to adopt the *Catechism of Vows,* published for and used by the Brothers of the Sacred Heart. This seemed to contain the explanations and examples of the vows that the new constitutions called for. To this end, Mother ordered enough copies so that each community could receive at least one, probably more. She indicated, as she sent these to the congregational houses, that they "should be thoroughly studied by the young sisters."

In 1904 Mother Florence had sent Sister Patrick Morrissey and Sister Bernadine Cassidy to Ireland to recruit young women. She had been in correspondence with Father Cassidy, Sister Bernadine's brother, for some time now, and Father had been interested in discovering good prospects. The recruiters returned

November 19 with fifteen young women, who were warmly welcomed and initiated into convent life. They slept in the dormitory of the original building, on the fourth floor.

In 1906 Sisters Joachim Sweeney and Sister Ignatius Sheehan went again to Ireland and returned with thirteen girls, the first to occupy the new St. Ann's Hall, with the new novice mistress, Sister Columba Friesenhahn. That Christmas it snowed, not very much, to be sure, but enough to stir up the feeling that something very special had been sent the Divine Infant on His birthday.

The facilities for the postulants and novices had long been inadequate, but now Mother felt that the construction of a formation center could no longer be postponed. She therefore made provisions for the construction of a complete new building, extending south at the west end of the academy. Initially it was planned to have two stories for dormitories and dining hall, but, as plans developed, it ended up having a large dormer-windowed third story, which would also be used for dormitory space. This building rose without much fuss and was overflowing with postulants and novices by the end of the year. It was called St. Ann's Hall. The first floor contained an auditorium, which the academy students later used for their recitals and other programs. St. Ann's Hall was filled very soon and the full academy cast longing eyes at it, even above the first floor. Mother Philothea, involved in both the academy and the novitiate, saw that, if the novices were to be separated from the students, the formation center should be at a greater distance from the students. Eventually she planted in Mother Florence's head the seed that grew rapidly into a next step in the building development—a separate mother house for the candidates, novices, aged and sick sisters, and the administration. This idea, already envisioned by Mother Florence since 1896, grew stronger as the months went by, until she saw that it was an immediate necessity. It could not be undertaken, however, until after several other projects, already begun, were completed.

The academy obtained the affiliation of the University of Texas in 1906 in English, mathematics, and history. There was some grumbling among the clergy that the sisters were going too far, encouraged by the "worldly Father Constantineau." It was not necessary to cater to the state, they felt. Bishop Forest, however, ignored these criticisms, so that no more concerted efforts were made to him against Father Constantineau and the sisters. But the Oblates' status and favor still rankled among them, and they had not yet had satisfaction.

In the meantime, Mother came across the small booklet *The Polite Pupil*. She believed firmly that a vital part of education was to teach morals and manners to pupils. No one was educated without them. She sent a copy to each community, telling the sisters to study it themselves and teach the children its contents.

Pastors were becoming more difficult to satisfy in several places. In August, before the beginning of the new school year, Mother received from Rev. William Shocek in Ellinger, Texas, an insulting letter concerning the sisters there and in Colorado Line. Quite angry, Mother immediately called her council together to discuss whether to withdraw the sisters from the two places. Then she wrote Bishop Gallagher:

> I have had an insulting letter from Rev. Shocek of Ellinger. I replied that if the sisters were there for "sacking in money," as he termed it, it would be better for us to withdraw from Ellinger and Colorado Line. The decision of the Council is to call the sisters home, and I shall see to it as soon as possible. . . . If the sacrifices which the sisters were called upon to make during the past years deserve reproach, it is better for Father Shocek to employ other teachers.

Although Bishop Gallagher did not take any stand, or else he did it quietly, Father Shocek sent a humble apology and begged for the sisters to remain. Mother wrote this to the bishop, adding, "The sisters confirm that they are wanted. We have decided to let them stay."

The priest in Quapaw was also asking too much of the sisters in the Indian school there, she told Bishop Meerschaert. "After all, there is a limit to what a few sisters can do." The laundry, for example, was done by them, standing in the flowing stream.

It seemed to Mother that congregational money was constantly being filtered into Oklahoma Territory. She told the bishop this in October: $100 for repairs in Quapaw, $225 for buildings in Antlers, $300 for Enid, and $200 for Ponca this year. The income to the congregation was still small, a salary for a regular teacher being $25 a month, with the cook and the music teacher not receiving any pay as a rule from the parish. Money from the Indian schools was even less. Times were hard, but, if it was in God's plan, He would provide.

But conditions were unsettled in Oklahoma, too. An Enabling Act was passed, admitting territories to the U.S. on the same footing as the original states. Formerly the Oklahoma and Indian Territory had territorial government under the Organic Act of 1889. Tribal government had been abolished by Congress in 1898, and the Indians were court governed until 1906. Oklahoma was now awaiting the proclamation of statehood to be announced; then the election of a governor would take place. There was unrest among the Indians as well as the whites until all this was settled.

In the meantime, summer was approaching, always an exciting time in the congregation, when all the sisters came in from the missions for educational and spiritual renewal. It was privately also a time to catch up on friendships, mission news, evaluations, and comparisons among the sisters. Father Constantineau, hoping to forestall the usual gossip and uncharitable conversation that sometimes happened at this time, wrote in the *Family Circular* in May:

> Only the sweet and pleasant events will be treasured up in store of his memory, so that on his return home, no word of recrimination or against charity are heard; there is no relating of the tales of unpleasant incidents that are inevitably the part of every life; in a word, everything disagreeable or injurious to oneself or to others is forgotten. Only the good works and kind actions of those who surround them are remembered. . . . Our love, our devotion, our filial obedience are the best means of showing how great is our gratitude to God for having given us such a good Mother.

Mother Florence wrote in the same issue, "You will find enclosed herewith a list containing the names of all the sisters with the course of study they will follow."

In March 1907 Mother Florence began to receive requests for sisters from Rev. A. J. Drossaerts, rector of the Church of the Sacred Heart of Jesus in Broussard, Louisiana. He had learned of the Sisters of Divine Providence from Bishop Meerschaert in Oklahoma, and he promised Mother a veritable Paradise for the sisters if she could send some. He said Broussard was the "Eden of Louisiana," inhabited by wealthy people of good spirits, with several millionaires in the parish. It was Evangeline country. The people were refined, with a French background. It was a healthy country, where only a few "adults" died each year. They had two good doctors in the town. It was a good location, and the sisters would deal "only with the white children. They are a choice people. I will donate the Sisters a lot 300' by 300' on a choice location and the people will donate $1,500 to build the convent." He wanted a music teacher and a French teacher, among others. It sounded tempting but Mother could not see her way to moving into Paradise for a few years. However, she kept the invitation on the back burner while Drossaerts kept the requests coming.

What she did have to give her immediate attention to was the school in El Reno, Oklahoma, that she had committed herself to for that year. She went to visit the place and evaluate it. She agreed that, if the school were renovated, made more modern and attractive, "to match the modern educational program we will set up, then we would be satisfied. It must be at least equal to the public school." She arranged to purchase the furniture for the sisters' quarters from the Sisters of Mercy, who had been there and were leaving.

Also the school in Alexandria had to be enlarged for $7,000, and possibly next year new buildings would have to be constructed in Natchitoches and Alexandria, as she had discussed with Bishop Van de Ven.

She was always glad to get back to Our Lady of the Lake,

where her artistic eye continually sought that which would beau-tify and adorn this spot. This time it was a large statue of Our Lady, which should be placed right in front of the main build-ing. Because this academy was dedicated to Our Lady, the statue must be given a place of honor. So she went about purchasing just the right statue for the spot, which was prepared for it in a circle in the entrance. On October 7, 1907, the Feast of the Holy Rosary, this statue was unveiled and dedicated with members of the congregation and the academy present. There it stood to remind both the campus residents and passersby that this place was under the special protection of Our Lady.

Plans were being firmed up for the building of the new mother house where the park was located. This meant that the park would be lost. Mother, remembering the park at St. Jean-de-Bassel and what it had meant to her, decided that there had to be a park. She began to look at the land adjoining the convent and academy on every side, with the intention of purchasing some of it for a new park. The purchase of thirty-five acres across from the academy was made that year. The ground was broken February 29, 1907, for the new four-story mother house, to be built at a cost of $70,000, of which $20,000 was borrowed from Amiens, France, and $40,000 borrowed from the Oblates.

By this time, constructing immense new buildings with little or no money was becoming routine. Negotiating debts and loans had become part of a regular administrative procedure, but Mother Florence felt much more secure with Father Constanti-neau at her side, helping make the decisions. The purchase of land was a good investment, she learned, especially since it meant that schools would be conducted in congregationally owned institutions on a high level, which they were able to maintain without too much interference. Therefore, Mother purchased property in Laurel Heights, San Antonio, for the construction of a school, and she offered to give Father Wack $100 to pur-chase the lease for the land in New Braunfels where the school was, or, if he didn't want it, to purchase it herself for the con-gregation. She loaned Father Van Hulse in Vinita, Oklahoma, $300 without interest, to be paid back if the sisters left there.

The Temple school, with only thirty Catholic pupils, she decided had no future and no support from the parish. It was, therefore, with permission from Rome, vacated and sold in 1907. This was hard, because so much in terms of money and human effort had been expended there over the years. But it was a part of growth, Mother decided. Do what has to be done, and then leave when the task is completed; move on, as the pilgrims that the sisters are.

Then it came! Happy was the news that May 28, 1907, brought. The constitutions had been given approval on a temporary basis for five years. Just in time for the summer homecoming! The whole mother house rang with jubilation. Bells rang, feasts were set, planning for a serious and thankful summer was under way.

Because of the new government structure, it was deemed necessary to have a canonical election according to the new constitutions. A chapter with thirty-two delegates and members of the present administration was called. Mother Florence sent out this letter to the sisters:

> We hope to conclude all the work in connection with the election and the promulgation of our Rules within about two weeks' time. . . . You will understand it is such a serious matter, we can make no exceptions, and every sister must be present to enjoy the privilege which our Holy Rule gives her of participating in the election.

All the sisters had to come together for at least two weeks of orientation. Mother felt she had to forewarn the sisters. In the May *Family Circular* she announced:

> The Constitutions are stricter, it is true, but closer to Rome. And from now on May 28 will be a feast of the Congregation.

Oh, Mother St. Andrew, how you wanted to see this day!

10

Fifth Term (1907-1913)

Mother Florence was riding high. The first canonical election unanimously chose her as superior general. Under the new rule a superior general could serve two six-year terms of office, and a possible third with an indult from Rome. Mother Florence had already served three six-year terms and one three-year term, but that was under diocesan government. This was her first term under the new papal approval. The superior general was no longer able to select her own council; the chapter delegates elected them. There were now four council members, not including the treasurer or the mistress of novices. The chapter had elected Sister Philothea Thiry as councilor and first assistant, Sister Joachim Sweeney as second councilor; Sister Scholastica Schorp as third assistant and secretary; and Sister Eugenia Kaiser as fourth assistant. Sister Constantine Braun was elected treasurer, and Sister Columba Friesenhahn was appointed mistress of novices.

As a pontifical congregation, the Sisters of Divine Providence no longer needed a "father superior" because the chapter was now the highest governing body in extraordinary affairs and the elected superior and her council the highest in ordinary affairs. The sisters were still under the jurisdiction of the bishops in the dioceses where they resided. But Mother Florence had profited so much from the assistance of Father Constantineau that the arrangement of "ecclesiastical superior" was allowed to continue during the experimental five-year period while the approval was still temporary. Father Constantineau was a firm support to Mother Florence in having the sisters understand and live the rule, because he did not mean to fail at this point. But some of the sisters began to tire of hearing "According to our holy rule . . . ," and "The holy rule says. . . ." In a way, it eased the burden of discipline for her when she could say "because our holy rule says it," as she used to say, "The bishop says."

Because Mother Florence found it hard to be objective, discipline for her was not easy. The congregation had grown to three hundred and fifty members, with Irish, German, French, American, and even a few Mexican sisters. Although a concerted effort was made to mold the novices and sisters into perfect, docile, and obedient subjects, so that "seeing one, you see all," it was not that simple. Even in their identical habits, they just did not look alike. Nor did their habits always look alike, as great as was the effort to keep them doing so. No one saw this so clearly as did Mother Florence. The slightest deviation from the pattern brought her wrath down upon the wearer. Decorum, so important to Mother, had to be monitored; discretion was sometimes violated; and, worst of all, sisters occasionally failed in obedience. Obedience was the key to religious life. She had stressed this from the beginning, and would hold to it to the end. If one were an obedient religious, she would be able and willing to do almost anything and would be a blessing to any community; moreover, she would be happy. Some sisters did not share her appreciation of this virtue, especially to the degree they sometimes had to practice it in their communities. Most, however, did take these admonitions literally, accepting as the will of God every wish and command of superiors, however unreasonable and humiliating, for they believed this was what they had freely agreed to when they requested membership in the congregation.

It was obedience that gave local superiors their power. If they were insecure themselves, or insensitive, or stingy, or partial, as sometimes happened, they made obedience hard. If they wished Mother Florence to discipline a sister or change her

from their community, they reported her as "disobedient." A few
sisters veered from the straight and narrow path and were dismissed from the congregation; a few disappeared without giving
notice, only to seek reentrance later or to request a dispensation.
Several, warned again and again, never considered relinquishing
the course they had chosen.

Almost without exception sisters had their difficult days and
years of struggle—with their particular mission, their superior,
their companions, their health, their school work, their faith.
But most of them took so seriously their commitment to Jesus
and the congregation that they survived the trials and grew old
gracefully, still zealous and active to the end. Mother Florence
yearned to comfort them and relax their burdens, which she
often did individually; on the whole, however, she was firm,
sometimes harsh, but always kind and loving at heart.

To be a person in authority for twenty-one years, to confer
with bishops and other persons in high places across the country,
to construct a group of buildings for housing sisters and students,
to get the rule approved—this alone was enough to put the
sisters in awe of Mother Florence, even if she had always shown
herself warm and gentle. But this was not her way. During the
summers she gathered her flock together in the pavilion, the only
place large enough to seat them all, and spelled out their failings,
sometimes naming the guilty persons but more often leaving the
sisters guessing who the culprits were. When Father Constantineau
was present, as he sometimes was, the sisters were doubly
humiliated.

When Mother visited the communities, as she did regularly,
often without an announcement, the sisters made every possible
effort to show themselves and their classes at their best. Each
little community seemed to work in heavenly harmony, and all
were delighted to see "dear Reverend Mother" and listen to her
words. But inwardly they trembled, for she missed not the slightest error in their classroom notebooks and recitations, their table
manners, their prayers said in choir, the cleanliness of the house,
and especially the altar linens of the church, which she never
failed to examine. Although the sisters truly loved and respected

Mother, it was a relief when she went away. Often, following her departure, a package came from the mother house containing altar linen to replace what she had seen in the poor parishes as "torrible" and "not fit for our Lord." The sisters in the mother house chapel, on hearing that she was home from visiting a poor mission, quickly hid the best altar linen, knowing that she would come looking for something to send back.

In the business of the congregation, this term did not differ greatly from the others. She opened and closed schools as usual, built and repaired houses, borrowed money and paid off debts, countered the dengue fever that swept across the Southwest, purchased thirty-five acres of land across the street from the mother house for a new park, installed electric lights in the academy, purchased machinery and equipment for the new laundry.

In October 1907 someone broke into the chapel and stole the Blessed Sacrament. Although this was not publicized, the administration thought of the Ku Klux Klan or some Satanic group as culprits. There were hours of reparation in the chapel for days and weeks following the theft.

Mother's feast was always a day of festivity, especially in San Antonio and Castroville. The presentation included an elaborate program, a festive meal, a prepared speech, and gifts of handwork that sisters had made for half a year. The other half year's fancywork was presented in a similar celebration during the Christmas holidays. The linen and fancywork were sold during the year to help pay the debts. In 1907, the last year Mother would be living at the academy, she gave the students a feast day treat of a trolley car ride into town and back on Commerce Street.

In Oklahoma Mother opened two new schools, one in Lawton and one in Union City. The Lawton sisters referred to their house as "The Cold Storage." They wrote home that they had an entertainment to raise money to buy wood for the stove. Knowing that Oklahoma would be incorporated into the Union any day, Oklahomans elected Charles Haskell as governor on September 16. On November 17 President Theodore Roosevelt issued the proclamation of statehood. Haskell took the oath of office as governor at Guthrie, the state capital, on November 17, 1907. If neighboring states believed that wars with the Indians ceased with statehood, they had only to wait a few years for the renewal of excitement, which they would make the most of when the occasion came, as it would come in 1909.

In December, when the new mother house plans were ready to go into action, Mother Florence became quite ill, so ill that she was not able to assist at Mass on Christmas Day. Communion was brought to her in bed, a humiliation for her, that her body was not able to cope. But she was up again in January, when the construction on the new mother house actually began. The following document was deposited in the cornerstone of the building for which the plans had been drawn by Mr. T. Galenolen and the contract let to Mr. Fuessel:

> On this day, the 29th of Feb. A.D. 1908, being the fifth of Pius X, Most Rev. Falconio, Apostolic Delegate to the U.S.; Most Rev. James Blenk, Archbishop of New Orleans; Rt. Rev. J. A. Forest, Bishop of San Antonio; Theodore Roosevelt, President of the United States; Thomas Campbell, Governor of Texas; Brian Callahan, Mayor of San Antonio; the 42nd year of the establishment of the Sisters of Divine Providence in Texas.
>
> *Providentiae tuae nos committimus.* In the name of the Father and of the Son and of the Holy Ghost. Amen. Confiding in God's help, we the Sisters of Divine Providence and humble daughters of Venerable Father Moye, our saintly founder, whose beatification is now expected, erect this building in honor of the Blessed Trinity, under the protection of our dear Mother Mary and St. Ann, our patroness, as our new mother house and novitiate, to be known by the name "Our Lady of Divine Providence."

One hundred men worked to complete the building from January until it was finally finished in the spring. Between the mother house and the academy was left place for the dream chapel to come.

With Mother Philothea no longer congregational secretary, Sister Angelique, who had sometimes been so upset by Mother

Florence's temperamental outbursts that she became physically ill, no longer wrote the *Family Circular,* which now deteriorated into a dull routine listing of events. Mother Florence, who was satisfied to maintain a good secondary school academy and summer normal, did, however, see the wisdom of beginning a college conferring degrees when Mother Philothea explained to her the coming requirements for teachers. Unless the sisters obtained degrees, they would in future be unqualified to teach. Now that Mother would be separated from the college building, caring for the entire congregation, she delegated to Mother Philothea, with the help of Sister Angelique and Father Constantineau, the major responsibility for developing the college. But she followed their efforts closely and gave support when it was called for.

In the meantime the rule had been translated into English from French and copies printed for each sister. When she distributed these, she also wrote, "It is needless for me to add what you know so well, that our Holy Rules are for us the only sure means of reaching sanctity to which we all aspire." She pointed out that St. John Berchmans attained sanctity by keeping his rule perfectly. She wrote the parish priests to read the rule so they would know what was required of the sisters, and she wrote the superiors to lend the rule book to the pastors.

The newfangled "airships" were appearing more and more frequently around San Antonio. The *Academy Review* of 1908 carried a history of the flying bird and ended with this observation:

> Opinions as to the future utility of the airship differ. The government, however, is making every effort to promote its use, and the probabilities are that not too many years from hence aerial navigation will be as common as present locomotion by automobile.

Indeed, in 1909, the oftspoken airship appeared over the school and the pilot offered a ride to the fairgrounds for anyone brave enough to go. But, although curious, nobody had the courage to get in, for fear of falling into the river.

The greatest event of 1908 was not a spur-of-the-moment decision. Two major anniversaries were celebrated in Europe that year: Pope Pius X's twenty-fifth anniversary of his ordination to the priesthood, and in France the fiftieth anniversary of Our Lady's apparition at Lourdes. Father Constantineau reminded Mother Florence that her doctor had recommended a sea voyage earlier in the year, when her health, still delicate, had been at a low point. She should go to Europe—visit her home, Lourdes, Rome, and St. Jean-de-Bassel. He was going himself and would be able to get an audience with the Holy Father. Mother Philothea would also go. It was agreed.

Both Mother Florence and Mother Philothea planned how they could best represent their congregation to the Holy Father. They wrote all the mission houses to have pictures taken of their student bodies, with the pastor and the assistant on the picture, but not the sisters. They were to send two pictures to the convent: one to be put in an album to be taken to Pope Pius X, and one to keep. While Mother Florence thought up ways to enhance the trip, and wrote letters regarding their plans, Mother Philothea studied how she could best serve the congregation by taking note of anything that could be useful to it in the future. For her it was going to be educational; for Mother Florence it would be therapeutic.

But, before this trip could take place, Mother had to deal with Father Heiring in Tulsa. His decision was that the sisters would allow boys to board at the convent. Mother told him:

> That is out of the question. The boys can board at the rectory, as they do in other places. Our Rule says we may take only girls. Do you understand my position?

He answered her immediately:

> I wish to say I do (understand your position) and I feel you are taking a wrong position. You must board both boys and girls who have not made their first Communion—regardless of age. Notwithstanding the ruling of the Chapter, this is what I will stand for and what will be included in the school work here.

"There will be no older boys boarding with the sisters!" Mother wrote Father Heiring in May, and she waited for word from the pastor for the sisters to pack their trunks and go home. But it didn't come.

Also, she had finally considered the "Paradise" Father Drossaerts had promised her in Broussard. But, as so often turns out when Paradise is just in sight, somebody intervenes to make it less heavenly than promised. In this case it was the people of Broussard. "If we give the sisters everything, they will have no vested interest in the place. If the pastor is changed and they can't get along with the new one, they will leave. How about the sisters building their own residence and keeping boarders?" This was certainly not a new concept; Mother had been doing this in many places. She wrote:

> We agree to your proposition. You build the parish school and donate the $1,000 land to us, and we will build the convent.

In April Sisters Joachim and Bernadine went to Ireland to recruit candidates. Mother Florence and Mother Philothea set out August 11 for Newport, Kentucky, to visit with the Sisters of Divine Providence there before setting out for Europe. It was Mother Philothea's first visit, and she went everywhere with her small notebook, indicating everything she saw of interest to write the sisters back home, even taking notes of furniture and equipment she might need. Mother Florence spent her time visiting with her old and faithful friend Mother Marie Houlne, the provincial superior. They had only one day to talk, so they left sightseeing to Mother Philothea and enjoyed the heart-to-heart talks they both so longed for. The two sisters set sail for France on August 13, and arrived in Paris on August 22. Then they went to their respective homes, Mother Philothea to Saaraltroff and Mother Florence to Surbourg. Antoine met Mother at Surbourg and took her home. She saw for the first time his wife Madeleine, and their daughter, Francoise. Antoine was as dear as ever, looking after her every need, inviting the neighbors and relatives in to visit with his famous sister.

"Our niece, Sister Cornelia, is doing fine now," she told him.

"She is timid and quiet, and for a time she seemed unhappy. It was a temptation, I suppose, for one who left home so young and never saw much of the world. Now she is happy and doing well, teaching music." She found her nephew, Eugene, established as a saddler and earning a living.

Mother Florence enjoyed every minute of this visit. She did not jog along on Antoine's grain wagon this time, as she had done on her first visit home. But, if anything could restore her ailing body, it was the clean, fresh air, the aroma of myriads of blooming flowers, the wooded area filled with singing birds, the beautiful French language, still spoken in her village. The shining walls and floors of the home and the beloved little family completed the picture that would remain in her mind for many years. Antoine was never so happy, and his little girl could not tear herself away from the dear sister-aunt she had heard so much about. It was a joyful week in Surbourg and one long to be remembered by all. At the end, the entire village accompanied the family to the train station with singing and fond adieus. She looked long and lovingly at Antoine in parting and saw that he was pale and thin. "I may never see him again," she told herself as she kissed him fondly. She remembered parting from her parents twenty-two years ago for the last time, and the tears of both brother and sister fell. Antoine had never ceased to help her, sending small amounts of money for her projects, and always alert to help the girls going to the convent.

She spent a few days at St. Jean-de-Bassel, visiting with her old friends, but she found a slight coolness at the same time, for they felt that she had been responsible for the separation of the Texas branch from the St. Jean-de-Bassel congregation. She was not able to make them fully understand what had happened. The next stop was Lourdes, where eighty thousand tourists had come to celebrate the fiftieth anniversary. It was a touching scene for the sisters, who prayed fervently for the sick at home, especially for Sister Victor Wienert, who had fallen and broken her back. They made the Way of the Cross on the hill behind the grotto. They prayed that Mother Florence's face, sore at this time from her allergies, might be cured. Although they did witness two cures, there was no instant relief for Mother's face or at home for Sister Victor.

Then they left Lourdes, stopping at Toulouse, Marseilles, Genoa, and Florence, and arriving in Rome on September 13. Here they met Father Constantineau, who had planned their itinerary. Nothing was too much for them. They heard Mass in the catacombs, visited the Mamertine Prison, where St. Peter had been imprisoned and had baptized his fellow prisoners. Taken from catacombs to churches to religious celebrations, where they prayed for countless intentions, Father Constantineau, who had been in Rome a number of times, told his companions he had never been forced to pray so much; he would not need to pray again for a long time.

They visited their Cardinal Protector, Cardinal Merry del Val, and finally reached the highpoint of their visit, the audience with the Holy Father. Both Father Constantineau and Mother Philothea sent home accounts of the visit, which later appeared in the *Family Circular* and the *Academy Review:*

> Mother Florence gave the Pope, Pius X, a jubilee present of a substantial purse, contained in a white skull cap. The Holy Father, with a pleasant smile accepted the offering, saying as he did so, "Thank You." Rev. Mother then said that an exchange of skull caps would be a very great favor. He accordingly took off the one that he wore and before handing it to Rev. Mother, placed the new one on his head. Finding it was a perfect fit, since the necessary precautions had been taken to purchase a skull cap from the religious community that does this class of work for the Holy Father, he exclaimed "Ecco" (Here) and with a kindly smile he placed his skull cap in the hands of Rev. Mother, and the new one remained on his head.

Both Mother Florence and Mother Philothea watched the expression on his face as he sat down at the table where the prepared album of institutions, children, and works of the congregation lay. He turned page after page of the entire album, commenting and questioning as he looked. When he reached St. James, Alexandria, and saw the sea of black faces, he was visibly impressed. He signed two diplomas giving the papal blessing, spoke to Mother Florence in French, and finally said, "I bless you, your congregation, your sisters, and all the children confided to your care—and all your intentions."

"Nunc dimittis!" the trio sighed after this happy visit, and they prepared for their departure on October 9.

As was the well-established custom in the congregation, there was a triumphal welcome home for the voyagers. Members, friends, and students heard for many months the glories that had been witnessed and experienced abroad.

At home again, reality bore down upon them. For several years there had been no war with the Indians in Oklahoma. Something romantic had passed from the American scene. Therefore, when the "Smoked Meat Rebellion" of 1909 occurred, Oklahomans themselves and neighboring states made the most of it. It frightened Mother Florence and the sisters in Oklahoma and kept them wary, but not intimidated, for some time to come.*

*The Creeks had always opposed the sale of land allotted them, and they organized to resist the law. They had Negro slaves, now free, who made up about one-fourth of the population of Eastern Oklahoma. Chitto (Snake) Hargo (Crazy), a member of the House of Kings, was the Creek leader, an orator of great ability. He adhered to ancient treaties and was peaceful, living on a farm and liked by his neighbors. The Hickory Grounds, held by the Creeks, had a restaurant on the premises. Around the Hickory Grounds were tents and shacks inhabited by the Negroes, whom the Creeks allowed to stay, although they disapproved of their stealing mules and horses from the nearby farmers. Trading centers were simply wide places in the road, and men riding along carried rifles.

In the early spring of 1909 it was reported that a thousand pounds of smoked meat was stolen from Macey Springs, near Pierce and Henryetta. The sheriff visited the council grounds where the restaurant was, to have a look around. He was ordered off the place. He returned later with a posse, of whom Timothy Fowler, a sixty-year-old preacher, was accidentally killed, and several more men were wounded. A second posse went to the camp grounds, found it abandoned, and burned it.

All of eastern Oklahoma, alarmed now and trigger-happy, set out to find the Creeks, especially Crazy Snake the leader. Two men were killed on this trip. On March 28, 1909, Governor Haskell ordered out the Oklahoma National Guard. Unofficial posses were everywhere. On March 31 one of

Considerations more or less weighty than the "Smoked Meat Rebellion" faced Mother Florence in Oklahoma. Father Heiring in Tulsa wanted the music department, the boarders, the school, the convent, everything under his direction and supervision. Mother sent him a contract that had been agreed upon in Broussard, Louisiana, by Father Drossaerts. The conditions were clear, and approved by Archbishop Blenk of New Orleans. She wrote to Heiring:

> The information that I give you with regard to our practice concerning our boarding school and music department must remain exactly as I stated in my letter.

Father Heiring finally accepted the terms stated by Mother Florence.

To Father Sevens in Enid she also had to clarify the congregational position:

> We cannot under any circumstances allow a sister to become the organist or the leader of a mixed choir, even for a brief period. But in case your organist were to fail you, it is always

---

the most extensive manhunts in the history of a nation was staged, with a hundred and one cowboys joining the hunt.

The April 2 *Vinita Weekly* headlines read, "100 Creeks Under Crazy Snake On Warpath." The national papers took up the cry and blew it out of all proportions. By April 22 the chase was abandoned, with the newspapers admitting, "1,000 men could not find Crazy Snake in the region where he was hiding," and the *Oklahoma Times* summed up the story thus:

> The Snake Indian uprising is but a ripple on the surface of a new commonwealth that has recently undergone transition from territorial government to statehood. The same number of men might be killed in Kansas City, Minneapolis, Chicago, or New York . . . in a saloon riot and . . . be only a commonplace incident. But here the name "Indian" figures in a story, and around that word is clustered a wealth of romance and sensationalism.

The Commission of Indian Affairs said only:

> Outside the so-called "Crazy Snake" trouble and the arrest of an occasional recalcitrant Indian for refusing to work the roads or pay his road or personal tax, there has been no trouble between the Indians and the state and county officials.

possible for a sister to have a children's choir trained to replace the mixed choir until a regular organist can be found.

The sisters of Quapaw, hardy of soul and body, wrote triumphantly that they had killed a cow and two pigs to augment their food supply. Besides this, they had taught the older boys to plow the ground and plant seeds for the grain and garden. Their educational work was not confined to the classroom any more than they were. About this time, too, the mines near Quapaw closed down, causing a run on the bank that upset the already limited economy.

In October 1909 President Taft came to San Antonio, where many students and sisters turned out to see him. Sister Eugenia, superior of St. Joseph's Academy downtown, told Mother Florence apologetically, "Although it was mortifying for the sisters to appear in such crowded streets in the city, yet for our pupils it proved to be a source of pleasure. The good president had a kind smile for each and every one." Perhaps it was not so mortifying to the sisters after all, but it was gratifying to think that this was so. Father Constantineau, never at a loss, had an audience with President Taft in St. Anthony's Hotel.

The bishops of the dioceses where Mother Florence had schools were always important to her. Bishop Forest's health had reached such a point that he was no longer able to fulfill all his duties, so Rt. Rev. John J. Shaw was appointed coadjutor. Bishop Forest left the administrative duties to him. Bishop Van de Ven of Natchitoches, Louisiana, the same year, 1910, moved his see to Alexandria. Bishop Patrick Lynch replaced Bishop Dunne in Dallas; Bishop Meerschaert was still in Oklahoma, and Bishop Gallagher in Galveston.

The Oklahoma state capital was transferred to Oklahoma City, but not without bitter controversy. By initiative process, the Oklahoma people chose a capital. The capital election was completed on June 12, 1910, while Governor Haskell was in Tulsa making a tour of the state to explain the government policies and practices to the people. Shortly after midnight Haskell received the results of the capital election. It was to be Oklahoma City.

He phoned his secretary, Bill Cross, in Guthrie, to meet him at the Huckins Hotel in Oklahoma City at 7:30 A.M. with the state seal. He and a group of his friends took the train to Oklahoma City, where they met at 7:30 as designated. Haskell found a secretary at that early hour to draft the proclamation declaring Oklahoma City the capital. Hearing of this, the Guthrie people were outraged, claiming that the capital election was not legal; indeed, they took the case to the supreme court, which upheld the claim. But Haskell called a legislative meeting at which the legislature declared Oklahoma City to be the capital. The supreme court stated that this procedure was proper and that now Oklahoma City was legally the capital. Feelings ran high in Oklahoma, especially in Guthrie, for years over the change, as the Enabling Act had promised that Guthrie would be the capital at least until 1913. There were now 32,000 Catholics in Oklahoma, with 86 priests, 29 brothers, and 234 sisters.

Father Willibrord in Perry had become very possessive of the sisters there. In August 1909 Mother Florence replaced Sister Cresentia with Sister Imelda, as she had told Father it would be necessary to do. He had written her irately that, if the change were made, Mother would take the consequences. Therefore, when Sister Imelda arrived in Perry, Father had her return ticket already purchased and put her right back on the returning train. Perry had one less sister that year.

In September Mother Florence and Mother Philothea went to Canada for the Eucharistic Congress. As usual, Mother Florence soaked in all the beauty, excitement, and emotion of the occasion, making it a rejuvenation experience, while Mother Philothea observed everything, taking copious notes to be able to tell the sisters and the students about it later. Mother Florence informed the sisters on her return that "in Canada most of the sisters in the congregations came from the schools taught by these sisters. Why does this not happen among our sisters?"

By the time the two travelers returned to Texas, things were happening that demanded their full attention. Sisters Joachim and Philomene had returned from Ireland with nineteen candidates; this was welcome news. They were disturbed to learn that the sisters were no longer permitted to teach in the public schools in Medina Valley. Mother deplored the fact that the poor Mexicans would be the ones to suffer most. But the Castroville parish was in the process of constructing its own free school. Mother also visited Beeville, returning from "the Bee City" with an orange branch "having twelve oranges suspended from it." Father Constantineau, visiting Mexico, returned with a beautiful picture of Our Lady of Guadalupe, which was given a place of honor. A telephone system was installed in Bernardo Prairie and Mentz, putting these two towns in communication with the world.

As usual, there were difficulties in some parishes. "Does the rule permit the sisters to ring the Church bell?" Father T. A. Bily of New Waverly wanted to know. "They do it in Granger, Corn Hill, and Frydek." "The rule says NO, regardless of what is done anywhere," came the answer. And Frydek, well, the sisters in Frydek were cold, but they wrote, "Someone stopped by and threw in a feather bed." The pastor in Stillwater wrote that, since he would have to pay the cook a salary, would it be all right for the sisters to prepare his meals. "No," came the answer, "we will not prepare your meals." Mother felt strongly about having the sisters do this.

In May the administration sent out statements to pastors asking for $200 a year for each sister. Father Netardus in Praha was furious:

> If priests were to look so much for the dollar and uniformity in financial matters as far as our salary is concerned, hell would surely in a short time be a more populated region than heaven.

He said he would have to try again to get a public school system that Mother had talked him out of five years ago. Mother answered him shortly:

> We have had the Bishop's approval of these contracts. Never before have we been judged mercenary or doubting of the priest's veracity for so doing. Please try to get other sisters.

He approved the contracts. In Burlington the pastor bought a piano so that Mother would send him a sister music teacher. He did not approve of having a Baptist teaching music.

Up to now, all sisters' deaths had taken place in the mother house in Castroville or on the missions. There was no cemetery yet at Our Lady of the Lake. In January 1910 Sister Theodore Feiler was the first to die in the new mother house, of spinal meningitis. Her body had to be taken to Castroville for burial. This death precipitated the question of a cemetery on the campus. But no action was taken at that time.

Again jealousy raised its head against the Oblates. Father Hume, chancellor to the bishop, had appointed Oblates as extraordinary confessors to all the Sisters of Divine Providence in Fayette County. Rev. Moirite on one of the missions wrote Hume that the pastors objected to having Oblates come for confessions:

> I would consider it a favor if your lordship would grant me an interview, since our teachers are situated in a peculiar condition, and it may be useful for the bishop to hear my statement before he makes any appointments.

Father Hume did not cancel or change any appointments he had made for that year.

In January 1911 was begun a custom very dear to Mother Florence's heart and continued throughout her life. The new mother house was now completed with a dining room and all the fourth floor dormitories ceiled. She invited the academy sisters over for a New Year's dinner. Nothing was missing. The best linens, silver, crystal, and food, with novices, twenty of them, serving at table. This was reciprocated later in the year when Mother Philothea invited the mother house sisters to dine at the academy. No one would dream of missing these festive occasions.

As most years had their highs and lows, so especially did 1911. The high was Mother Florence's twenty-fifth anniversary as superior general. The low was the canonical visitation of Bishop Shaw. Bishop Forest died on March 11, 1911. He had been a real friend to Mother Florence, and she mourned his passing.

Most of her relationships with him had been positive; he had stood by her when she needed his help, had encouraged her, but had not imposed his opinions or leadership on her. Bishop Shaw now took over the government of the diocese. One of his first acts was to make a visitation of his diocese, including Our Lady of the Lake Convent and Academy, and the other houses in San Antonio.

Mother and the council did not know what to expect. They did know that there must be a backlog of negative reports about the Oblates' influence on the congregation and about the University of Texas approval of the educational system at Our Lady of the Lake College. But they did not know Bishop Shaw's position. Mother briefed her council in early April to get all the reports in order, for their standing with the bishop for many years to come might depend on this visitation. Bishop Shaw brought with him the chancellor, Very Rev. Wm. W. Hume, and a co-visitor, Rev. Louis Tragresser, S.M. The bishop's report a few days later was very favorable and gratifying, but the chancellor and co-visitor were not so complimentary. Belonging to a different school of thought from that of Father Constantineau, Mother Philothea, and Sister Angelique, they were very diligent in ferreting out the other sisters' opinions about these persons as well as about Mother Florence, who obviously supported the system in operation. They gave their report to the bishop with recommendations.

Although they found a good family and religious spirit among the sisters, they said the sisters had placed themselves too exclusively in the hands and under the direction of the Oblates of Mary Immaculate:

> As a congregation there is a tendency to cater too much to the worldly spirit. They have obtained the approval of the State University rather than the spirit of the Church.

Their report as a result of their interviews turned up the following items and responses: Although several sisters complained about Mother Florence, the priests did not consider these complaints serious. But they suggested the bishop visit the other houses of the congregation for more light on the subject. The congregation, they found, was in debt, and they said it ought to sell some of its property. Interviewing Mother Florence, the visitors concluded that Father Constantineau had been conducting most of the congregational business, and that she was in favor of the state affiliation. She did not agree with what she thought were too frequent visits to the convent by the priests in Castroville, but she said that she herself would not interfere with community life there. Their visit with Mother Philothea indicated to them that she was concerned only about the school, but Sister Scholastica said that Mother Philothea governs Mother Florence. In her usual outspoken way, Sister Scholastica pointed out what she would like to see changed: The sisters would like a change of government; they consulted Father Constantineau before the last election, but he advised them against electing too many "outsiders." The visitors concluded that he had too much influence. They said that the sisters were taught to look up to him and, if they were unfavorable to him, they were sent on the mission. Father sometimes attended spiritual reading when Mother made all kinds of remarks, and he also made remarks, which the sisters didn't like. The districts were formed last time to give a favorable delegation at chapter. Even the election of a confessor was not free, as the handwriting on the ballots was recognized.

Most of the sisters expressed satisfaction with Mother Florence: "Mother has no favorites." "She is very kind." "The sick get good care." "There is nobody like her!"

In their report the visitors observed that

> the young sisters have no opinions of their own. They have been brought up to regard the mother superior and the Oblates as all-perfect and all-wise. I am of the opinion that Sister Philothea is a stronger character than the superior and dominates the entire community. If this sister were removed, I believe it would be for the good of the whole community.

The discipline of the house was good, they reported, except for priests coming for spiritual reading and recreation; books for novices and postulants should be censored so as not to allow "promiscuous reading" by young persons; and rooms should be for one or three, not for two. The report indicated agreement with Sister Constantine that the Oblates had introduced a commercial spirit, and the visitor found an intangible air of worldliness or lack of simplicity that had perverted at least the higher superiors. The superior general, he said, no longer needed Father Constantineau, and it would be well to sever the relationship.

Sister Angelique, the report stated further, was strongly in favor of affiliation, which was Father Constantineau's idea. She would also welcome affiliation with the Catholic University of America. As for affiliation with the University, they stated, it was an "unmixed evil. It produced feelings of pride and exclusiveness that were altogether incompatible with religious life."

Bishop Shaw read all these observations and recommendations with interest, but not with alarm. In his next visit with Mother Florence he gave her a little fatherly advice, especially about her relationship with the sisters, as a few of them had asked him to do. It hurt her to learn that they had turned to the bishop as mediator. But she, always obedient to the bishop, took his advice seriously and mitigated her behavior, of which she had been entirely unconscious, in the future. He also did not reappoint Father Constantineau as ecclesiastical superior that year; the constitutions did not require such a person anyway. In May Father Constantineau was appointed by the council as business advisor to the congregation, who wanted to liquidate their debts. The bishop, in fact, had suggested to the pastors of the diocese that they buy the property that the sisters owned in the parishes.

Then one day came the message that Mother Florence dreaded: "Antoine is dead." He was the last of her immediate family, so loving, so devoted in all ways during his entire life. This time she could not contain her sorrow. Many sisters had received help at his hand. Priests who had gone to France had been received in his home. He was a known friend of the congregation. The announcement of his death was made in the *Family Circular*. Bishop Van de Ven offered a requiem Mass for him. Messages of sympathy came from priests and sisters everywhere. This loss cut deeply into Mother's personal life and left a scar difficult to heal.

That summer the congregation went all out to give Mother Florence a memorable celebration on the occasion of her silver jubilee as superior general. Nothing was spared, and she was happy in spite of the sorrow of the recent past.

The year 1912 rocked along with the usual catastrophes and rejoicings. Sister Sylvester Fikac, on her way home from Westphalia to San Antonio, died in Yoakum as she was changing trains there. The people of Yoakum, who had never met Sisters of Divine Providence before, took charge of everything. Mother was so touched that, when they later asked for sisters, she sent some immediately. Spinal meningitis hit Dallas, closing the schools. A twister in Perry, Oklahoma, blew the steeple off the church; San Antonio suffered a hailstorm around which the inhabitants later dated events as "before" or "after" the hailstorm. It caused unusual damage and expense. It was night. Lights and telephones were out. To cap the climax, the lime sacks where the foundations were being laid for construction took fire. But no one became hysterical and the sun shone again in the morning.

The Little Office of the Blessed Virgin, to be used by the sisters, was presented to Bishop Shaw for approval, as were the *Directory* and the *Book of Customs.* Because the Catholic University of Washington had arranged to conduct a Sisters' College, the bishops encouraged the sisters to build houses of studies on that campus. Mother Florence complied with that request, for there were a number of sisters who had completed as much education as was offered in the normal and now needed higher education in order to teach in the college on campus.

The people in Castroville were suddenly in a state of excitement because the construction of Medina Dam, a mammoth production, had begun. A few bodies were said to have been accidentally and tragically mingled with the cement in the pouring of walls, but this rumor was vigorously denied. A deserted Mormon village was inundated with the filling of the lake, its chimneys still visible when the water level fell. Many of the laborers on the project, imported with their families from Mexico, settled in the neighborhood after the construction was completed.

It was becoming more and more inconvenient to bury sisters in Castroville. It was not so difficult in 1910, when only three died, or in 1911, when one died, but, when in 1912 nine sisters, none of them retired, died, the decision was made to erect a cemetery near the convent. For the first time in her twenty-five years of administration, Mother Florence proceeded with this project without applying for permission or approval of the bishop. This was simply an oversight and was not intentional. When she realized her omission, she sent profuse apologies to Bishop Shaw, who accepted them very graciously.

The feast of Our Lady of Guadalupe, December 12, 1912, was doubly blessed. First, it was celebrated in honor of Our Lady of the Americas, becoming better known each year as the Mexican population increased in San Antonio; but, more immediately, it was the day on which Mother Florence received a cablegram from Rome, saying that the constitutions were permanently approved. This was the crowning event of an eventful year!

As early as February the council was hard at work preparing for the coming chapter. The sisters were grouped for election of delegates; the convent basement was made temporarily into a dining room because the first floor dining rooms were not adequate to accommodate all the sisters. Mother Florence, a little less imperious after Bishop Shaw's admonition, visited all the houses, familiarizing the sisters with the contents of the rules. On March 2 she wrote the sisters, stressing two matters of importance: (1) approval of the institute, and (2) final approval of the constitutions henceforth to be celebrated on December 12, 1912. Two special graces coming from this were: (1) a general absolution from all infidelities since the beginning of the sisters' religious profession, and (2) a plenary indulgence for all members and all students on March 13, 1913. She concluded, "Now each one of us without exception should look at this book as the infallible expression of God's holy will in our regard."

Before the business of chapter actually set in, Mother Florence was annoyed by numerous intrusions upon her time and preparations. When St. Francis Parish in Alexandria was divided, Bishop

Van de Ven agreed with Mother Florence that the boarding school would be transferred to the more elegant Providence Academy. This was done in 1913, with Sister Blandina as principal. When Mother traveled from one house to the other, she was a news medium, keeping all the sisters up to date on what was happening throughout the congregation. At this time, Bishop Shaw asked Mother to repay now if possible the debt she owed to Father Kirch, now deceased. It was to be used to rebuild a boys' orphanage that had burned. Also, Father Sevens, having been transferred from Ponca City to El Reno, said that Father Stillman did not give him information about the parish. He found a debt of $4,000 that no parishioner knew about. He could not find out about the two lots the sisters owned, and about the arrangements of the sisters themselves. He would negotiate a salary for the sisters, he said; moreover, the sisters would remain there during the summer while he went to Europe and his housekeeper had a two-month holiday. Mother wrote to him in her usual vein:

> We don't know anything about the debt. The pastor made all arrangements. We accepted the arrangements. Two sisters will stay during the summer.

Finally, as summer traveling approached, Mother wrote to the sisters in Oklahoma and northern Texas:

> A special coach will be put on MK&T at Dallas, and the sisters are to send their half fares to the convent, which will then pay the complete fares.

The "special" coach was exclusively for the sisters, who boarded the train all along the route. In it took place fond reunions, picnic lunches shared, chanting of the office in choir, violin music and singing, and little sleep for the travelers, weary after packing trunks and closing mission houses.

The stage was set. One small item had to be taken care of before summer activities began: Sister Liboria and Sister Madeleine would go to Germany to recruit young women. Veteran recruiters that they were, they had no premonition of what was to occur on this last of all recruiting trips to Germany.

11

Sixth Term (1913-1919)

Mother Florence was worried. Sister Madeleine Sheltein, who had been recruiting in Europe twice before this, was having a hard time of it. On each previous trip she had gone armed with credentials: letters from the bishop of San Antonio, Mother Florence, and priests and bishops in Alsace. But she never had needed them, and she had always returned with a large number of candidates. This time she had taken no credentials. All summer she had traveled about in Alsace and Lorraine, where she recruited sixteen young women, one below the required sixteen years of age. Sister Liboria Thiemann recruited in East Prussia and Westphalen.

When it came time to leave, Sister Madeleine, who had a very masculine appearance, being tall and thin, with a long nose and a low-pitched voice, was apprehended by government officials as a male hustler in disguise. She was held in custody and transported out of Alsace by two policemen, thus failing to meet her recruits at the designated places. Disappointed, they returned to their homes. Sister Madeleine's brother was able to inform the guardian of two of the girls to take his charges to Bremen, where they could meet Sister. Two other girls came independently to Bremen, one from Bavaria and one from Lorraine. Thus, from her sixteen recruits, she salvaged only four, later known as Sisters Anita Schwartz, Leonarda Gebhard, Estelle Marie Hauer, and Clarita Rudloff. Humiliated and frustrated, she completed her last recruiting trip in disappointment. Sister Liboria arrived at

Bremen with ten young women without incident. It was the last group to come from Germany or France, because the war broke out the following year.

Mother Florence had been informed of these difficulties. She also knew that two girls in the group were under sixteen, and there would be trouble disembarking in Galveston on this account. She asked the sisters to pray. Sister Madeleine did have trouble in Galveston. When the others disembarked, Sister Madeleine, Margaret Schwartz, and Annie Fitkar were retained on the boat. After a great deal of questioning, during which Sister Madeleine sat saying the rosary fervently, she was allowed to take the girls off, but only after having sworn to be their guardian and educate them.

When the group arrived in San Antonio, on October 11, 1913, they took the streetcar as far as Twenty-fourth Street, where they were met at the footbridge over Elmendorf Lake by forty-five other young women in a merry mood. As usual, Mother Florence and her council stood on the front steps of the convent, with arms held wide to welcome the newcomers.

Mother was now embarked on her sixth term of office, the second under the new constitutions, and things looked fairly good. The election of the general council had taken place Saturday, June 21, with Bishop Shaw presiding, and Father Antoine, OMI, assessor. This time the number of delegates had increased from the thirty-six of 1907 to forty-eight. Looking out over this group of women that Saturday morning, Mother saw the strongest, most powerful, and most vocal members of the congregation, some of whom had complained earlier to Bishop Shaw about her treatment of the sisters. Bishop Shaw was very cordial, and the sisters were friendly and supportive. Her change of attitude since her talk with Bishop Shaw had pleased the sisters, and she sensed a good spirit among them. She was grateful to the bishop.

The first ballot gave her a unanimous victory, with the only dissenting vote her own, going to Mother Philothea. To assist her as counselors were elected Mother Philothea Thiry, Mother Joachim Sweeney, Mother Scholastica Schorp, and Mother Eugenia Kaiser. Sister Gonzaga Menger was elected secretary, and Sister Constantine Braun treasurer. Bishop Shaw indicated his pleasure at the harmony that prevailed at the election, and he imparted his blessing on all the newly elected.

The largest block of time at the chapter of affairs was devoted to reorganizing in more detail the complete course of study to be followed from grades 1-12 in all subjects taught in all the schools of the congregation. It included examinations to be given, the marking procedure, and suggested texts to be used. The music program was also outlined.

Mother Florence wrote her dear friend, Mother Marie Houlne, that chapter was over, and she sent her a book of the chapter decisions. She concluded her letter:

> If only the distance were not so great, how I would wish to have a long talk with you heart to heart. If God has blessed our work here in the Southland, the seed of privation, humiliation, and manifold persecutions, has been sown in Calvary's soil.

Mother Florence, now fifty-five years old, meditated long hours on her official description as given in the constitutions:

> The Mother General should have a spirit of recollection and prayer, great regularity of life, true self-denial, a judicious mixture of firmness and sweetness, of calmness and activity, and that prudence according to God which is based upon supernatural motives. She should have a lively sense of the importance of her charge and her responsibility before God. She shall consider herself the mother of all the members of the Congregation, shall treat them with charity, love them as her daughters in Jesus Christ, honor them as His spouses, and be of easy access to all, not allowing herself to be carried away by preferences or predilections. She shall help her sisters in their troubles, and do all she can to encourage them, and lead them to perfection.

She, of course, agreed with this and actively worked at fulfilling it perfectly. She felt that the young sisters particularly needed her encouragement. She listened to them for hours, telling about their work and their life on the mission. She took a personal interest in every sister and remembered each in a special way. Although they might be frightened by her at a distance, they loved her close up. In the summer evenings they gathered around her, singing, laughing, and telling stories; she was always simple and happy.

It was the custom in the congregation to celebrate the feast of the Holy Innocents, December 28, by making the youngest sister in the community "Superior for a Day." Father Constantineau added to the fun by introducing for the convent and the academy communities a "Peanut Party," where all sorts of humorous activities took place, and peanuts overflowed the tables. No one enjoyed these moments of relaxation more than Mother Florence, who congratulated the performers and laughed heartily at the ingenious performances. She did not consider this "the spirit of the world," which she emphatically termed as "torrible," and from which she tried to shield the sisters. This was innocent fun to be enjoyed.

Mother Philothea was now relieved of her duty as mistress of studies because of the pressure of other responsibilities she had as superior of the academy and head of the college and high school, besides being first assistant on the council. Sister Angelique Ayres was then appointed as mistress of studies.

In June and July Mother was deluged with requests from Oklahoma. Father Heiring in Tulsa requested in his brusque manner "a qualified" commercial teacher. The classrooms were crowded. Sister Hugo had seventy-five pupils and Sister Hedwig sixty-five. He did not object to this, but he complained about the music teacher:

> I will not stand for any sister trying to teach classes and then shall teach music also. If you want to shovel off on us a music teacher and have *me* pay for the same, you are laboring under presumption or erroneous views. If I find this attempted, you will hear from me.

This was not quite the case, as Mother pointed out to him:

> Sister Marcia taught classes six hours each day. Only after the arrival of a teacher to replace her did she take charge of a music class exclusively.

Father Sevens in El Reno was trying to get his parish organized. He told Mother that he had convinced the parishioners to assume the debt, although "it is really yours, since you signed the contract." Then he complained that Sister Chrysostom still had "too much Father Stillman about her." He overlooked the fact that he still had a great deal of "Ponca City" about him.

"You will notice," Mother Florence told him, "if you read the contract, that we have fulfilled our part."

Always careful to maintain harmony between the pastor and the sisters, Mother was upset about conditions in Cleburne, Texas, which Bishop Lynch, consecrated Bishop of Dallas in 1911, promised to investigate, and in Quapaw, where the pastor was said to have spoken against the sisters. In St. Patrick's, Missouri, she objected to the sisters living over an amusement hall, where they had "sleepless nights," but "principally on account of the effects that may be produced in the minds of the young religious."

For many years now Mother had been pressured into investing in property in three states. Not only had the congregational debt increased dramatically during the last few years, but the responsibilities attendant upon keeping such property and buildings in repair consumed more time than she could give. During the past term she had systematically attempted to sell property where possible and liquidate the congregational debt, which in 1907 was $141,000. By 1913 the debt was only $85,000. This had been achieved in spite of six years of building amounting to $192,000. This achievement had called for the united effort of the entire membership, whose personal sacrifice of time, energy, and comfort they gave freely. Even students were sometimes asked to help in the efforts.

A plan was made at this time to give the individual houses responsibility for their own constructions, repairs, and debts, with the mother house only "lending" funds when necessary, to be repaid at a later date. This placed a larger responsibility on the shoulders of local superiors and communities and less on the superior general.

Mother was able to close out the year 1913 in thanksgiving to St. Joseph and to Father Constantineau for the city's decision to build the bridge on Twenty-fourth Street in preference to one at the east end of the lake. This would allow the street from Commerce to the Old Castroville Road to be completed and would give easy access to the campus from the end of the car line on Commerce. It was an important decision that Father Constantineau had been working to bring about. This decision also prompted the council to make plans to improve the property adjoining the park by forming a meadowland and planting trees thereon.

Perhaps the concerns of greatest importance in 1914 were three: the outbreak of World War I, with its attendant repercussions in the States; the persecution in Mexico, which made it necessary for many Catholic missionaries to leave Mexico; and the failure of the education department of Fayette County, Texas, to honor the sisters' certificates, thus causing their withdrawal from several schools in the county.

As former members of St. Jean-de-Bassel community of Lorraine, now a German possession, the Texas congregation followed the activities there very carefully. Mother Marie Houlne, superior general at St. Jean-de-Bassel, came to the U.S. in 1914 to make a visitation of the Kentucky province. During her stay there Germany became embroiled in the war, and she was unable to return. She was to have a long period of exile in the States while her congregation in the buffer zone was right in the middle of the fighting. The first thing the sisters did at the mother house was to move the novices away. Then the facility itself was transformed into an "Ambulance," where the sisters remained to care for the wounded. They never knew when the convent might be blown to pieces and all lives be lost, but they remained to give what help they could. During this time, the sisters in the United States from German territory suffered for their families and for the sisters there, about whom they heard little. Mother Florence kept in contact with Mother Marie in Newport.

In August 1914, after Mother had recovered from a rather severe illness, she and Mother Philothea went to Washington, where they were making the House of Studies there livable. She had the occasion then to visit together that she and Mother Marie Houlne both wanted. When she returned, she found the urgent request from exiled sisters from Mexico to seek refuge in Texas. Her motherly heart responded positively and she presented the case to the sisters in Castroville. This was to be the beginning of a much larger project. Six sisters came from Mexico in September. But also from Mexico came a stream of clerics: an archbishop, two bishops, and a number of priests. The house of one of them in Mexico had been turned into a post office, another into a telephone office, and a third into a commercial house. Their chalices had been confiscated and were being used for table wine by the rebels. In October ten more sisters came. They were given refuge in the house of the former chaplain at Castroville and they ate in the convent. The sisters in the community and the boarders gave up blankets and quilts for them.

Father Constantineau, a good friend of Father Francis Kelley, head of the Catholic Church Extension Society, had invited the latter to speak to the college and convent communities on "The Marvels of Womanhood." While in San Antonio, Father Kelley, along with Bishop Lynch of Dallas and Father Quinn, OMI, looked into the situation of Mexican immigrants and the facilities at Castroville. Father Kelley was receiving requests for housing Mexican seminarians unable to pursue their studies in Mexico. An arrangement was drawn up with the approval of Bishop Shaw, Mother Florence, and Father Kelley, and signed January 26, 1915, turning over the main building in Castroville with all its furniture to be used by the Mexican seminary for a period of one year, with the option of extending to two years. Actually, because the persecution lasted for more than three years, they remained longer. This was to be a traumatic time for the inhabitants of the old home.

But, before the movement could take place, Mother had to make, with the bishop and the superintendent of Fayette County, arrangements for the school year of 1914-15. As early as July, Bishop Shaw had informed Mother that Fayette County would no longer pay sisters' salaries. The county did ask, however, to use the school buildings. The bishop told Mother Florence and the pastors that the public school could *not* use the congregation and parish property. Some pastors asked to take the case to court, because they wanted to keep the sisters in the public schools, but the bishop was opposed to this step, and, especially, he warned Mother Florence not to get involved with the courts. It was, in fact, an opportunity to establish parochial schools instead of public schools—something Mother had wanted for years. "The people cannot blame us, as we did not take the initiative in this matter," the bishop told Mother.

Mother wrote the priests that the sisters would no longer sign contracts, which would be contested in court. The districts, however, varied about enforcing the law. In Wallis, State Superintendent William Doughty, said, "There is no law in the state prohibiting members of the Catholic Church from teaching in the public schools." But G. A. Sterling of La Grange said, "I beg to say I can no longer approve it." The Wallis pastor told Mother Florence, "This is a test case. Will you stand with us to fight it in court if need be?"

Mother said no. No contracts would be signed under these circumstances, even though it meant losing the public salaries in all these schools. It would really be a hardship on the congregation. Because the parishes in Fayette County did not agree to establish parochial schools, Mother had to withdraw the sisters from High Hill, Dubina, Sedan, Ammansville, Halman, and Bluff. These were all small country places where usually only two sisters taught. The new directive from Rome said that there should be three or four sisters in a house, and there was no way Mother could send four or even three sisters to some of these places anyway. This significant shift in personnel was completed only in October. At this late date Mother agreed to staff one or two new schools on the waiting list.

Usual and unusual demands, complaints, and incidents continued to occur. One of Mother's "girls," Sister Vincent, on vacation in Kansas City, wrote that she was not coming back and that she wanted to apply for a dispensation. Mother recalled how the council members had complained to her that Sister Vincent looked very disorderly in her habit. Mother should speak to her. In the meantime, Sister's novitiate companions, noticing the same thing, had taken her in hand, had washed, ironed, and mended her habit, and dressed her in the proper manner. When Mother Florence called her to her office, she was amazed at the transformation. "Na, Nan," she said kindly, "go, it's all right." Sister Vincent probably never understood why she had been summoned and dismissed. The application for dispensation was made and a document was on its way when Sister appeared back at the convent after three months away, saying she did not wish to accept the dispensation after all. She returned it herself when it came, giving an explanation, and she offered to make amends for her thoughtless actions.

In Oklahoma Father Van Hulse wanted to discontinue the high school in Vinita, but Mother would not permit it. In Durant the pastor wished to establish a high school there, which request Mother also failed to grant. Father Paul Nemec in Sealy begged for a music teacher because "the people here are 'crazy' about children's singing," and he demanded a Polish sister. Father Heiring, besides complaining that the boys were relegated to the background, said there were

> too much levity and loose remarks in the presence of the children (which applies as much to the superior). When speaking to a person, I am told a matter once and that is sufficient and all I want and I do not want it rehashed and rehashed until it is tattered and I be a heap of indignation.

Several pastors asked Mother to cancel their salary debt because of hard times. She found times hard too, but she agreed to cancel part of a parish's debt occasionally for good reason. The Stillwater and Bison pastors asked for a complete change in teaching staffs, and she complied. Some pastors wrote letters of high praise for their entire staffs or for individual sisters. This was like music to her.

Pope Pius X died on August 20, 1914, a sad announcement to Mother Florence, who recalled her glorious visit with him six years ago. She requested the sisters to pray for him, whom she doubted really needed prayers because of his holy life.

In September Mother announced by letter that Latin classes begun in summer would be continued by correspondence during the year. "Send in the lessons every two weeks," she instructed. Latin was a requirement for a B.A. degree in college. Then she gave her undivided attention to Castroville.

It was no small project uprooting the sisters from the old home in Castroville to make room for the Mexican seminary. The January 26 contract that Mother Florence and Bishop Shaw signed with the Catholic Church Extension Society (1) placed at the disposal of the Catholic Church of Mexico the convent at Castroville, (2) offered without rental, but the party of the second part agreed to pay for maintenance, upkeep of buildings, fences, and waterworks, (3) for one year with right of option in favor of the party of the second part for a second year only, when the convent and its contents would be handed back in good condition to the party of the first part. An inventory of all furniture and equipment was attached.

The sisters in charge of the parochial school and the boarding school in Castroville were to occupy the former house of the convent chaplain. A dining room and kitchen were added to this building to accommodate the sisters, the funds being furnished by the Catholic Church Extension Society.

In late January Mother Florence put on her apron and helped the sisters move. Relics of forty years were rescued as from a fire, carried from the old home into more cramped quarters. The Mexican sisters stood helplessly by, cheered occasionally in their exile by Sisters Gonzaga and Isabella Menger, who were able to converse with them in Spanish. The old sisters still in Castroville were moved to the mother house in San Antonio with the few personal possessions they had accumulated over the years. They knew they would never see the old home again, the only permanent home they had ever known since they had left Europe.

The poor old home now began to bloom. The former infirmary became Bishop Herrera's apartment, and the chapel was transformed into "a veritable cathedral." The Mexican bishop took a great interest in the sisters and boarders, offering the first Mass in their new home and inviting them for services in the seminarians' chapel. The Mexican sisters, in lay clothing, had not received their luggage and were without supplies. But all was furnished for them. Never before, the bishop said, had anyone ever shown them such a favor.

"We are preparing martyrs," he told the sisters, "who are to go back and perhaps suffer death."

Throughout the year Castroville swarmed with dignitaries from Mexico and from the States. Many brought gifts for the sisters and offered the Holy Sacrifice in their house. Reverend Mother herself brought them a statue of the Sacred Heart, and they had Forty-Hours Devotion for the first time. The sisters felt that God was rewarding them for the sacrifice of leaving the old home.

Providence in Alexandria, now ready to be furnished, was another occasion for Mother Florence to put on her apron and go to work. She loved doing this. It reminded her of her first happy years at St. Joseph's. She mingled with the workers and ate with them, black and white, at their work benches. At vespers time the sisters gathered for prayer on the second floor, where they used nail kegs as seats. At night they slept on mattresses in the art room, using their suitcases as wardrobes. A three-by-six-inch board placed on chairs served as a washstand, and the building at night was lit by candles. In such a situation Mother felt real achievement.

But she felt the need also for spiritual and cultural growth of the sisters and students. The *Sentinel of the Blessed Sacrament,* a new spiritual magazine, Mother considered worth sending a subscription of to all the houses, and she recommended that each house purchase and use the books *True Politeness for Religious* by Demone and *Christian Politeness and Counsel for Youth* by McVey.

In September a hurricane hit Galveston, always vulnerable to the weather. Devastation did not compare with the flood of 1900, but it was serious. On September 16 the water and wind kept rising, until by 5:00 P.M. all was dark. The sisters tried to be brave, but by 10:00 P.M. the wind won over the house. Blinds broke first, followed by panes. Nothing could stop the flow of water into the house, which began to rock like a boat on the ocean. Finally the sisters struggled through the water to a neighbor's house. When the storm subsided at 5:00 A.M., the sisters returned home, but there was no light, no drinking water, no heat, no gas. The only place to go was to bed. The following days were truly pioneer. A cook stove was erected in the yard under an umbrella. All provisions in the stores had been ruined by the seawater, and the baker's shop had washed away. "But whatever was smoky, burned, or half raw tasted as good as a feast day dinner on another occasion," the sisters later said.

Whether it was the hurricane experience or something else, Sister Johanna Feger, the superior at Galveston, sent Mother Florence a telegram in November: "Send somebody to take my place. My brother came and got me." Later she wrote to explain that she had to help her brother, and she asked for a dispensation. Several other sisters, unable to live up to the stricter new rule, also left or were dismissed.

Two dear friends informed her about their lives. Bishop Van de Ven was celebrating the twenty-fifth anniversary of his ordination to the priesthood. Mother directed the Louisiana sisters how to participate in the celebration. Mother Marie Houlne, still in Newport, wrote that she was ill and unable to regain her strength. She had planned to come to Texas but she was not able to do so.

Because 1916 would be fifty years since the Sisters of Divine Providence had come to Texas, Mother decided to make it a great occasion. According to her usual elaborate planning, she began early, asking all the missions to have school pictures taken, as they had done for Pope Pius X's Jubilee. They were also to prepare the exhibits of school work and fancywork of the sisters. Nothing would be spared during this celebration. The book *Memoirs of Fifty Years* would be published, even though its author, Sister Joseph Neeb, had died this year without having finished the work. Completed by Sister Angelique Ayres, the *Memoirs* were published the year after the Jubilee.

All across Texas, Mother was preparing to withdraw sisters from the public schools. Father Held in Nada, whom Mother had won over after the infamous *Rundschau* articles in which he had caustically criticized the congregation for obtaining approval of the University of Texas, appealed to Mother to show him how to organize a parochial school. The people of his parish wanted to keep a public school. "It is a question of breaking in a very few wild and stubborn German and Bohemian horses. They say they pay taxes, so they should benefit." Father himself lamented losing the $1,000 from the state, although he had been paying each sister only $200 a year. Mother instructed him to have each pupil pay $5 a year, and said the sisters would send out the bills. When Sister Hildegarde was sent to head the school, he was relieved: "Sister Hildegarde is right for the place. She will win the old grumblers and kickers over."

Life was not allowed to become dull in San Antonio or elsewhere.

In October, the Liberty Bell, on its way from the San Francisco Exposition, to Washington, D.C., stopped over in San Antonio. A wave of patriotism moved hordes of people to view it. The sisters in Tulsa sadly left their humble old home to move into the new penthouse apartment on Eighth and Boulder, a worthy dwelling provided by the zealous Father Heiring, who had finally won the affection and loyalty of the sisters and his parishioners.

Except for the worsening war and the Golden Jubilee celebration, the next year was comparatively uneventful. The Mexican Seminary, St. Philips, was progressing well. A group of five priests were ordained in February and quickly departed for Mexico. This was the second ordination in Castroville. Miss Stella Carranza, a niece of the president of Mexico, came to board with the sisters in Castroville in January. In February another Miss Carranza came to fill the last place in the boarding school. Never before had the sisters attended Holy Week services as they did that year at the seminary chapel—"so long and inspiring!"

In spring two perpetually professed sisters left the congregation, one from Perry, Oklahoma, without any notice, and one in summer after having requested a dispensation. The Golden Jubilee came off as planned with Mother Florence at her most gracious and exuberant. Bishop Lynch gave the sermon at the High Mass, and the day passed off as one long to be remembered. A statue of Our Lady of Providence, a Jubilee souvenir, was purchased and placed on the center stairs of the convent. Likewise a massive statue of the guardian angel was purchased for Providence in Alexandria. It was unveiled and blessed there in the presence of the bishop and clergy in September.

The school in Okmulgee, Oklahoma, was accepted for this year, Mother having ordered the desks and blackboards earlier. Father DeHasque had done a splendid work for the schools in Oklahoma by gaining recognition from the state department. Mother urged the sisters to augment by excellent teaching the good opinion already held by state officials. It was Mother's personal interest in each sister that made them willing to extend themselves. She came into the classrooms and heard the lessons. She examined the pupils and praised them and their teachers for doing a good job. She spoke to the sisters in detail about their efforts and encouraged them. They felt that she appreciated what they were doing and that she really loved and respected them. They were ready to do almost anything for her in the way of sacrifice and effort because their life was worthwhile.

In Alexandria the sisters who taught the Negroes at St. James had to commute from St. Francis School, a long walk each day. This year Father Cronenberger informed Mother Florence that Mother Katherine Drexel would pay the rent for a sisters' residence across the street from the school. St. James parish was not able to furnish the house, so Mother instructed Sister Jane at St. Francis to do it at congregational expense.

The pastor in Broussard, Father Cassel, was giving the sisters a hard time. When he wished to punish them for provoking his ire, he was in the habit of turning off the water or the electricity, and correcting them in the presence of the students. Several times during the next two years the administration was on the point of withdrawing the sisters, but the bishop always urged patience, sometimes a difficult virtue to practice. Father Cassel, summoned by letter, came to see Mother Florence about the deteriorating relationship. He offered to correct his mistakes but he refused to give the sisters back the choir and their pew in the center of the church, thus indicating to the parish that the situation had not changed. Father Drossaerts, who had been responsible for obtaining the sisters in the first place, met with Father Teurlings and the Broussard people about the problem. The people said the sisters must stay in Broussard. Father Drossaerts offered himself as their pastor again, but he was not assigned, for there were greater things in store for him. Father Cassels blamed Father Teurlings for putting him in a bad light. He said that the gas ran out, causing the lights to go off, and that he was doing everything to please the sisters. Some among the people, he said, had no more use for the sisters than they had for the priests. "And nothing pleases them more than to see differences existing among them. This time they caught us unawares and are rejoicing." Because Father seemed determined to comply with most of the requests Mother made, she wrote the superior to give him another chance. Not much later Father Cassels was transferred, a new pastor assigned, and harmony was resumed in Broussard.

While outwardly Mother Florence attempted to go about work as usual, converting the garden north of the building into a park and replacing the white picket fence in front of the college with a low cement one, she was concerned about the negative attitude toward all Germans in the U.S., including the sisters. There was a concerted move on her part to get the sisters naturalized before any real trouble arose. To this end the sisters were studying and discussing American history, the Constitution, and the government, learning patriotic songs, and participating in recommended war projects. The flu of 1917 struck violently for the first time. Mother Philothea, always susceptible on account of her low resistance to infection, was quite ill. Even Mother Florence was briefly incapacitated, but worse was to come. Foreseeing what might be expected from them, Mother Florence wrote:

It is fitting that the spouse of the crucified God embrace willingly, nay joyfully, the crosses inescapable from their state of life and learn the lesson of humility, resignation, and entire trust in God. Having suffered with and for Christ, we shall also reign with him and partake in the triumph of his glorious resurrection. . . .

On April 6, 1917, the United States declared war on Germany. The European sisters did not dare to speak of their homeland. In the villages, parishes, and schools, and even within their own communities they were sometimes made to suffer for their nationality. Most suffered in silence; a few hated the fact that they were German, because of the suffering Germany was imposing on them.

Mother wrote the sisters to be very careful in speaking of the war. "Because we teach many nationalities, we must be careful in speaking. We need to pray for peace and safety." Cards were sent out by the government, asking the people to do all in their power to observe the "Food Preservation Law." Mother urged the sisters to sign these cards and observe them "especially since we have the vow of poverty." As the atmosphere became more strained later in the year, Mother warned the sisters, "If agents come selling books, they cannot be authentic history. If people ask questions, just say, 'We do not discuss war.' " She continued to press the sisters to pass their examinations and obtain their naturalization papers. There was a great effort to do this. In the meantime the sisters began what they were to continue during the rest of the war: knit warm clothing, send care packages to the soldiers, and wrap bandages for the Red Cross. The German sisters worried about their families in the immediate danger zone, but spoke little of their concerns.

The Mexican seminary in Castroville was moving along smoothly. One incident, however, marred the established operations. A can of gasoline, left too close to the engine in the pump house, exploded, causing the pump house to burn and the pump to cease functioning. While it was being replaced and the pump house being rebuilt, the seminarians formed a bucket brigade from the river to the seminary in order to supply the water needed for the large building and the parched grounds. It worked so well and the students enjoyed it so much that little suffering resulted. All was restored to order in a few days.

In New Waverly the water situation was not so quickly settled. The pastor issued a command not easily circumvented. "As I have very little water in the cistern, you will please take each day two buckets only. In my absence, Lizzie could not get any water for the cow."

About this time Father Constantineau's father died. Both Father and his sister were beside their dying father in his last illness.

During this year the Oklahoma Church was hard put to cope with the "Dry Bone Law," being enforced in the dry state of Oklahoma. Because no alcoholic beverages were being legally sold in Oklahoma, altar wine had to be transported across the border. But now the line was drawn tighter to prevent this exception. For a brief period of time, while this subject was being negotiated, the Oklahoma Church suffered great inconvenience. Pure flour was difficult to obtain in Texas for altar breads. Bishop Shaw wrote, saying it could be purchased from Mr. Dittlinger in New Braunfels. "Please see about getting it from him and use the pure flour only for altar breads."

Inconvenience and lack of income hardly ever influenced Mother to withdraw sisters from a place. It was service she wanted to offer, as she wrote Sister Lydia in Durant:

> Our Mexican schools and colored schools would never have been accepted, and some of our country schools would share the same fate, but it was the numbers of students and not the money. If I were to look only at the compensation, many a school of ours would be closed. If Father insists the sisters return to Durant, they shall do so and give it another chance.

The Ku Klux Klan made a show of patriotism by harassing Germans. They took a San Antonio man of German forebears, from St. Henry's parish, for example, and asked him to sing the "Star-Spangled Banner" as proof of his Americanism. He sang the first verse perfectly, and then he asked them to sing the second verse. They were unable to do so. People locked their doors and turned off their lights when the Ku Klux Klan were around burning crosses and using the tar-and-feather method of intimidation. Their efforts were directed against the Catholic population, along with the Negroes and the Germans. In Perry, Oklahoma, and elsewhere in the state, the woman who described herself as "Sister Ethel, an Ex-Nun," went about giving lectures against Catholics, and sisters in particular. The sisters associated her with the KKK.

All schools in Alexandria, Louisiana, closed on account of meningitis in January 1918. To complicate matters, ice and snow covered Louisiana, and two sisters fell on the ice, breaking arms and legs. Word also came to Mother Florence that Father Pefferkorn had died in Europe. Father had long ago redeemed himself for his part in the deposal of Mother St. Andrew. At Mother Florence's request he had served as chaplain at the mother house at Our Lady of the Lake when he was ready to retire from parish duty. Here he took great interest in the girls in formation, teaching them, romping with them in the halls at recreation (for his living apartment was adjacent to the main entrance in the original building), laughing and singing with them, and throwing candies for them to catch. They had all loved him, for he had lightened their days. When he retired, Mother Philothea told the novices they would have to stop this light play, for the new chaplain was a "religious priest" not accustomed to such levity. He was Father P. F. Parisot, OMI.

Mother Florence remembered very well that Father Pefferkorn had lent her money during one of her building projects, and he had returned to Europe without having asked payment of the debt. But relatives were to request payment to them, and she had to go to some pains to make a proper settlement the following year.

In March 1918 work was completed on the new cemetery back of the convent. Sister Lucretia Engelberg was the last sister to be buried in the Castroville cemetery, and Sister Evangelista Butler was the first to be buried in the new Providence Cemetery in San Antonio.

While Mother was taking care of all the minor necessities,

her heart was aching over the war and its effects. She was fearful what it might do to the sisters. In April she wrote to them that all persons of German descent, except those from Alsace and Lorraine, had to register and fill out a questionnaire. "Do this to the best of your ability, remembering that nationality is not an issue with you as heaven is your true home and you are loyal to your adopted country."

The Mexican seminarians moved out of Castroville in April, happy to have been so well taken care of in their time of trouble. The Catholic Church Extension Society asked for a list of repairs to be made and equipment replaced. They were as generous as possible in recompensing the congregation, sending a check of $1,000 for repairs. With the big house now empty, Mother remembered how the European sisters helped their country by using their convent as an "Ambulance," and she wrote to the president of the United States, offering the Castroville building as a convalescent hospital for soldiers at a rental of $1. The president responded cordially to "this patriotic and generous tender," saying that he had referred it to the secretary of war. Because the war came to an end before it could be processed, it was not accepted. The convent, now empty, seemed to the new bishop of San Antonio, Bishop Arthur Jerome Drossaerts, formerly of Louisiana and well known to the Sisters of Divine Providence, an ideal place for a diocesan seminary, because it had served so well as a Mexican seminary. He would pay the congregation $75 rent a month. The council agreed, but this plan was not to materialize.

Mother continued to be concerned over the registration of sisters. She asked them to register in the towns where they were teaching. "This will include photographs, which you should be able to have taken in the habit as it was done in San Antonio." Whether to attempt to bring the sisters home this summer was a difficult decision to make:

> It will be difficult to come home this summer on account of the war. But the benefits are innumerable, so we ask you to be ready to face hardships. Teach the children to make sacrifices and to be obedient.

The sisters did find traveling hard that summer, standing long hours in the stations and on the trains, sitting on suitcases during the night, crowded together and jostled about. But they came. That year, 1918, Our Lady of the Lake College was recognized by the State of Texas as a junior college. A student completing five college courses, one being education, was eligible to receive a First Grade Certificate good for four years' teaching. It was worth struggling home for.

The flu, which had touched down briefly in 1917, returned in full force in 1918, causing a national epidemic. About a hundred boarders at Our Lady of the Lake were stricken, and three died. The sisters worked day and night, bringing them all the relief they could. Among the stricken was Mother Philothea, whose condition was critical. Sister Ladislaus Friehan, already ill, learning of Mother's condition as well as that of several boarders, begged God to take her and leave Mother and the girls. Her request was heard. Both Mother and the girls recovered, but Sister Ladislaus died. An appeal was made to the sisters to assist in nursing the poor in the city hospital. Four sisters went to take care of the most abandoned, but Mother did not permit the young sisters to volunteer for this work, because their health was too precious to jeopardize. Ever solicitous, Mother wrote the sisters in October:

> Because of the terrible flu, many schools had to be closed. We ask all those who can to make a Holy Hour every day. Take care of your health, and when you feel the first effects, follow these directions if you cannot get a doctor: calomel, castor oil, quinine, asperine, phenocelene.

Father Urban DeHasque of Oklahoma wrote that he carried the Blessed Sacrament in his bosom for three weeks in camp. All day and all night he ministered to the sick. Schools were closed. Sister Cresentia Fitzpatrick, thirty years old, who had just earned a master's degree at the Catholic University of America in Washington, D.C., with a major in Latin, was teaching at Our Lady of the Lake. With every ounce of energy, she gave to the health and welfare of the sisters and the pupils boarding there. But it was too much for her young strength. She contracted the flu and, on December 10, she passed away, to the extreme sorrow of her friends and pupils, and especially her three sisters in the order. Sister Berchmans, one of her sisters, was herself grievously ill in the convent infirmary, so ill that the superiors questioned the wisdom of telling her of the death of her sister. But Sister Berchmans recovered.

An Armistice was signed on November 11, 1918, and the U.S. soldiers began coming home. It took a long time to heal the wounds that war had inflicted on those left behind in all the countries involved in the global conflict.

The flu continued in 1919. Sister Flavienne Braun, so zealous in health care even before the sisters had moved to San Antonio, having taught the sisters the Delsartean method of physical education learned in Alsace and which the sisters introduced into the U.S. schools, died in February 1919. Sister, who had been ailing a few years now, was a close and trusted friend of Mother Florence for all the years both had spent in Texas. Sister Luca Denniger, one of the group who had come from Europe in 1880 with Mother Florence, apparently at the point of death, promised that, if she recovered, she would devote the rest of her life to the teaching of the poor Mexicans in Castroville.* She recovered and carried out this promise. In Antlers, Oklahoma, not a large town, some two hundred people died, so that it was difficult to find enough coffins for all to be buried in. In many Indian families there were two or three deaths. Thirty Quapaw pupils were ill, but none among the boarders died.

With the war over and traveling restored, Mother Marie Houlne was finally able to end her exile and return to St. Jean-de-Bassel. She had promised during the long war that, if the mother house in France were spared, she would spread devotion to the Sacred Heart. She now sent Mother Florence a picture of the Sacred Heart, and Mother Florence sent her $100 for congregational work, especially for the children "that you will give shelter to." Mother Florence's devotion to the Sacred Heart of Christ was no less than that of Mother Marie's, because they had shared for so long their common aspirations. She was later to name the dream chapel the Sacred Heart Chapel.

Before the end of Mother's second term under the approved constitutions, she saw the college approved as a four-year college issuing degrees. Mother Philothea, with Father Constantineau as college president, and Sister Angelique a dependable assistant, had forged ahead in every possible way to raise standards, enlarge the program, achieve accreditation in educational associations, and improve the faculty. With the need for more classrooms, dormitory space, private rooms, and dining area, the administration decided to go ahead with the building of a classroom/dormitory construction to be named Providence Hall, but later changed to Moye Hall. Mother Florence stated in her April message:

> The states have passed laws regarding certification of sisters teaching in private or parish schools. We have to get ready.

Mother Florence had other concerns to prepare for—concerns that sorely rent her maternal heart and left her wounded for many weeks and months to come. She sensed their coming but was not quite prepared when the actual day of reckoning came.

12

Seventh Term (1919-1925)

"I would gladly die to maintain unity and loyalty within the congregation," Mother Florence told her two councilors, Mother Joachim and Mother Eugenia, as they sat together one spring day in 1919. The bluebonnets were in full bloom on the campus, and leaves were multiplying daily on the young trees. Mother looked out the east window of her office of the convent second floor, across Twenty-fourth Street where cars were steadily flowing past, across the newly landscaped park with its young trees beginning to show signs of life, across Elmendorf Lake, and straight east where the city's skyline was rising higher every year.

"I have always said that I would be ready to go when the congregation and the constitutions were approved by Rome. Now they are, and the college is established. The congregation has grown beyond all my dreams. I don't want to see anything happen to all this. It would truly break my heart."

"Mother, except for you this would not be here," Mother Joachim told her. "It has taken a firm hand, and at times a firm voice, and there has been occasional grumbling; but the sisters have been happy with your leadership and what it has brought about. No one else could have done it."

These two sisters decided that they should gently tell her that, in spite of all this, there would not be a consensus in this year's election, as there had usually been. They recalled the one time when Sister Scholastica had received a number of votes and how Mother had considered it a division in the congregation. They believed that this time the votes would be more numerous for someone else, and they did not want it to come as a shock to her. Mother Florence brought up the subject herself.

"Although I feel that nothing could ever be so difficult again as the times we have passed through already, I sometimes think it would be wrong for me to accept another term. The constitutions say that the superior general may be elected to a second term; it doesn't say a third. I know that it is possible to get an indult, but I think of the example it gives the sisters to ask for exceptions."

"Mother, you know very well that we have asked for exceptions before, in the case of superiors' terms, and we will do it again. Besides, Bishop Drossaerts is the one who actually applied for the indult when we requested it. You know he would like to see you reelected, as would most of the sisters, who would not dream of having someone else."

"These 'most' that you speak of tells me that there are those who would have it otherwise. I have had a feeling that there is such a movement. Tell me about it."

"Some of the delegates are close friends of Mother Philothea, who was their novice mistress, their superior, their mistress of studies, and now is in charge of the college. As you know better than anyone, the college has become a very important part of the congregation, the sisters having worked so hard and so long to build and furnish the houses, and now to obtain their degrees from it. Mother Philothea is the heart of the college, and as such is quite powerful and influential. Some of the sisters believe she should now have a chance to be the superior general before she is too old. They believe that Father Constantineau and Sister Angelique could run the college, with Mother Philothea still advising as part of her greater role."

Mother Florence was silent for some time. She considered that during her thirty-three years as superior general Mother Philothea had been very close to her. She was experienced in all the areas of the congregation, as well as the college. She would be the logical one should she, now sixty-one years old, decline the election. But she could not bring herself to say "I will not serve again" if she were elected.

When the council had asked for an indult, it was well understood by all that the election of Mother to a third term would require a two-thirds majority instead of the simple majority of the other elections. This, they felt, was no problem, because in only one of her six previous elections was she even mildly opposed.

"And Father Constantineau, how does he feel about this?" Mother Florence had had Father Constantineau at her side ever since he came as delegate superior. The sisters used to seek his advice, and he would say frankly that he was in favor of reelecting Mother Florence. But Father Constantineau was not delegate superior any longer, and he had not been near her lately, so absorbed was he in his work at the college.

"We do not know," they told her, and it was true, but they felt that he might now be leaning in favor of Mother Philothea. Mother Florence had this premonition, too.

"I will not decide yet," Mother said. "I need time to watch the weather." Mother Florence herself felt, and so did her advisors, that Mother Philothea had no ambition, no desire, to be superior general. She was so completely absorbed in the work that she loved. It was enough. She had no thought but to support Mother Florence for another term.

So Mother Florence listened and observed as the time drew near for elections. And, as she watched, she saw that it was true. Several of the superiors were speaking favorably of this change, even pushing it, she thought, among the delegates. As the sisters gathered for chapter, she detected a restlessness among them. Their attitude toward her was guarded, and a few kept at a distance. She took this as a negative sign. She herself had several times mentioned the possibility of resignation, rather to receive the reaction than to make a statement, but she had taken no definite action.

After night prayer on the eve of elections, she returned to her room as usual. There was a light knock on her door. "Come!" she said, and one of the delegates entered, visibly distressed.

"Is it true that you will no longer be our superior general?" she asked breathlessly, anxiously.

"I do not know, my child. Why do you ask?"

"I was told you have resigned and I will have to vote for someone else," she confided.

"We shall see," Mother said, outwardly calm but inwardly perturbed. So it was spread about that she had resigned. Then Mother Philothea was practically elected already. She would have to pray for light.

"Divine Providence will guide us tomorrow," she assured the sister. "Ask Him to help you make the right choice. Goodnight."

She spent a sleepless night, and, when morning came, she sought out Bishop Drossaerts before the morning Mass.

"The sisters want to elect another superior general; therefore I wish to resign as a possible candidate."

"Mother Florence," he told her kindly, "you are a real mother to the sisters. They love you and need you. That is why we have obtained the indult."

"No," she said, "I can't divide the sisters, and I need to give Mother Philothea a chance. If I agree to accept the election, the sisters may feel that they have to elect me out of loyalty. You must tell the sisters that I withdraw as a candidate."

"You are a strong woman. Can I go against you? I will tell them, but I am sorry."

And so it happened that Bishop Drossaerts stood before the sixty-two delegates, on August 1, 1919, with Father A. Antoine, OMI, as assessor, and told the sisters,

"Your Reverend Mother, Mother Florence, wishes to withdraw her name from the possible list of candidates for superior general. She asked me to tell you not to vote for her."

There was a genuine gasp of dismay and surprise throughout the chapter hall. Mother Joachim stood up tall and straight and in her firm, loud voice addressed the bishop:

"Your Excellency, are we not free to vote for whom we wish?"

"You may," he answered. "Yes, of course, you are free. I am merely delivering Mother Florence's message."

"Thank you," Mother Joachim said as she seated herself determinedly. The business of the chapter proceeded. But some of the delegates were confused. Should they respect Mother Florence's wishes and not vote for her, or should they take Mother Joachim's cue and vote for her anyway? The ballot was taken and counted. The result was Mother Florence thirty-four and Mother Philothea twenty-seven, with Mother Joachim one. This, of course, was not a two-thirds majority. Mother Florence thought her wishes should have been respected. "Since I do not have the required two-thirds majority, let it go to Mother Philothea," she said.

"We will follow the procedure outlined in the rule," the bishop said. When a second vote was taken, it showed that only sixty-one delegates had voted. The votes were discarded and a third ballot was taken. This time the vote was Mother Florence forty-one and Mother Philothea twenty-one. It was still indecisive. Mother Florence, deeply humiliated before the bishop, Father Antoine, and the sisters, could scarcely remain in the room, although in face and actions there was little indication of her turmoil. The bishop was less restrained. He stood up.

"Sisters, if you cannot elect a superior on the next ballot, I will have to be your superior myself." He sat down.

"My God," Mother Florence said within herself, and she knew that others were thinking as she was, "we have returned to 1886, Mother St. Andrew, and Bishop Neraz!" Mother Joachim stood up, sending her piercing glance over the assembled delegates.

"Sisters," she said in no uncertain terms, "use your common sense, and elect your superior!"

A fourth ballot was taken, which read Mother Florence forty-seven and Mother Philothea fifteen. Mother Florence closed her eyes. Would it ever be the same again? To have this bitterness in her heart for six years would be a burden. How could she charitably interact with the sisters responsible for the commotion? She wanted to hide away with God alone, and never see them again. But it was not that easy.

The bishop declared Mother Florence canonically elected

superior general, and the election proceeded. The newly elected council members were Mother Philothea, Mother Joachim, Mother Scholastica, and Mother Eugenia. Sister Gonzaga Menger was elected secretary and Sister Constantine Braun treasurer. Receiving the homage of the delegates this time was a real cross.

In spite of the agony she felt, Mother stoically led the sisters through the following days' business with simplicity and humility. When the delegates passed the resolution "Sisters are not allowed to go to the opera at night for programs other than those of students of their own schools" and "Sisters who are visiting their neighboring sisters should not visit persons in that place unless accompanied by the superior of that place or a sister delegated by her," it seemed to Mother for the first time that this was nit-picking, unworthy of a chapter's deliberations. One topic, however, restored her to partial life. It was the discussion concerning the raising of funds to build the chapel. If there was one reason for her to be in office this term, it was to build this dream chapel, conceived twenty-three years ago. Every edifice on campus was built penny by penny with sacrifices of the sisters. And this chapel was left until last, for it was to be the crowning glory of them all. The chapel fund had already begun, but on a small disorganized scale. Now it would be a priority with every sister involved, and the chapel would actually get under way in a short time. She had once said, "If I could but see the four walls of the chapel, then if death would come to me, I could go, knowing that my sisters worship God together in one chapel." She would see this chapel completed before she left this office in six years. This one hope sustained her. It was right that the delegates had not accepted her resignation after all.

And yet Mother could not bring herself to face immediately the people she had to work with, those in whom she had placed implicit trust and confidence, with whom she had borne the burden and the heat of days gone by and who had failed to support her in this election. Father Constantineau was among them. She felt imprisoned by a feeling of bitterness of which she was ashamed. She determined to go away to a place of solitude where she could clear her mind and forget her bitterness, where she could renew her spirit before taking up the chapel project with the religious purpose and enthusiasm it deserved. The chapel was to be a bright and happy place, the culmination of all her dreams. It could not be conceived in sorrow, but in joy and love. So she set September aside as her time of healing, to be spent in Hot Springs.

In a letter of August 1919 she asked the sisters to consecrate themselves and their schools to the Sacred Heart. She also said that she would be away from home during September. But, before she left, she removed Sister Mary Pia Heinrich, whom she had appointed mistress of novices three years ago, and sent her to Enid, Oklahoma. Sister Pia had been swayed by Sister Jane Berringer to vote for Mother Philothea, and she knew that seeing her daily about the convent with the novices would be apt to stir up all her pain again.

By the end of September Mother had purged away her bitterness of spirit and had regained her health and strength, so that she could scarcely wait to return to her duty, free and clear of the past. She felt an urgency that even in her active life was more pressing than usual. It had to do with the construction of the chapel. She would have been happy just to exert her energies on this project alone. She wanted to begin now, but there was not yet enough money to start. Besides, all other business had to flow as usual. She chafed under the delay.

Delighted with the new Broussard pastor, she sent him the sisters' contracts. She approved linoleum flooring for the academy, a door at St. Joseph's, San Antonio, a new radiator in El Reno. She asked the pastor for better accommodations for the sisters in High Hill, asked the pastor in Chapel Hill to teach a religion class so that one of the sisters could prepare the sisters' noon lunch, added to the building in Abilene, appointed Sister Callista Baltz as mistress of novices, and reappointed Sister Angelique Ayres as mistress of studies for the congregation. She arranged for the poor children in Cistern to attend school. She approved repairs at St. Francis in Alexandria and purchased new pianos in Palestine, St. Henry's, and Enid.

"No," she told Father Notofer in Alexandria, "the sisters

may not attend the movies in the parish hall." Because the Castroville cottage, which had been offered for sale, had no buyer, it was taken apart and moved to the San Antonio campus. A sleeping porch was built onto the residence in Ponca City, and new radiators were purchased for St. Joseph's. There was always something.

When she saw that the chapel could not be begun yet, she decided to get as many congregational houses visited as possible so she could devote herself completely to the chapel when the time came. She told the sisters she would not be home until December and not to send their reports in until then. She also decided to discontinue *The Family Circular* for the year, because the sisters were not showing sufficient interest in it, and she had no one with time to edit it.

A young lady entered the convent at this time, a niece of Father Lefevbre, provincial of the Oblates of Mary Immaculate. The future Sister Louis Joseph Lefevbre was from Canada and spoke only French. Mother Florence had a great love for this sister, to whom she spoke French and who she supposed would be a great leader in the congregation some day as her uncle was in the Oblates. She was solicitous about her every need, seeing that she had the best English and music teachers because she had a rich, full singing voice and musical ability. She began early to groom sister for a leadership role in the congregation, and she later confided in her more than in any of her own contemporaries. "Come," she would say, as they entered her room and closed the door, adding, "we have to talk. I may be going soon, but you will be here. You need to know some things about the early days." And she would talk about what was on her mind: her treatment of Mother St. Andrew, her regrets, her strong belief in religious obedience, her disappointment at Mother St. Andrew's disobedience, but her joy at Mother's final return. She spoke of her dream for educating the sisters to be cultured and refined religious teachers, of helping the poor and under-privileged in poor country places: the Indians, Negroes, and Mexicans. She spoke of the chapel and its influence on the city of San Antonio and on the sisters themselves. She spoke of her hope of some day having hospitals and a fitting infirmary here at the convent. Sister Louis Joseph listened and wept and venerated the "queenly presence" in her simple bedroom, but she had no aspiration to be a leader in the congregation. She wanted to be a simple missionary sister who would occasionally sing. Mother Philothea did not see the possibilities in this young sister that Mother Florence saw. She was to remain a simple missionary sister and a music teacher, but a devoted friend of Mother Florence to the end.

The agreement had been reached between Mother Florence and Mother Philothea that they would support each other's projects. Mother Philothea would be in charge of fund raising for the chapel if Mother Florence would approve the construction of a classroom/dormitory building for the college. So in actuality Mother Philothea had her hand and heart in both buildings, while Mother Florence left the college building completely in Mother Philothea's care and she hovered over the chapel construction once there was enough money to begin. As usual the sisters of the congregation extended themselves to their limits to finance both constructions at once.

The chapel fund had begun as far back as 1911, when the sisters had celebrated Mother Florence's silver jubilee as superior general. Such an amount of needlework had been displayed at that celebration that the decision was made to start a chapel fund with the proceeds of the sale of this fancywork. It went so well that a Moye Guild was formed to make and sell needlework that would be done during the sisters' recreation. The cash donations came from candy given to the sisters and sold, eggs candled and sold in crates, dime books filled by sisters and friends, money sent from relatives and friends to buy a "gold brick" for the chapel, and anything else the sisters on the missions could come up with.

If Mother Florence had ever doubted the unity of the membership, she had only to look about her from 1919 to 1925 to see how the sisters in every house cut back on butter, desserts, candy, milk, and clothing to save money. The long black serge skirts had a tendency to wear out near the bottom and in the front, where they got the hardest treatment. The practice evolved of ripping the skirt from the waist, turning it upside down and around for another few years' wear. Ample sleeves received the same alteration. Darning and patches appeared on the fine veils imported from France and on the capes. Black dye restored many a browning and greening veil and cape to its original hue.

Each year Mother Philothea came up with new money-raising projects, and results from the various houses were published. In March 1920, Mother Florence announced the following income:

Cash donations from houses and parishes	5,957.95
Father Moye Guild	3,105.00
Total	9,062.95

Emulation among communities was strong, and the fund grew rapidly. But, as the houses competed and superiors asked sacrifices of the members, life sometimes became burdensome for the sisters, who were constantly deprived of every relaxation and delicacy they longed for. But they all wanted the chapel, and they wanted Mother Florence to see it finished before she left office.

There were now some 480 members in the congregation; the salary was being raised, not without parish complaint, from $200 to $250 per sister per year. Music teachers, not paid by the pastors, earned more than $250 a year by giving private lessons.

"Sisters, your stipend earns our bread," Mother often told the sisters, "but the music teachers put the butter on the bread." The music teachers stood well in the congregation, if they were good teachers and no complaints came about them. In 1920 the congregation purchased pianos for St. Michael's, Natchitoches, St. Henry's, Fredericksburg, Our Lady of the Lake, and Marlin. Pianos were a good investment.

When Mother Florence was not out on visitation, she often came to the novitiate with a handful of letters she had received from the missions.

"If you would just know what is in this letter!" she would

exclaim in exasperation. Or "Some sisters are not doing their share!" What scared the novices most was the vehemence of her feeling about discipline. "Children, you must have discipline in your classrooms. You cannot teach without discipline!" Whatever discipline was, the novices were determined to have it, so as not to put their superior general through such agony.

But she had her light moments, too. On a Sunday afternoon, the families of the sisters came to visit them. All the parlors were overflowing with parents, children, sisters, and brothers. They sat under shade trees on the campus and walked in the park. Mother knew most of them. She would come to the parlors to visit briefly with the families. Mrs. Kotula, whom she had taught at St. Joseph's, had a teenage son, who had just taken a car apart. If he could put it back together so it would run, his father would let him keep it. His mother was afraid he would succeed. "Don't worry, Lena," Mother told her. "He'll be all right." She gave him a St. Christopher medal for safety. He put the car together and wore his St. Christopher medal for many years in safety.

Buying, selling, and construction went on endlessly. In April it was decided to sell the property, house, and furniture in Castroville to the Oblates for a scholasticate. The $25,000 would go for the new chapel. It was hard to part with the old home but it was vacant and a worry now, so this seemed best. In May Sister Cunegunda Kuhn died in Plaucheville, from a fire begun from a gasoline iron she was using. The house was destroyed. An annex for the sisters' residence in Dallas, Texas, was built, a wooden structure with dormitory upstairs and a dining room and community room downstairs, for $6,570; a new car for the convent was purchased at $2,800.

Mother had to tell Father Plutz in Campti in October that she could not supply sisters for his mulatto school in spite of his plea:

> These poor people are discriminated against in many ways by their white neighbors, and it seems too bad to deprive them of the only chance they have of acquiring an education.

But to have a white, a black, and a mulatto school, all small, could not be managed. In December Mother was ill, but she recovered before Christmas and was visiting the missions again. She was overjoyed to learn that Mother Marie Houlne had been reelected as superior general of St. Jean-de-Bassel community. She wrote:

> God has deigned to find you strong enough to carry, as you have done so nobly in the past, the heavy cross of the congregation and to be for so many chosen souls the safe pilot while crossing the ocean of life. May God's choicest blessings be yours, and may His Sacred Heart be your strength and your consolation. . . . I still hope to see you once more in our dear United States. What a consolation this would be.

Moye Hall was now under way, almost completed, in fact, with its unique octagonal rotunda, railed in on the three upper floors, with a skylight in the central top. Mother Philothea, with the architect, Mr. Waharenburger, and the contractor, Mr. Fuessel, looked forward to the festive assemblies in this rotunda with students on all four floors participating. Her vision was of candles glowing in the dark all around the rotunda from first to fourth floor while students' voices rose in song and prayer. There was a wide stairway in the center from the first to the second floor, where the choir could stand. Of course the students would not use these privileged stairs any more than the sisters would use the center stairs in the convent or the original academy building. Moye Hall matched the main academy building and the mother house, built of blond bricks.

At the request of Mother Philothea, Mother Florence sent Sister Inviolata Barry and Sister Pia Heinrich to the Catholic University of America in Washington, D.C., to earn Ph.D.s, and she told them not to waste any time in getting finished, as they were needed at the college. The two sisters took the admonition so seriously that their days at the university were a time of real stress and anguish. No sister of the congregation had earned a Ph.D. before, and Mother Florence did not realize what it would require of them. In each of her letters she pressed them to get on with it and come home. In each of their letters to family and friends they begged for prayers in order to hold up under the strain and to succeed in fulfilling the expectations laid upon them.

"Now we can begin to work on the chapel," Mother Philothea at last told Mother in 1921. "We have enough money to start, and we can sign out contracts." Mother Florence was delighted.

The architect was Leo Dielmann, whom both Mother Florence and Mother Philothea knew from St. Joseph's parish, San Antonio. It was decided that the congregation could bear $200,000, and the chapel would be dedicated to the Sacred Heart. Mother Florence had always dreamed of a two-spired chapel, such as the ones she knew in Munster, Metz, and Strasbourg. She had even had a postcard printed with the artist's conception of such a church portrayed. But, when the architect, the contractor, Mr. Fuessel, and the council considered the cost of the two spires and the effect produced, they agreed that one high spire would not only be more in keeping with the projected cost but also more effective in San Antonio, which at that time did not have such elaborate churches.

Mother Florence felt more than a slight tug at her heart as she made this concession, but, as the plan developed, she saw that it would be more beautiful than the two spires.

In the meantime, Mr. Fuessel, who was quite ingenious and who extended himself to meet the expectations of the two powerful women of the congregation, devised a system for watering the gardens on the campus. This was important, because the grounds and gardens were as much a part of the campus plans as the buildings themselves.

On August 5, 1921, the birthday of Mother Florence, the ground-breaking ceremony took place. It was impressive. Mother Florence knew it was going to happen; she knew the outline of the chapel had been marked off in its place between the convent and the academy, but she did not know, as she went out for the ritual, that along this outline the sisters would form what they called a wall of "human bricks." She was touched as she had not been in a long time, and tears of joy fell as they had when the document of pontifical approval was ready to mail to Rome.

"My children," she told them in a broken voice, "I almost feel that the chapel is really standing there, as I know you are making it possible every day to be. This chapel rising here will be a monument to God and to the Sisters of Divine Providence long after you and I are gone, and God is still here. God bless you for all the sacrifices you have already made and will continue to make until it is completed."

While the sisters sewed and saved, Mothers Florence and Philothea planned and prayed. The $200,000 would not be enough after all. The building itself would cost $268,000 without stained glass windows, altars, statuary, and furniture. There was, besides, the ground floor under the chapel, to be an auditorium now and overflow-chapel some day. This also had to be furnished. Both superiors reeled under the financial burden, but they never doubted that it could be accomplished, for there was a Divine Providence.

Glass and marble companies in St. Louis and Deprato Statuary Company in Chicago were contracted for windows and statues. Schroder and Sons of Italy were designing a main altar of Carrara marble in the form of a Gothic cathedral, with a carved replica of Leonardo da Vinci's *Last Supper* in front below the altar table. This altar was the gift of 15,000 students taught all over the Southwest by the Sisters of Divine Providence. But the furnishings were to come later.

On June 22, 1922, the copper steeple cross was blessed by Bishop A. J. Drossaerts and elevated above the tower to the pinnacle of the new structure, the highest construction in San Antonio at that time. The cornerstone was sealed into place at the entrance of the chapel. The sisters were home for this occasion, and enthusiasm ran high.

Every step of the construction now sent a thrill of joy through Mother Florence. At sixty-four, she was not quite so agile as in her 1885 days of building at St. Joseph's school, or finishing of the mother house at Castroville in 1886. Her greatest strength and ingenuity in building were shown in 1896, when the first academy building went up, and in 1908, when the convent mother house was built; but never was she so dedicated to any building project as this one. She watched it by day go up brick by brick and she dreamed of it by night. She could not tear herself away from it.

Pastor and businessmen from various places came to see it rise. Some donated money for the construction. Few disapproved. An indult was obtained from Rome to borrow an additional $75,000. Nothing could stop this construction. Somehow God would provide. Mother spent longer hours in chapel and knew it was right to do this. Efforts were stepped up to obtain income. Mite boxes were placed in the mission classrooms, and jewels were donated for the monstrance to be placed on the altar. A published list of contributions was always issued. Father Depreitre made a donation, which was earmarked for the side altar of the Sacred Heart.

Congregational business, as usual, would not stop. A school was accepted in Pecos, New Mexico, and one in Texarkana, Arkansas, two new states and dioceses; and a second school in Houston, for poor Mexicans, was accepted. This was to be the cradle of a new branch of the congregation in years to come, begun by a Belgian sister partially educated in Mexico, whose compassion for the unfortunate Mexicans was limitless. She was Sister Benetia Vermeersch, who would later organize the Catechists of Divine Providence to work with poor Mexicans in Houston and San Antonio. Also the golden jubilee of the Galveston school was celebrated in the usual fashion. The Indian school in Antlers was in financial trouble, with only fourteen Catholics in attendance. When Mother was planning to withdraw the sisters, the bishop persuaded Mother Drexel to come to their aid; they remained there at the insistence of the Indian Bureau. Father Neudling in Alexandria complained that the only recreation that the sisters had was sitting on the porch every evening sewing and embroidering; they needed more activity. Father P. J. Crane in St. Leo's, San Antonio, on the other hand, said, "The sisters must not go around and associate with the women of the parish." He asked for sisters, "good disciplinarians." They could have only two entertainments a year—for the sake of the school.

The chapel construction went on under Mother Florence's vigilant and eager eyes. She could look out her office window and see it all the time. It was hard to believe it was really so beautiful, as she had dreamed it all these years. It would be perfect, she thought, as a mother thinks, watching her infant growing from one stage to the next. In August 1923 the council agreed to purchase three hundred chairs for the auditorium at $1,150. Later four hundred additional chairs were purchased. Spiritual reading and congregational meetings would be held there in the summer, although everything was still unfinished—even downstairs.

While the chapel was progressing, Mother also gave her attention to myriad other problems in the congregation. Broussard, Mansura, and Devine required extra attention in 1923. The Broussard pastor wanted a colored school:

> Please send me two additional teachers to teach the colored in Broussard. Any sister who knows a little French and has sufficient control over the children could teach in the extended school, as far as I can see. Mother Katherine Drexel will finance it.

But, if she took the school, Mother wanted to do better than that. She wrote:

> No, we don't have any more sisters. I suggest that the colored sisters take charge of it.

Things were not going so well financially in Broussard anyway. She had asked for a sister's salary of $30 per month. Father Massebiau wrote her that "the parish is financially very low." In order to provide more room, the sisters moved to the attic so that their sleeping quarters could be used for additional classrooms. Mother Florence wondered what had happened to the millionaires in the "Little Eden" that Father (now Bishop) Drossaerts had promised her years ago.

Texas had its own hardships. Father Planchet in Devine bemoaned the fact that the former pastor had said Mexicans were entitled to worship with the white people in the same church. The old church was now abandoned and could be renovated for a Mexican school. He told Mother, "Don't send a third sister. It would only aggravate the situation and cripple the parochial school." Mother was shocked that the pastor would object to this small favor to the poor Mexicans. She sent Sister Mary Rose, saying to the pastor, "She can help the superior; since the Mexicans are migrant workers, they come late anyway. She can teach them when they come."

Many of the missions, Mother found, were still primitive and very poor. It was surprising that so few conveniences had been provided for the sisters in some places. Sister Cordula wrote from Mansura, Louisiana.

> We have no modern conveniences here as bathrooms and light, but the sisters are all trying to make the best of it, and are saying, "This is real mission life."

Rev. R. E. Frei confided to Mother Florence in July that Sister Assumpta in Palestine had been given a warning by the Ku Klux Klan. Just in case anything happened, he did not want it to come as a surprise. Mother thought Sister Assumpta could handle it, so neither she nor Sister Assumpta ever mentioned it.

Finally the time came to send out the invitations in the diocese for the dedication of the Sacred Heart Chapel. It could not be consecrated because of the debt on it. Besides, it was far from finished. But it was standing, and beautiful to behold, with the tall steeple extending into the blue Texas sky, and bridges running to the convent on the south and the academy on the north, for it was to serve both the sisters and the students.

Although the number of people that November 21 at the dedication was limited, Mother saw, in her mind's eye, as she sat in the last pew, every seat filled with a black veiled presence, chanting together the *Little Office of the Blessed Virgin* and assisting at the Holy Sacrifice of the Mass. What more could she ask! The bishop and her many friends among the clergy expressed their amazement over the size and perfection of the edifice. The chapel was almost pure white: the walls, except for the stenciled borders among the beams and pillars; the tile floor in the center aisle, except for the gray and green design; the white marble altar; the steps; the communion railing; the white light coming through the clear glass windows; the ivory brascolite hanging lights! It was dazzling in the November sun. It was almost too much to bear, and Mother Florence wept. What more had she to live for?

She had photographers make pictures of the chapel both inside and outside, which she sent to the missions, saying,

> You are receiving a picture of the interior and the exterior of the new chapel. Frame it and keep it, for it is the fruit of your efforts. It is not completely furnished yet, but that will also come.

When she sent the same pictures to Father Depreitre, she said, "Midnight Mass was a foretaste of Heaven for us. Everyone says it is beautiful. The stained glass windows are to be installed in June."

A few days after the dedication Mother Florence and Mother Philothea were returning from San Antonio in the convent car driven by Peter Lagutchek along Commerce Street. As they came to Prospect Hill, Mother asked Peter to stop. They looked across the lake, which clearly reflected the long row of cream buildings— the rectory, Moye Hall, the academy, the chapel with its single spire reaching into the sky, and the convent mother house.

"Do you remember the first time we saw this sight?" Mother Florence asked.

"I do indeed. It was a prairie covered with flowers. Mrs. Kelly's horses stopped as this car has stopped today. What did you see on the hill that day?"

"I saw then what I see today—a long row of majestic buildings, hundreds of sisters going into the chapel to worship—a chapel with two spires instead of the one I see now. This was what I saw. What did you see?"

"I saw the academy extending almost to the lake, with young women sitting in the lawn drawing on their sketch pads and walking in the park with their books. It must extend still further —to the end of the block on the north."

"And the end of the block on the south, for an infirmary."

"Are you happy, Mother Florence?"

"Now I like the single spire. It will be beautiful with bells that sound out over the city, telling the people God is here, and ringing the Angelus to remind them of Mary's humility and obedience. A clock will show them the passing hours, and our chapel doors will be open to God's people."

"Would you believe that it would come to pass?"

"To think that we passed through a world war and hard times besides. Divine Providence held us in His hands. We must do great things for Him. Not big things, just small great things, in gratitude."

"Yes," Mother Philothea said, "yes."

Glancing at her, Mother Florence thought, You will have to carry on. It won't be easy, but what ever was? They drove on.

No time was lost. In early December the council decided to change the convent chapel into an infirmary and a small chapel for the sick and aged sisters. A little later the decision was made to transform the academy chapel into a library and assembly room, and a third story should be built above it for dormitory space. This new dorm would have semiprivate rooms and would be called St. Theresa Hall. At the year's end the college had obtained the following memberships: Catholic University of America, Catholic Education Association, Texas State Department of Education, Texas Association of Colleges, Senior First Class College as approved by the Texas State Department of Education, and Southern Association of Colleges.

Still the push was on to complete the chapel. It seemed providential to Mother Florence during the following year to be able to complete the arrangements to sell the congregational property in El Reno. St. Francis, Alexandria, also wanted to purchase the congregational property there, but the parishioners were not able to close the deal that year. Property sales allowed more funds for building at home.

Father Francis Kelley, the head of the Church Extension

Society and a good friend of Father Constantineau and Mother Florence, was appointed as the new bishop of Oklahoma. Rev. Emil Depreitre was named the vicar general. Mother was extremely pleased and told them so.

Father Urban DeHasque had written to Mother, his first ever complaint, to remove the Okmulgee superior, who had rumored about that her trunk was packed and she would not return. Father would be pleased to see her leave, but she had not taken into account Mother Florence, who believed strongly in obedience. Mother at first said that she would send her back in spite of the packed trunk, but in the end she gave in to Father DeHasque and reassigned Sister Jane.

In March, Mother informed the mission sisters that the stained glass windows were being installed and the chapel was "also becoming completely finished and is God's own work." In May she wrote, "We want to complete the altar of the Sacred Heart in 1925." Everything should be finished before she left office. This was done. The altar was purchased for $6,000 and installed in January 1925.

This was not the end. Everything, it seemed to Mother Florence, was starting over again, and she was tired. It was necessary to build an annex to the convent on the west side—a large dining room with dormitories above it, at a cost of $20,000. Besides this, Bishop Kelley in Oklahoma persuaded the council to purchase land and build Newman Hall near the University of Oklahoma in Norman. This would entail a $57,830 outlay. Along with this they agreed to purchase twelve acres of land on the west side of the campus for $9,288. Mother Florence was weary of debts, loans, and construction of buildings. During her thirty-nine years she had completed her last of seven buildings. It was a relief. Mother Philothea would have to take care of all this, with Father Constantineau's advice.

Mother St. Andrew had recruited 151 sisters and postulants from Europe and Ireland during her time. Mother Florence had added 239 more from the same source, making a total of 390 sisters from Europe and Ireland who remained in the congregation. In recent years a large number of young women from the

States had entered, although a majority of the sisters were still foreign-born. Recruiting had stopped in Europe with World War I, and she saw that from now on the membership must come from the States. Conditions were changing so fast that native sisters would probably adapt better, she decided reluctantly, as she considered the untold sacrifices and dedication of the pioneering German, French, and Irish sisters in the past. The entire congregational membership at this time numbered 554 in spite of the deaths and departures during the years. There were also many young women in formation, so the future looked bright.

Chapter of elections would take place June 6, and she would be free at last.

13

A New Role (1925-1931)

Mother Florence was numb. In the few minutes' break between the election of superior general and the election of the council members, she escaped the chapter hall and fled to the chapel. She wasn't needed anymore anyway. Mother Philothea would take over the leadership of the congregation from now on.

Of course, she had known in her head that she would not be reelected, and yet, in her heart, she had expected something to clear away the obstacles that would prevent her election. But not a single vote! She was stunned. Even Bishop Drossaerts, who had greeted her so warmly, had expected the sisters to vote for her.

"We can get another indult. Your case is different." And for a wild, glorious moment she had believed it. Distressed now, she lifted the lid of her pew in chapel to take out a handkerchief. But her hand came in contact with an envelope. She took it out hesitantly and slit it open. It read:

> Dear Mother Florence,
> Much as some of us would like to reelect you, you will not be reelected this time. We just want you to be prepared and not to feel that we have abandoned you. It is because of Canon Law and is no reflection on you. Perhaps it would be well for you to officially state your resignation before the election. It will make it smoother for you and everybody else. That is why we are informing you tonight.

The letter was signed and dated July 5. She had not opened her pew last night. She wished she had. Maybe she would have given in her resignation; but she had done so at the last election, and it had not been accepted. In fact, it actually made little difference. She could bear it, she thought; but she was not so sure anymore that she would be relieved of the thirty-nine-year-old burden. It no longer seemed a burden—only a labor of love. Carrying a burden for thirty-nine years leaves an impression on one's back and shoulders that feels void and empty when the weight is lifted. She swallowed her tears and returned to chapter, light of shoulder but heavy of heart.

The ballot for first councilor was soon taken, and Mother Florence received fifty-three of the fifty-eight votes. Her breath came a little more easily as she accepted the position graciously. She would share the burden with Mother Philothea after all, much as she had been doing now for some years. Her old friends—Mothers Joachim, Antoinette, and Eugenia—were elected as the other councilors. Sister Gonzaga was elected secretary and Sister Constantine treasurer.

Bishop Drossaerts believed the sisters had not shown proper appreciation for Mother Florence. In his mind, she should have retained the highest position in the congregation as long as she lived. After the election he accosted several of the sisters, "Are you one of the sisters who put Mother Florence out?"

But Mother Florence, who had accepted the office thirty-nine years ago in obedience, was determined to give it up with the same degree of obedience. It was now time for her to do what she had been asking the sisters to do all these years. "They will not hear complaints and criticisms from me," she promised herself, "nor will there ever be a task too humble for me to perform. It will cost me dearly, I am sure. I feel it already. But I will be equal to it." "Be a woman!" she had told the sisters many times. Now it was her turn.

Mother recalled the day when Bishop Neraz had burned Mother St. Andrew's records. In a way, it seemed to her now that it hadn't been so bad after all. Mother St. Andrew had been a prolific and emotional writer. She herself had in her possession letters of sorrow, confessions, petitions, reprimands, admissions, even though she had always chosen to take care of personal matters face to face rather than in writing. She did not want anybody rummaging through her own or other people's lives after she was gone from office. She sifted through the files, removing all sensitive material and took it quietly to the burner. She did not in any way tamper with official records, however. She felt relieved when the last page went up in a wisp of black smoke.

Mother Florence was immediately assigned as superior of the mother house. Although her dear and long-time friends came frequently to visit her, bringing small gifts and tokens of their love and appreciation, she often felt that it was simply to ease her into a lesser position rather than a real desire to visit with her. She began to realize shortly that the special treatment, the deference, she had received for so long, went with the office and not with the person. She was not the one they came to see anymore. It was the superior general. They simply stopped by to see her. It was thus with bishops, pastors, and business executives. They now went to Mother Philothea. Being a first assistant was a far cry from being superior general. Giving an opinion or voting in council was quite different from having the final responsibility for the action.

Immediately she tried to adjust to her new role, but she was depressed. However, she wrote to Mother Marie in France on June 17, 1925:

> Only a few lines to inform you that in our general election June 6 Mother Philothea has been elected superior general to our dear congregation. Your humble servant has been elected her assistant. The election passed off nicely, to the edification of our good bishop. The Chapter of Affairs took place right after and lasted two days, and on the 9th the summer school opened with over 500 sisters and ladies in attendance.

Mother Philothea delegated to Mother Florence some important business with which she was familiar, but she kept for herself charge of educational matters of both the academy and the college. She continued to live at the academy and work closely with Father Constantineau, the president of the college, Sister Angelique, and the other college faculty. Mother Florence had never become actively involved in the college, and only superficially involved in the academy. Her interests had been with the sisters in the entire congregation, with the academy as only one of the houses, albeit a main house on account of the college.

Even during her administration the mission sisters had complained that the fruits of their many sacrifices to raise money went to Our Lady of the Lake campus rather than to the mission houses farther away and the sisters assigned to them. The sisters at the academy were special, they said, and those at the convent next in importance, then the houses in the city. She realized it was true, and she wished it could be otherwise, but she felt it would be even more so now since the college was Mother Philothea's chief interest. Even now a new dormitory at the north end of the campus was being planned, a loan having been negotiated for $150,000 from a Houston bank to be used for this building and a Newman Center in Norman, Oklahoma, where Oklahoma-based sisters would be studying at the university there in the future. Later Bishop Kelley helped negotiate a new loan in Oklahoma for Newman Hall. Along with these acts, the new administration reorganized the college corporation, changing Mother Florence from president to vice-president. The first piece of business was to purchase ten acres of land adjacent to the present property on campus at $775 per acre, and in September eight more lots adjacent to the convent for $3,000.

Mother Philothea believed that Mother Florence was enjoying her freedom and her leisure time. She wrote Mother Marie, superior general at St. Jean-de-Bassel, in July:

> Dear Mother Florence is very happy to have been able to lay down the burden. She, however, is still well and active, and is keenly interested in everything, so I feel grateful for her election as First Assistant.

Mother Florence had had her home base at the convent ever since it was built in 1908. As much as possible she had noticed what was going on in the house.

When it was first constructed, "Our Lady of Providence Mother House" had appeared as its title. But some of her friends had soon told her that an unsavory connotation had been associated with the words, "Mother House," where people expected to find small children. She had changed the official title to "Our Lady of the Lake Convent," carved above the main entrance, where it still stood. She began a systematic review of the entire convent. She found that the "Glass House," a title she hated and forbade the sisters to use, which was built in 1915 at St. Joseph's Infirmary for tuberculosis patients, was not too effective in producing cures. The sisters were not happy to be confined to this torrid area, where they were completely isolated. It was now in need of repairs and renovation. She called this to Mother Philothea's attention. It was given a general overhaul with a thorough cleaning. All-new bedding and beds were purchased.

She studied the sisters who had become mentally incompetent over the years. Miss Mary was the Marie Metz she had brought to Texas in 1886, but who gradually lost the ability to function independently. Miss Mary was very agreeable, obedient, and dependable if supervised. She assigned her to specific duties in the infirmary. In August she wrote her friend, Mother Marie:

> You may have been surprised at my silence. What could I write? My news are not many. I spend my year as assistant and local superior of the mother house, filling my post the best I can and happy to gain the merit of obedience and giving to our dear sisters the good example of a true religious. May God grant me the grace to finish my days setting this example, of virtue by deed more so than by word.
>
> As to the news of our dear congregation, all works peacefully. Our Reverend Mother Philothea is loved and revered. She has my sympathy in all the difficulties she faces and my warm support as also my poor prayers.

Sister Beatrice Bind, who had been an efficient music teacher in her youth, had become deranged, so that in 1922 she had been committed to St. Paul's Sanatorium in New Orleans. She was no longer violent, so that Mother requested she be returned to the convent. She personally would see that Sister was properly cared for. Her release was approved for early 1926. A new infirmary was needed, and she began to speak of it to Mother Philothea.

In the summer of 1925, Archbishop Drossaerts, looking over the diocesan records, found that, although Mother St. Andrew had purchased property in St. Joseph's parish from Bishop Pelitier, she had never received a quitclaim from the diocese. Because the question arose about selling the property, Archbishop Drossaerts gave it to Mother Philothea now. Looking at this claim reminded Mother Florence anew of the good days at St. Joseph's when she and Father Pefferkorn had built the new school, with the support of both Mother St. Andrew and Bishop Neraz. Indeed, as the days passed and she worked alongside the sisters she had known for many years, history was relived daily for her. Sometimes, seeing sisters in their final illness caused her great anguish as she recalled the hardships of their simple lives.

When Sister Madeleine Sheltein died, Mother recalled the last difficult recruiting trip to Europe when Sister had been taken for an impostor. Sister Ermelinda Phillips, a native of East Prussia, refused on the point of death to take any pain-relieving drugs, just as Mother St. Andrew had refused an anesthetic in her operation. She died in great pain. Sister Liguori Huber from Alsace, who had worked with the Oklahoma Indians for many years, died in Joplin, Missouri, where she was transferred from Quapaw with pneumonia. This year, too, they were able to transfer Sister Beatrice from the sanatorium in New Orleans to San Antonio, where Mother Florence took her on as a special project. Sister behaved like a small child, standing with a finger in her mouth, not moving until someone came to take her by the hand. Mother Florence, grasping her hand, walked with her on the campus, reciting the rosary, examining the flowers and vegetables in the garden. Mother tried to draw her out—to make her talk. She was never too busy to assume this self-imposed duty. By now she was also going about her self-assigned work in the convent kitchen, where one of her "girls," Sister Prosper Ehrmann, was in charge. Sister Prosper, in spite of her rough-and-ready ways, was always loyal and faithful to her superior.

Mother worked with the preparation of the salads, allowing a little free time for the regular staff. She also found her way to the laundry, where, in the intense heat, the sisters were working all day at the machines, hanging out the clothes behind the laundry, and putting sheets and pillowcases through the steaming mangler. She set herself the task of folding and shelving the sisters' and students' clothes as they were dumped on the table dry.

It was a change from being superior general. It was dull and boring, but it was not humiliating. She felt that now she had to take her turn at what she had hardly ever had to do. She felt near her sisters and she came to know them as she had not known them before, especially the household sisters. They lost their awe of her and loved her devotedly.

In August 1926 Mother Philothea asked her to go to Washington to make needed repairs on the house there. She loved this. She wrote to Mother Houlne from Washington, congratulating her on her reelection, and telling her what she was doing. Mother Marie answered, writing of their large novitiate. Somehow Mother did not receive the letter written to her by Mother Marie, and it seemed to her that now not even letters could find her in her poor insignificant setting. She wrote:

> Your letter to me never reached me, but I felt compensated by reading Mother Philothea's. What a future for your dear congregation! Our number is far too small for our needs. Our Southern people are not yet ready to make sacrifices, and our young people are too much for *having a good time.*

When the college corporation met in June 1927, Mother Florence was replaced as a member, and her feeling of rejection increased. It was made up now of Mother Philothea; Father Constantineau, president of the college; Sister Angelique, superior of the academy and dean of studies; Sister Inviolata Barry, dean of students; Sister Mary Pia Heinrich, registrar; and Sister Clarence Friesenhahn, treasurer. But the year did bring some consolation.

That year there appeared at the convent a Miss Leona

Foelker from San Benito, Texas, sent by Father Yvo Timon, OMI, her pastor, "To my dear friend, Mother Mary Florence." Miss Foelker had been superintendent of the North Houston Independent School District, but, more important, she had almost completed her nurse's training in Houston when she was called home to take care of her sick father. Mother Florence, no longer being superior general, did not even see Leona for a few days. Mother was in the kitchen paring vegetables when Leona first saw her, dispelling the young lady's illusion of grandeur that she had been led to expect in the venerable superior. It soon became clear to Mother that this young woman was an answer to her prayers. She was a nurse, the first one to enter the convent from the States. Although she had little dealing with the young people in formation, she was delighted, for she felt that this woman was a providential gift to her personally and to the congregation.

As Mother went about her convent duties, she found it very difficult herself and saw that it was also difficult for the older sisters to walk up the four flights of stairs. She proposed installing an elevator in the convent, at least to the third floor, and this was effected at the cost of $4,200. In April the altar of the Blessed Mother in chapel was finally purchased with $5,800 of the sisters' "sacrifice" money. Now the main chapel furniture was in place, and the debt on the chapel was gradually decreasing. Mother Philothea, loyal to and solicitous about Mother Florence, came regularly to the convent to see her. She instructed the novice and postulant mistresses that the young women in formation were to show Mother reverence and respect in every instance. If she heard that was not happening, she did not spare the guilty ones. This also held true for all the sisters no matter what their position. Birthdays and feast days were still celebrated much as they had been when she was superior general.

In spite of all this, the gleam was gone from Mother Florence's eyes and the spring from her steps. She felt herself being systematically pushed aside, given only token consideration, and listened to halfheartedly when she spoke in council. She voted to send sisters to Ireland and Germany to recruit when the subject was proposed; but, when the two sisters—Sister

Callista Baltz and Sister Inviolata Barry—were selected, no one sought her counsel on how to proceed. She felt that she could have worked out an effective program for them, because she knew exactly how former recruiters had succeeded. They left, however, without having discussed the subject with her at all and returned with few results—no German girls and only three from Ireland.

She made another trip to Washington in August, where she always enjoyed her reunion with the St. Jean-de-Bassel sisters stationed there. Being on the council gave her at least a fair insight into what was going on in the congregation. She eagerly voted with the council to sell the property in Cleburne, to get the San Antonio City sewerage system installed on campus, and to purchase five acres of land for $7,500 for a school in California. She felt she was still alive when she was contributing to congregational progress, making history.

What transpired outside the council she was less and less aware of. She resented this neglect, for she felt that, if anybody had an interest in and right to know, it was she. But, although the sisters noted her sad expression and lack of vivacity, they never heard her complain.

About this time, one of the household sisters in the academy, Sister Nicholas Hinkes, in her eagerness to be of service to Mother Philothea, slipped and fell in the freshly waxed corridor, breaking her leg. The doctor put it in a cast, but Sister complained constantly of the intense pain. "Take off the cast," she begged him, but he told her it was only healing. Finally, when the pain continued to increase, and she could bear it no longer, the doctor removed the cast and found the leg irreparably infected. "The leg will have to come off," he told her.

"No! No!" she cried, thinking of the helplessness that would result. Believing she was concerned about her appearance, he told her brusquely and insensitively, "What's the matter with you? You are no fine society lady." Mother Florence never left her side during the agonizing days in the hospital after the operation. She also succeeded in obtaining for the sister a wooden leg, which she was to wear the rest of her life.

At a congregational corporation meeting Mother Florence was amazed and grateful to learn that the total assets of Our Lady of the Lake, both convent and academy, totaled $2,958, 668.93. But it still did not satisfy the accrediting agencies, who were requiring an endowment toward which they were willing to credit the $63,260 contributed services of the sisters on the staff. It was decided at the next meeting, therefore, that the congregation would assume the complete debt of the college so that it would be considered debt-free to receive financial aid from the General Education Fund of New York. The debt was $223,000. The college would compensate the congregation each year by paying $5,000 normal school expenses for teacher instruction.

In May 1928 Sister Victoria Lindemann died, leaving a void in the congregation never to be filled. Sister Victoria was a significant and colorful person, strong in body, mind, and faith. She had early given herself to the most difficult of manual work in the fields and gardens of Castroville. She hitched up the horses, drove the wagon, and pitched hay in the fields. She tended the animals and the garden, milked the cows, and transported the sisters in the wagon to and from their missions across the raging or merely trickling Medina River. When the congregation moved to San Antonio, she continued the work there, without the responsibility of taking the sisters to their missions, for now there were cars and a driver. Her days were spent with her animals and her garden, and she was happy, offering her prayers and her labors for the release of the poor souls in purgatory. Although sixty-five years old and slowed down considerably by her heavy labor, she worked almost to the day of her death, followed everywhere by her faithful dogs. When she died, the dogs mourned long and loudly, keeping the congregation awake at night. After her burial, the dogs never left her grave, where they tried to unearth her body. They eventually died beside the grave, heartbroken from grief.

Mother Joachim Sweeney was soon to follow Sister Victoria. An Irish woman, powerful in faith and works, Mother Joachim had served on Mother Florence's council from 1904 to 1925 and continued to serve in this position during Mother Philothea's administration to the end of her life, in August 1928. Mother Joachim was fearless in right, never hesitating to give her opinion or stand for her strong beliefs. Mother Florence and Mother Philothea both felt her loss deeply.

Early in 1928 Mother Philothea had begun to work for the paying off of the chapel debt so that the House of God could be consecrated on the occasion of Mother Florence's golden jubilee. When Mother Florence learned of the plans, nothing pleased her more than the coming consecration.

"You need not, in fact, should not, celebrate my jubilee. I am content to remember this quietly, as I am no longer superior general. But the consecration is something else. Let it be."

"You know, Mother, that all your friends would be disappointed if they were not invited to celebrate with you. You have not had occasion to see some of them for several years, and this will be a happy time for you as well as for the entire congregation."

Mother Florence saw it as a last fling. She would submit in obedience. Besides, she would probably enjoy it. And she did. The sisters spent, according to rules for such a ceremony, the entire day preceding the consecration in prayer, silence, and fasting. It was such a glorious celebration as Mother had helped to arrange on many occasions before. This time all attention was centered on her. She was lauded and feted before her friends and acquaintances, her accomplishments reviewed. Bishops and priests, religious of many congregations of women, all her sisters and business acquaintances, lay friends and former pupils came to rejoice with her. She was at her regal best, greeting and conversing with them, graciously accepting gifts and compliments. But best of all was the consecrating of the chapel, a touching and beautiful ceremony, with the sanctuary filled with church dignitaries.

Archbishop Tritschler Cordova of Yucatán blessed the interior and exterior of the church. He blessed and opened the door, sprinkling the middle aisle with ashes in the form of a St. Andrew's cross. He blessed and fixed the twelve crosses on the wall, each under a bracket holding a candle, which was to be lighted on each following anniversary. Bishop Van de Ven of Alexandria was the main celebrant, and Archbishop Drossaerts delivered the sermon.

When it was over and she had written about it to her friend, Mother Marie, she felt that life would all be downhill from this time on:

> I can hardly realize that 50 years have passed since I had the happiness to pronounce my first vows. . . . If obedience had not imposed the celebration of my 50th anniversary of my vows, I would have been more happy, but I had to submit. His Grace, the Archbishop and Reverend Mother Philothea had their reasons for imposing this ordeal on me. My 48 years spent in Texas was no path covered with roses; on the contrary, our congregation has taken deep root on Calvary and our first foundations have a great resemblance with those of our first schools in Europe. God has made use of a poor instrument to do this work. I do thank you for the loving invitation to see once more the cradle of my religious life. I sometimes long to see it, the Chapel where I pronounced the cherished vows, the classrooms, the recreation rooms, where I spent the many happy hours, and oh, last but not least, to have a heart-to-heart talk with you, dear Reverend Mother. How much I would like to tell you, but I doubt that this will be my happy privilege for 1929.

It was not. There was to be no trip back to Europe, and Mother understood that she was not to have exceptions denied to the other sisters.

Business resumed as usual. Mother Florence was slightly concerned over the arrangement in Dallas not only to make it a high school, with which she would have no problem, but to make it a central high school for boys. There were several other Catholic high schools for girls in Dallas, but none for boys, and Bishop Lynch urged Mother Philothea to accept the challenge. On the advice of Father Constantineau, because St. Joseph's was in an Oblate parish, and because the congregation was already teaching boys in a number of places, Mother Philothea was in favor of doing this.

A move with which she was more in sympathy was to place in St. Francis Retirement Center Mr. William Wiedermann, who had been on the convent premises for many years and had previously given his money to the congregation. The congregation bore the expense of his care at St. Francis. The community also undertook to place a blind girl, Ofelia Rodriguez, in a home for the blind in Jersey City and to be responsible for her should she need further help.

A new building project in 1929 was the construction of an elementary demonstration school on the campus, to be used in connection with the education program in the college. This would especially help the sisters in formation, because they could do their practice teaching on campus rather than be assigned to the public schools for this practice. The building was to be named St. Martin in honor of the founder of the Sisters of Divine Providence, and the cost would be $71,000.

Because her own life and activities were so circumscribed, Mother came to look forward more and more to the council meetings. It was here that she felt involved in congregational affairs and learned what was going on. She heartily supported the building of the grotto in 1930, modeled on the one at Lourdes, at a cost of $5,000. The chapel was becoming more beautiful and more dear to her every day. She approved the writing of a new *Directory,* which was compiled by Rev. F. Thiry, OMI, the brother of Mother Philothea. Mother Philothea wrote to Mother Marie in France:

> Mother Florence, whom you will remember, is still quite active. Mother joins me in sending most cordial greetings to you, Reverend Mother, and to all the dear sisters at St. Jean-de-Bassel.

The great vacation school push began in 1930. Not only did the congregation send out sisters to many places during the summer vacation to teach religion to public school children, but in San Antonio hundreds of poor, mostly Mexican immigrants and migrant workers, were taught during the summer and during the year. The sisters at the academy were especially diligent in training high school and college students to take small groups of children for instructions once or twice a week. These classes on campus took place under the shady trees in good weather. Mother Florence was especially happy to see this missionary work going on all around her.

The year 1930 ended with a fire in Beeville school. Insufficient care taken in disposing of oily equipment had been responsible for the fire, and the sisters felt a responsibility for it. They came to San Antonio during the Christmas holidays. Because the congregation was unable to rebuild the school, Mother Philothea and Bishop Emmanual Ledvina agreed that the congregation would return their lease and the insurance money for the fire to the diocese, and the diocese would rebuild with this help.

In the convent Sister Aquinata Tolksdorf, always nervous and a bit scrupulous, was becoming greatly disturbed. Mother saw that her mental aberration was steadily progressing. The doctor recommended that she be institutionalized in New Orleans, at St. Paul's Sanatorium. Mother recalled how in 1912 she had come from West Prussia by herself. Although twenty-six years old, she was unfamiliar with American ways, and she spoke no English. When she arrived in Galveston, after having suffered an illness between New York and Texas, she was retained on the boat for a day or so. The sisters in Galveston were expecting her but did not know the exact time she would arrive. When she was released by the ship doctor, she took her luggage and disembarked. A man approached her and indicated that he had been sent to bring her to the convent. She soon found herself in a house of ill repute. Terrified, she wrote and dropped onto the sidewalk below her window a letter calling for help. Fortunately her call was heeded, and she was soon rescued, but the traumatic experience affected her sensitive soul the rest of her life. Mother felt the weight of this sister upon herself and hesitated to send her away, but, in the end, she asked Mother Philothea, for the good of the sister herself and the rest of the community, to make the transfer. Sister Aquinata remained in New Orleans until some years after Mother Florence's death, when she was finally able to return to the convent.

Two major projects were inaugurated during Mother Philothea's first term and Mother Florence's term as first assistant. Mother Philothea was bent on fulfilling the requirements of the Southern Association of Colleges and Universities, which required an endowment of $300,000. It was decided to place the sisters' patrimony, $18,000, into this fund, and borrow $30,000, thus making a beginning of $50,000, which would be increased each year. Sometimes Mother Florence chafed under the demands that the college was making on the congregation, but she had long ago left this management to Mother Philothea, who, she knew, was an astute businesswoman, not now just in charge of the college but of the entire congregation as well. It was with a more positive feeling that she approved the installation of a series of bells for the chapel tower, purchased with a gift of $5,000 from J. D. Culligan of Houston to Sister Benetia Vermeersch. The bells would belong to a clock system. Sister Benetia was working among the poor and neglected Mexican children in Our Lady of Guadalupe Parish and surrounding areas. She begged from local businessmen for the most needy of God's children—illegal immigrants and families unable to speak the English language or obtain work in these hard times. Businessmen found her irresistible and gave her whatever she asked, deeming it a privilege, as she told them, to help the poor. It was this spirit of charity and humanity that later prompted Sister Benetia to assist a young man aspiring to the priesthood, a migrant worker named Patricio Flores, to enter the seminary and become a priest. He was later to be the first Mexican-American bishop and eventually Archbishop of San Antonio. The $5,000 gift for bells was a silver jubilee present to Sister Benetia, who was better known to the Sisters of Divine Providence for another of her outstanding abilities. She was instrumental in obtaining free passes on the railroad, so that many sisters traveled on "Benetia's passes" for years.

The bells were a complicated system. There were five: a large one called the Ave Maria Bell because it sounded the hour with the Lourdes Hymn, and four smaller ones. The clockwork, skillfully made of copper and bronze, was placed on the floor above the loft in the choir, with bells arranged on different levels above the works. The faces of the clock were installed on three sides of the tower. The fourth side, the west, was left blank because it was thought that San Antonio would not extend farther west. But, before the installation took place, Archbishop Drossaerts, assisted by Father Thiry and fifteen other priests, baptized the bells, giving each a name, and blessed the bells and the clock mechanism. The new organ was blessed at the same time.

When Mother Florence heard the chapel bells that spring of 1931 ring out the "Ave Maria" day and night on the hour, and the lesser bells striking the quarter hours, and when she heard the full melodious organ strains accompanying the sisters' full and well-trained choir under the direction of Sister Mary Henry Ehlen and Sister Mary Hortensia Gaertner, she said again, as she had said on several previous occasions, "What more have I to live for? Everything I have dreamed of has come to pass."

But summer came, and chapter of elections with it. She believed her zeal and her mental capacity had not been impaired by age. Her love for the sisters had grown rather than lessened. Mother Philothea was occupied with the college. She herself could be again elected without any indult. She could govern the congregation still. She spent much of the night in prayer. What she asked was to be able to do what she was called to do. She went to chapter in fear and trembling. This event could restore her to full life or cast her down.

When Mother Florence entered the chapter hall on June 3, 1931, she was greeted warmly by Archbishop Drossaerts and the sisters. But there was a difference. Eyes were no longer on her. They were on Mother Philothea, calm, prim, and organized; and upon Sister Angelique, her staunch supporter, who seemed to read Mother Philothea's thoughts and put them into words when it was appropriate to do so. Mother felt a slight foreboding that this competent, collected sister, no longer so young as Mother would like to believe, would be pleased to occupy an administrative post beside Mother Philothea. Sister had, in fact, been the right hand of Mother Philothea ever since Mother had been made secretary of the congregation and she had assisted her as subsecretary. She had actively supported Mother for superior general in both 1919 and 1925. Mother Philothea had never spared Sister Angelique, and Sister had borne the discipline well, keeping her smile and becoming more firm in her devotion as years passed. She understood Mother Philothea's delicate health better than anybody and she tried to shield her as much as possible both physically and emotionally from the stress of the position. The sisters consulted Sister Angelique about administrative policies and anything pertaining to Mother Philothea, and she was equal to anything. Like all the capitulars, Mother saw that Sister was necessary to Mother Philothea.

Before the voting began, the Archbishop praised the work of the past administration and asked God's blessing on the future. "She will be reelected," Mother Florence told herself. She was. The only dissenting vote, Mother Philothea's, went for Sister Angelique. Mother Florence knew that she was thus indicating her preference for a first assistant, and it cut her to the heart.

The vote for the first assistant, Mother Florence's present post, went to Sister Angelique on the first ballot, in which Mother Florence received only twenty votes. It was a bitter, bitter moment.

For the second councilor her name surfaced again, only to give way to Mother Antoinette in the second ballot. She felt her administrative position in the congregation slipping away. The vote for third councilor again showed her a strong opponent of Mother Eugenia, who received a majority on the second ballot. Only one position remained, that of fourth councilor. Again her staunch friends fought for her, but the majority went to the Irish Sister Vitalis Tracy, who was replacing the recently deceased Mother Joachim Sweeney.

This was the day she had hoped never to see—when she would be completely displaced from the council of the congregational government. Nor did it help her when at the close of the chapter of elections the sisters gave her a rising vote of thanks for her forty-five years of arduous and self-sacrificing work for the congregation. The image fleeted across her consciousness of these women tossing flowers into her grave. She was henceforth to be buried and forgotten. She was not named to any committee, not given responsibility for any action during the remainder of the chapter. She was buried and forgotten. She went to her room and wept long and privately for her own demise. Oh, that she might now rest in peace!

14

The Meeting (1931-1944)

Mother Florence looked out the east window of her second-floor bedroom. It was fall and the days were growing colder. Dusk came early. She saw the Mexican children, barefoot, shabbily clothed, and gaunt-looking, passing the convent. There was no laughter among them. "Poor children!" she said. Her motherly heart bled. It was depression and the people everywhere were out of work. The line was longer every day at the convent kitchen door. Joe, so long employed at the convent, told her that many parents in his neighborhood had no food for their children. She must work out something with Mother Philothea so that they could help their neighborhood in an organized way.

The novice knocked timidly and entered to draw the bath water and turn down the bed, for Mother would retire early tonight. But first she must meet with the sisters in chapel for night prayer. Remaining a few minutes when prayer was over, she saw Mother Philothea leaving chapel, and she went into the vestibule to meet her.

"Mother," she said softly, for it was the time of the great silence, "how can we help the poor? God has been so good to us. We have our gardens, chickens, and fruit. We must share it with the poor."

Mother Philothea agreed: "I will have food brought to the convent every evening from the academy. You can distribute it from there."

"And I will have the sisters cook more than we need in the

convent. Then each morning I will have the Mexican sisters help me distribute it. They can speak a few words of comfort to the people."

She returned to her room and found everything ready for her to retire. A sheet had been stretched taut over the steaming water in the bathtub so that it would not become cold if she were late. We are indeed blessed, she thought. Who else has plenty of food, hot water for bathing, and Our Lord under the same roof?

The next day she called together the sisters in the community and gave them instructions. The Mexican sisters were to go among the people and learn who in the neighborhood needed additional food, especially the children and the old people. They were to invite one member of each family to come in the mornings with a container or containers and wait at the edge of the long cement porch, which was waist-high. The sisters would fill the baskets, not mixing the foods but using wax paper to keep them separate. While the baskets or pails were being filled, one of the Mexican sisters would give the waiting people a short instruction in Spanish and pray briefly with them.

As the lines grew longer and longer, the food multiplied. The people learned to pray along with the sisters, and sometimes they sang a hymn in Spanish. Mother supervised the distribution, being sure that the dignity of each person was preserved, that the food was carefully distributed, and that a cheerful atmosphere prevailed. Eager hungry faces looked up to the sisters on the porch each morning. The sisters said a few words as they received the containers and another few as they handed them back full of food. They asked about the children and the sick. Tears of gratitude flowed. Mother thought of the multiplication of the loaves and fishes on the lake shore of Galilee. The day of miracles had not passed.

This was no small operation, nor one that grew less as the weeks passed. It went on for years, efficiently planned and organized until the people were again able to provide for themselves and the crisis was over. The congregation did not suffer. It seemed to Mothers Florence and Philothea that a providential

God filled the empty food pots and the empty coffers in spite of the lessened income.

Requests came during the early thirties to cancel or decrease the sisters' salaries in the parishes—in Frydek, Texas; Broussard, Louisiana; Union City, Oklahoma; then in Lindsay, Pilot Point, and Brenham. Everywhere the people were suffering.

Somehow, during this depression period Mother Philothea continued to beautify the chapel with additional pews, repaint the statues, and make new altar linens. As much as possible she kept the neighborhood people at work. At Mother Florence's request the convent basement was repaired and lighted, with trunk rooms added under the novitiate. The construction of a retirement center was also being planned.

One heavy trial distressed the administration and Mother Florence equally. Mother Florence loved Sister Louisa Plauche, a charming sister, an excellent teacher, and a superior for a number of years. Sister Louisa had requested and obtained a dispensation from her vows. Now living in Yoakum, she sued the congregation for $150 per month for a period of twenty-six years. Because Sister had signed a contract on entering the congregation that she would never claim any remuneration, her case did not hold up; but it simmered for some time, causing anguish to the sisters in Yoakum and to the administration. Mother Florence could not understand what had brought this talented and attractive woman to this point. She had not been mistreated in any way during her years in the order, had held the position of superior, and had a sister who was still a member. Sister Louisa, now Etna Plauche, was later to devise another plan. In 1939 she threatened to sell to a publisher the book of rules and the directory unless she was paid $2,000. Lawyers assured Mother Philothea there were no secrets in these documents to hide and that no publisher would buy them. Therefore, no action was taken and no further attempts were made to extract money by force.

Mother Florence's activities were limited to the convent. Her little Marie Metz, "Miss Mary," now sixty-five, had grown quite feeble in recent months, and in 1932 hers was the only death in the congregation. Mother wept as she accompanied her "little Marie" to the cemetery. She wrote Marie's brother in Alsace, telling of the simple but happy life and how it ended. Sister Beatrice was still strong in body, if helpless and dependent. Mother continued to look after her as a personal responsibility.

Trusting again in Divine Providence in the deep depression, Mother Philothea went ahead with the construction of the retirement center, St. Joseph's Hall—basement, four-story, fireproof structure, built at a cost of $102,000. But first the "Glass House" had to come tumbling down at the hands of August Fuessel and a wrecking crew. Mother was glad. It was too hot in Texas for all that glass, and it had not served its purpose very well during its seventeen years of existence. She thought of all the sisters who had died there. Perhaps with a new, well-equipped infirmary and a registered nurse in charge, more lives could be saved or prolonged. In the meantime she gave herself with great devotion to the sick. Many sisters were cheered by the bouquets of flowers she gathered and brought to them, the words of comfort she spoke, her loving hands, kind smile, and her sad eyes full of concern.

Among the retired was Sister Mechtilde Bader, a native of West Prussia. Mother vividly recalled how in 1900 Sister, aged thirty-nine then, was returning from her mission in Cuero for the summer. She was alone and without identification of any kind, but this was not unusual. As she stepped from the train, she glanced right and left for oncoming engines before she crossed the tracks. Then she picked up her heavy suitcase and began to move, not noticing the approaching locomotive. It caught the long skirt of her habit, drawing her leg back under the wheels. Her leg was completely severed below the knee. Railroad attendants were unable to identify her, but, seeing she was a sister, rushed her to Santa Rosa Hospital. From there inquiries were made at all the convents. Mother Florence quickly made a trip to the hospital, where she identified the sister and made arrangements for her care. She later had a wooden leg fashioned for Sister Mechtilde so that she was able to return to duty for twenty years. Occasionally her false leg gave way and had to be taken to the repairmen. On these occasions Sister Mechtilde remained behind closed doors in the house while two sisters carried the extra leg to the shop and waited anxiously while the repairman did a fast job on it so that they could take it back to its owner. Here she was, after twenty-four more years of quiet service in the convent, weak now and hardly ambulatory, but she was to outlive Mother Florence by five months, dying at the age of eighty-five.

As Mother Florence watched Mother Philothea walking through the partially completed halls, giving suggestions and criticisms to the workers, she thought of the energy she had put into the constructions she had been responsible for. Each new building was like bringing to birth a child—the anxiety and labor involved, but the joy of achievement at its completion. She envied Mother Philothea but realized that she really would not have the strength to do it herself anymore. She saw that Mother Philothea, even though not strong and well herself, was absolutely self-giving and forgetful of her own pain. And she was an organizer.

As Mother Florence looked around this year, she saw things happening, things she did not always quite understand or know the details of. She saw the future adoration chapel in St. Joseph Hall being planned, frescoed, installed with stained glass windows, furnishings, sanctuary decorations. She saw the former convent chapel changed to a sewing room. The road in front of the convent and college was tarviated for passage of automobiles on campus. Mother Philothea told her she had purchased additional land in Dallas for the Central Catholic high school for boys and that Bishop Lynch had sent a priest, Father Thomas Zachary, to help with the educational program. Then Mother Vitalis, who had replaced Mother Joachim on the council, died. Sister Angelica O'Neill was appointed to finish her term.

Finally St. Joseph Hall was completed, with the exception of the chapel. Mother Florence was appointed superior of the new house. She took great interest in the arrangement of the dining room on the ground floor, the community room on the first floor and her own first-floor bedroom, small and simple, but adequate. It would be very convenient with the adoration chapel

on the second floor. The elevator was almost across the hall
from her room, so that she never had to walk the steps.

Sister Annella Foelker had been sent to Santa Rosa Hospital
to complete her nurse's training. She now came to care for the
sick in St. Joseph Hall, where Mother leaned heavily on her
young shoulders. Father Constantineau, a diabetic, and Mother
Florence, both still suffering from allergies and other complica-
tions, sometimes spoke of the relief they had found at Hot
Springs. It was inconvenient for them to go there now. Maybe
some of the baths that had helped them so much could be
installed in St. Joseph's Hall for the sisters. Mother Philothea
sent Sisters Annella and Ernestine Stecker to Wisconsin, where
the Franciscan Sisters operated a system of water treatment.
They were favorably impressed by what they saw and heard.
Soon equipment began to arrive at St. Joseph Hall basement,
which was promptly renovated to accommodate the machinery
and treatment process. The five kinds of treatments provided
for were (1) "wicker"-ice treatments followed by rolling in a
blanket, (2) "hot packs"—with hay flour, (3) "salt rub"—
for circulation, (4) "electric cabinet"—with feet in cold water,
and (5) "medicated baths"—hot water spiced with pine needles.

Two Franciscans from Milwaukee came for two weeks, as
soon as the equipment was installed, to teach the sisters how
to administer the treatments. These were all active therapy involving both the therapist and the patient. The treatments were
for all kinds of joint pains, nervousness, high blood pressure,
and fatigue. The patients came out relaxed and refreshed. The
therapists came out tired.

No sooner were the treatment rooms and the therapists ready
than Father Constantineau began to come for therapy. Mother
Philothea had assigned him a suite of two rooms on the second
floor of St. Joseph Hall, where he slept at night, leaving in the
morning to go about his duties elsewhere. Sister Annella was
assigned to administer the treatments to him, which were given
at a time when none of the sisters was in the vicinity. It was
Sister Annella's responsibility to see that the sisters did not learn
about these ministrations, lest they be shocked. As Father

became weaker and more helpless, the therapy became more and more exhausting, especially because Sister had to undertake the entire process by herself at a time when she was already fatigued.

Mother Florence was having bad days, too—hardly ever confined to bed, but slower, more painful, and more forgetful. Still superior of the house, she delegated many of her responsibilities to Sister Annella, in whom she had complete confidence.

It was this year that Sister Prosper Ehrmann died, one of Mother's dear and loyal "girls," who had been governing the convent kitchen ever since it was built. She died of dropsy, sixty-eight years old.

Dear Sister Prosper! Even though she appeared ferocious among her butcher knives and meat cleavers, she had a heart of gold. Mother recalled how in Alexandria she had welcomed a large black man into her kitchen, where she was preparing him some food. Creeping up behind her, he put his hands on her neck to choke her. With a quick turn, she leveled him with one terrible blow and kicked him out the door. Then she went back to her usual duties. In Galveston each morning on her way to church she met the ghost of an old lady. One day she stopped and asked what the lady wanted. The spirit said she had promised money to the church, but her brother did not allow it to be given. She wanted her promise kept. Sister reported this to the proper place and met the spirit no more. Surely Sister Prosper would not fear meeting her God. There were seven of Mother's "girls" left now.

Mother was informed now that preparations were in progress in Rome for the beatification of the congregation's founder, that a branch of the Catholic University of America was being held at Our Lady of the Lake College, that summer religious education classes were increasing, that a new science building was being planned, and that the Our Lady of the Lake orchestra was presenting its final concert in the chapel auditorium. She attended and thoroughly enjoyed the concert, as she did her feast day celebration held in St. Joseph Hall.

The adoration chapel, a gem and the dream of Mother Philothea as the Sacred Heart Chapel had been her own dream, had come true. The sacrament was exposed night and day. Mother had moved to the second floor, and her room was almost directly across from the chapel; she spent many hours daily there in prayer.

Outside of her small world, a process of redecorating and ventilating the main chapel was going on, and novices were carrying on their practice teaching in the new demonstration school, St. Martin Hall, just across the road from the convent. Within her small world of St. Joseph's Hall, equipment for minor operations was being installed on the fourth floor. Such surgery as tonsillectomy and appendectomy would be performed there by physicians on certain days. When the numbers of patients scheduled for surgery was large, outside nurses were hired to help care for them. What with therapy, surgery, and care of the sick, the little world of St. Joseph's Hall was a hub of activity, almost too much to keep track of the first few years of its existence.

In 1936 attention in Texas was focused on the Texas Centennial Exposition in Dallas. All the Texas schools of the congregation participated, producing projects, booklets, displays for the Catholic Exposition Building. Everybody tried to go to Dallas for a day or two. The display, set up so carefully by Mother Angelique and some sisters from the college, was kept in order all year by the sisters in Dallas. St. Joseph Hall, no longer new, lost the center of attention and became quieter.

Father Constantineau, quite ill and partially bedridden, took up permanent residence in St. Joseph Hall, where he offered Mass more or less regularly first in the chapel and later in one of the rooms of his suite from his wheelchair. Sister Electa Schlueter, not a professional nurse but a natural one, trained by Sister Annella, ministered to Father Constantineau, who had utter confidence in her. When he required around-the-clock care, a male nurse was hired to perform this duty. Again, as for such a long time in former years, Mother Florence and Father Constantineau were closely associated. But it was not the same. After he had ceased to be ecclesiastical superior and had become the president of the college, and she had left the office of superior general, they moved in separate worlds. They occasionally met now, both still holding in fond memory the early difficult but pleasant times, as they remembered them at this point.

"Would you like to see the congregation repurchase the Castroville property?" Mother Philothea asked Mother one day.

"Of course, I would. It could never really belong to anybody else except for a little while. Surely our dear Lord has kept it to give back to us." The $5,000 the congregation had to pay the Holy See, to whom it had been sold, seemed a small price for the congregational cradle in Texas, shifted these past years from one congregation, seminary, and religious order to another, but never satisfied to be in other hands than those of its first love. Now at last the first convent and the congregation were together again. But, before it would be ready for its new purpose, that of a military school for small boys, it would cost the congregation an additional $85,000 to renovate.

Later in the year Mother Florence wrote to her friend, Mother Marie in St. Jean-de-Bassel:

> This may appear a surprise to receive a few lines from Mother M. Florence, who at present is leading a retired life at St. Joseph Hall, an annex to the Motherhouse. This building was put up four years ago and serves as an infirmary with the treatment and operating rooms, also quarters for the sisters who are over 72 years old, and an adoration chapel.
>
> The retired sisters have their adoration hours in the day time and some sisters from the College and Motherhouse with novices at night. I never expected to spend my declining years so quiet and so close to our Eucharistic God. What blessings in return for the spiritual privations we faced in the primitive days in Texas. God is so Good! What a consoling preparation for our final summons. May we make ourselves worthy of it.
>
> P.S. Please find enclosed a check of 52 francs as a remuneration to satisfy the conscience of a worried mind.

In 1937, Mother Florence, having been superior general, was automatically a chapter member, but going to chapter was a real penance for her, and she wished she might be excused. She asked Sister Annella to walk with her to the chapter hall and to come for her when the meeting was over. She did not trust herself with her memories alone. It was during these long slow walks to and fro that she relived again briefly and vocally her hours and days of bitterness caused by the last three elections, spilling over in choked voice as she passed her bedroom and the community room where the chapter was held. She did not think she could bear sitting through it all again, remembering everything from the last nine chapters. But her faith and her self-discipline carried her through another ordeal when she was satisfied to see Mother Philothea reelected for a third term. Mother Philothea, she knew, was suffering from cancer, about which she refused to do anything. However, she saw the strength of character holding her erect and firm. She prayed for her and hoped that she would hold up under another term's demands. She returned to her St. Joseph Hall room after chapter, weary and depressed. She had found during chapter that she was no longer able to think fast, to keep up on discussions concerning modern educational, social, and theological issues. She was beginning to feel her age. Other aged and ill sisters felt as she did. She would simply give her remaining energies to prayer and service to the sick and elderly. This brought her peace of mind.

Mother Marie Houlne had been replaced as superior general at St. Jean-de-Bassel. Mother Philothea wrote the new superior:

> Mother Florence, who often speaks of and loves our cradle, St. Jean-de-Bassel, is now in her 81st year. Although she is still able to be about, she is now growing rather feeble. The consolation of her declining years is the nearness of her room to the Perpetual Adoration Chapel. We are confident that through her prayers, and those of all our dear retired sisters, many blessings will come to the entire community.

It was true that, in spite of all the years of authority and responsibility, when she had exercised power not only over all the sisters but over bishops, priests, parents, young people, workmen and women, she prayed with the innocence and simplicity of a child, speaking to God intimately as a dear friend. She looked forward to these long friendly visits with Jesus, when she would complain, beg, tease, and thank Him alternately. She also prayed with the sisters and they looked forward to her visits. She had grown stout these last years with the relative inactivity of her life, the strain and burden lifted from her shoulders. But her regal bearing never changed. With hands folded and resting on her ample middle, she glided along the polished corridors into the adoration chapel and the dining hall, where she immediately detected the least speck of dust, withered flower, or crushed linen. Whoever was responsible for this carelessness was called to task.

One day when a young girl came to work looking weak, Mother asked her, "Have you eaten any breakfast?"

"No, Madre," the girl replied. Mother dispatched one of the sisters to bring her some breakfast and waited until it arrived. But seeing the arrangement on the tray when it came, Mother said sternly to the young sister, "Is this the way you learned to serve breakfast?" Taking the tray, she returned to the kitchen, where she rearranged the tray with a complete breakfast of fruit, cereal, toast, eggs, and coffee, surrounded by correctly placed silver, china, and napkin. "Here, child," she said kindly to the girl, whom she seated at a table. Taking the embarrassed sister aside, she said, "That is the way you prepare a breakfast tray."

The Texas Centennial had been extended through 1937, and Dallas was concluding this second year of celebration, which ended with the New Year. It was here, the last night of 1937, New Year's Eve, that Sister Angelina Marie Murphy, who had been responsible for keeping the centennial displays in order for the last two years, was sitting in the convent community room. Suddenly a bullet, fired through the window from across the alley where the slightly inebriated revelers were preparing for the New Year, struck her in the head. Anointed and rushed to St. Paul's Hospital, Sister was not expected to live through the night. Her friend and former teacher, Sister Seraphina Weinert, sitting beside her bed during the long night, offered her own life in exchange for the life of this young sister. In the morning there was hope for her recovery, which grew stronger each day. Mother Florence hardly knew this sister, who had entered the convent after her term of superior general was over. She barely recalled meeting her here and there. But her prayers were offered daily in the chapel for her recovery. She did know Sister Seraphina very well, from Germany, a music teacher; and, when Sister Seraphina died of pneumonia a few weeks after the shooting, saying that God was exacting His payment for the young sister's life, she praised God for the untapped generosity in the hearts of her sisters, while she mourned the death of her friend.

Mother Florence retired in 1940; that is, she was relieved of her duty as superior of St. Joseph Hall. Sister Gonzaga Menger was assigned as superior. Mother Philothea, who believed that she was doing Mother a favor, wrote to the European mother house:

> Dear Mother Florence, who is now in her 82nd year, is growing feeble, although she is still able to be about and attends all the exercises of the day. She sends a special message of sympathy to the sisters.

Mother had written a similar letter in 1925; but even now Mother Florence had plenty of life left in her, although her once firm handwriting was becoming heavy and shaky, so that correspondence was more difficult.

Again in May of the same year Mother Philothea wrote to Mother Ignace, the superior at St. Jean-de-Bassel:

> Our good Mother Florence is failing in health. Several weeks ago she was so seriously ill that the last sacraments were administered at her request. At this time, however, she is somewhat better. She was able to assist at Mass in the Adoration Chapel on the Feast of the Ascension of our Lord. News from the dear convent in Europe always interests her but when your recent sorrow [Sister Gertrude's death] was announced to her, she was much affected.

This was by no means the end. Mother was up and about, seeing everything and interested in everybody. She had been eager to have sister nurses in the congregation. She had pushed Sister Annella's training and leaned heavily on her. Now she heard that the congregation was purchasing a hospital in Abilene and that Sister Annella would go there to administer it. She was torn. Sister was needed at St. Joseph Hall. She herself needed her, but not so much as she had when she was the superior. Sister Annella was assigned to Abilene, leaving Sister Ernestine in charge of the upper floors and Sister Electa of the lower ones. Father Constantineau was in the care of a male nurse. Sister Electa still supervised his room to a certain extent and gave him all the tender loving care that she was capable of. One day in 1940 when the male nurse was wheeling Father down the ramp in his chair, the nurse's hold slipped and the chair went whirling down the ramp at great speed, to crash at the bottom. Father was thrown from the chair and injured somewhat. Because he was already in an almost critical condition, the fall hastened his death. The night before he died, he bid Sister Electa goodbye, thanked her for her devoted care of him, and promised to help her after his death. She was with him at his death, July 9, 1940, when he calmly breathed his last. Mothers Florence, Philothea, and Angelique saw that every honor was paid to this great priest, who had contributed so much to the success of the congregation and the college.

Another significant sister in the congregation was to pass on before Mother Florence. Sister Callista Baltz, also of Alsace, had been mistress of postulants and novices from 1909 to 1940. She had suffered quietly for many years. This year Mother Philothea sent her with Sister Ernestine to St. John's Hospital in St. Louis, where she was under the care of Dr. George Stecker, Sister Ernestine's brother, and several specialists. Her case was found to be too far advanced to save. She died on December 17, 1940. The autopsy showed her brain to be like glass, and scientists marveled how she could have lived so long. Because she was so saintly, the room where she died was treated as a shrine.

Mother Florence did not know why God had prolonged her life so far, except, perhaps that it would not make that much difference. She considered that she was practically in Heaven right now. All that was needed to complete her paradise were her dear friends and family who had preceded her in death— Mother St. Andrew, four San Antonio bishops, two Louisiana bishops, bishops in all the dioceses, priests with whom she had had long and warm relationships, friends, and even pupils—all gone. Here she was, keeping vigil with her dear sisters, right in God's presence. She felt humble and privileged. She would not rush this ending or hold it back when it came. Besides, she was afraid to die. Her fear had to do with her thirty-nine years in authority. She had held the lives of many people in her hands. She had sometimes been hard and demanding with the sisters so that they suffered because of her decisions and reprimands. Would God still hold this against her? In spite of her confidence in the Sacred Heart, she knew that God had to be just.

Browsing through the Psalms, which she had come to prefer to *The Imitation of Christ,* she paused on Psalm 71, consoled by what she read:

> *I have trusted in you since I was young,*
> *I have relied on you all my life.*

It was true; there was no other reason for her works, joys, and sufferings during seventy-two years. She read on:

> *Do not reject me now that I am old;*
> *Do not abandon me now that I am feeble.*

No, she prayed, do not let me be a burden to my sisters. Let me go as I am about my daily routine, walking and alert. Then she came upon the passage in Psalm 90:

> *Seventy is the sum of their years,*
> *Or eighty for those who are strong.*

She had suffered from physical illnesses and allergies all her life. Her years should not have exceeded seventy. But she had long since reached eighty, the limit for those who are strong! Strength, she decided, was more than physical; it was spiritual and mental. It was God in whom she had trusted all these years who was her strength. She looked about her. It was true with other sisters as well.

Sister Benetia Vermeersch, who had worked diligently and enthusiastically to form catechists in Houston for teaching the poor Mexicans, had been transplanted in San Antonio. She sometimes came to speak to Mother Florence. She now told of her new work: "I have to start over in San Antonio. My Houston catechists have almost disbanded. They needed formation and motivation to keep going." Mother knew this only too well, as Mother St. Andrew had known it before her, but there was nothing she could do. She still believed in obedience, which she had taught Sister Benetia and all the sisters.

"God writes straight with crooked lines," she told her friend. "If you are obedient, all will come out for the best." Sister Benetia was already beginning to see a new branch of catechists growing in San Antonio, where they had the support of the congregational administration and Archbishop Lucey, who was himself very zealous in social work and catechetics among the poor. The congregation, too, was moving into a social work program, and she approved of it.

Another chapter, 1943, was coming up. Mother was still an ex-officio delegate, being an ex-superior general. It no longer bothered her. She would simply go as an observer. Others could make the decisions, govern the congregation. She would pray.

Mother Philothea had completed her third term and was ineligible for an indult. Besides, her health was becoming more and more frail. Although Mother Florence had no close affection for Mother Angelique, as she had always had for Mother Philothea, she recognized her unusual abilities and felt that, because Mother Philothea had trained her well, she would be elected to replace her. Dr. John L. McMahon was president of the college and was doing very well, she understood. So she had no strong objection to Mother Angelique's election. After this chapter Mother Philothea was free to spend more time in St. Joseph Hall with her and the other sick and retired. They often sat and reminisced, Mother Florence speaking of the past and Mother Philothea speaking of the present and future. The membership of the congregation had increased to almost 700, with sisters living longer and more young women entering all the time.

Life was very slow and even now. She read of the war building up again in Europe. She thought of her brother George in Napoleon's army; she thought of the ravages of World War I and the needless loss of lives. She didn't want to see another war. She prayed for peace.

On February 18, 1944, Mother Florence rose as usual, assisted at Mass, ate her meals, read the newspaper, and spent some time in evening prayer; she said that she was tired and would retire early. She went to her room, undressed and lay down on her bed. Sister Ernestine brought her medication and a glass of water, propped her up on her pillows, and told her to take the pills. She saw that Mother was paler than usual and was breathing with difficulty. One of the sisters came to Sister Ernestine and told her that Mother Philothea wanted to see her, so she left. Sister Gonzaga, superior of St. Joseph Hall, had a bedroom in the south end of the convent adjoining St. Joseph Hall. On her way to the academy to see Mother Philothea, Sister Ernestine passed this room. In her hurry she knocked on the door, which she believed was that of Sister Gonzaga, but it was actually the one adjoining Sister Gonzaga's. In this room were two young sisters, who had returned to San Antonio from their mission in order to keep medical appointments—Sister Lauriana Gravel and Sister Bonaventure Jordan. Hearing the knock, they answered.

"Go to Mother Florence at once," Sister Ernestine called as she sped down the corridor. They hastily responded. As they hurried along the corridor, Mother Angelica, on her way to the adoration chapel for night prayer, a green washcloth laid neatly over her uncorneted head, surmised that something was afoot. She followed the sisters into Mother Florence's room, where they saw immediately that Mother was about to leave them.

"Go and call the priest," Mother Angelica told Sister Bonaventure, who quickly departed.

"The candle," Mother Florence, propped on two pillows, said briefly.

"Where is it?" Mother Angelica asked.

"In the drawer," she pointed. As Mother Angelica lifted the candle from the drawer and lighted it, she recalled having heard Mother Florence say more than once, "When Mother Florence meets her God, that will be SOMETHING!" She placed the candle carefully in Mother's hand and began to pray. Sister Lauriana stood at the foot of the bed. Mother Florence grasped the candle firmly and opened her eyes wide as she directed her glance to the corner of the room. It was as though in that place, standing with open arms as she herself had stood so many times, were Jesus indicating His glowing Sacred Heart just as she had fondly pictured Him; Mary and Joseph; members of her own dear family; Mother St. Andrew; and all her departed sisters and friends.

"I, Sister Mary Florence, renew my perpetual vows to God . . . ," she began. Her face was radiant with a joyful smile. Her fingers relaxed on the candle; the unswallowed pills lay on the table. Mother Florence had gone to meet her God, and that SOMETHING she had expected had finally come to pass.

Table of Foundations

*Still conducted by Sisters of Divine Providence.
**Still in ministry in this parish.
***A new diocesan school replaces this.

Date of Founding	*Place*	*Name of School*
1888	Natchitoches, La.	St. Mary's Academy**
	Natchitoches, La.	St. Joseph's
	Pineville, La.	St. Joseph's
	Temple, Texas	St. Mary's
1889	Cloutierville, La.	St. Mary's
	Cloutierville, La.	St. Joseph's
	Isle Brevelle, La.	St. Joseph's**
	Many, La.	St. John's
	Longview, Texas	St. Mary's
	Weimer, Texas	St. Michael's
1890	Tours, Texas	St. Martin's**
	Schulenburg, Texas	St. Rose's*
1891	Jefferson, Texas	
	Muenster, Texas	Sacred Heart
	Corn Hill, Texas	Holy Trinity
1893	San Antonio, Texas	St. Henry's
	Lindsay, Texas	St. Peter's*
	Pilot Point	St. Thomas'
	Pisek, Texas	St. Anthony's
	Praha, Texas	Assumption
	Windthorst, Texas	St. Mary's
1894	Campti, La.	St. Cecilia
	Campti, La.	Sacred Heart
	Moulton, Texas	St. Joseph's
	Industry, Texas	Immaculate Conception
1895	Denton, Texas	Immaculate Conception
	Gainesville, Texas	St. Mary's
1896	San Antonio, Texas	Our Lady of the Lake*
	Beeville, Texas	St. Mary's Academy
	Cameron, Texas	St. Anthony's
	Cleburne, Texas	St. Joseph's
1897	Cuero, Texas	St. Michael's
1898	Westphalia, Texas	St. Mary's*
1899	Lockhart, Texas	St. Mary's
	West, Texas	St. Mary's*
	Burlington, Texas	St. Michael's
	Plaucheville, La.	St. Joseph's
1900	Perry, Okla.	St. Joseph's Academy
	Devine, Texas	St. Joseph's**
1901	Granger, Texas	SS. Cyril and Methodius*
	San Antonio, Texas	St. Michael's

Date of
Founding   *Place*   *Name of School*

	Ponca City, Okla.	St. Mary's Academy*
	Selma, Texas	Our Lady of Perpetual Help
	Red Rock, Texas	Sacred Heart
	Norma, La.	St. Joseph's
	Bluff, Texas	Holy Rosary
1902	Antlers, Okla.	St. Agnes's
	Holman, Texas	Pecan School
1903	Tulsa, Okla.	Holy Family***
	Vinita, Okla.	Sacred Heart Academy
	Schulenburg, Texas	St. Anthony's
1904	Enid, Okla.	St. Joseph's Institute**
	Quapaw, Okla.	St. Mary's
1905	Dallas, Texas	St. Joseph's Academy
	Marlin, Texas	St. Joseph's
	Nada, Texas	Nativity
	Ammansville, Texas	St. Martin's
1906	El Reno, Okla.	Sacred Heart Academy
	Hobson, Texas	Hobson
	String Prairie, Texas	String Prairie
1907	Lawton, Okla.	St. Mary's Academy*
	San Antonio, Texas	St. Anthony's Institute*
	Union City, Okla.	St. Joseph's
1908	San Antonio, Texas	Our Lady of the Lake Convent*
1909	Broussard, La.	St. Cecilia**
	Frydek, Texas	St. Mary's
	St. Patrick's, Mo.	St. Patrick's
1910	San Antonio, Texas	St. Mary's Parochial*
	Stillwater, Okla.	St. Francis's
	New Waverly, Texas	St. Joseph's
	Lake Providence, La.	St. Patrick's
1911	Bison, Okla.	St. Joseph's
	Ennis, Texas	St. John's*
	Lott, Texas	Sacred Heart
1912	Washington, D.C.	Providence House of Studies
	Houston, Texas	Immaculate Conception
	Canton, Mo.	St. Edward's
1913	Yoakum, Texas	St. Joseph's*
	La Coste, Texas	St. Mary's
	Honey Creek, Texas	St. Anthony's
1914	Alexandria, La.	Providence Academy***
	Mansura, La.	Our Lady of Victory

Bibliography

Archives of the Archdiocese of San Antonio

Archives of the City of Surbourg, France

Archives of the Diocese of Galveston-Houston, Texas

Archives of Our Lady of the Lake University, San Antonio, Texas

Archives of the Sisters of Divine Providence, St. Jean-de-Bassel,
    France

Archives of the Sisters of Divine Providence, San Antonio, Texas

    Membership entry books

    Memoirs written by the sisters in 1926-28

    Chapter books

    Constitutions of the Sisters of Divine Providence, all editions

    Directories of the Sisters of Divine Providence, all editions

    The council meeting books

    The corporation meeting books

    All correspondence available

    Mother Florence's circular letters

    The necrology from 1870 to 1944

    The *Southern Messenger,* a diocesan newspaper, all copies

    The *Family Circular,* a congregational publication, all copies

Callahan, Sister Generosa, C.D.P., *A History of the Sisters of Divine Providence, San Antonio, Texas,* Milwaukee, Bruce Publishing Company, 1954.

_____, "The Road Taken," *Our Lady of the Lake University Magazine,* Vol. 4, No. 5, 1978

_____, "Our Lady of the Lake Conventual Chapel," *Our Lady of the Lake University Magazine,* Vol. 4, No. 1, 1977

Kempis, Thomas à, *The Imitation of Christ,* n.d.

Kuehne, Rev. Cyril Matthew, S.M., *Ripples From Medina Lake,* San Antonio, Taylor Publishing Company, 1966

Neeb, Sister Joseph, C.D.P., *Memoirs of Fifty Years, Congregation of the Sisters of Divine Providence, San Antonio, Texas, 1866-1916,* San Antonio, Nic Tengg, 1916

"Roman Catholic Church in Oklahoma, the Second Hundred Years,"
    Chronicles of Oklahoma, Oklahoma Historical Society, XXXI,
    No. 2, 1912

Strebler, Msgr. Joseph, *Alsaciens au Texas,* Strasbourg, Culture Alsa-
    cienne, 1975

Valdez, Sister Mary Paul, M.C.D.P., *History of the Missionary Cate-
    chists of Divine Providence,* Dallas, Taylor Publishing Company,
    1978

White, James D., *Tulsa Catholics,* New York, Carlton Press, 1978

Wilhelm, Abbe J., *Congregation des Soeurs de la Providence de St.
    Jean-de-Bassel,* Bar-le-Duc, 1927

Woods, Sister Frances Jerome, C.D.P., *Marginality and Identity,*
    Baton Rouge, Louisiana State University Press, 1972